A VOICE FOR JUSTICE

A Voice for Justice

WRITINGS OF DAVID SCHUMAN

Edited by Sharon J. Schuman

Oregon State University Press   Corvallis

Published in cooperation with the Wayne Morse Center
for Law and Politics, University of Oregon

Library of Congress Cataloging-in-Publication Data

Names: Schuman, David, 1944-2019, author. | Schuman, Sharon, 1946- editor. Wayne
    Morse Center for Law and Politics, sponsoring body.
Title: A voice for justice : writings of David Schuman / edited by Sharon J. Schuman.
Description: Eugene and Corvallis, Oregon : Oregon State University Press, 2021. |
    Includes bibliographical references.
Identifiers: LCCN 2021018398 | ISBN 9780870711107 (paperback) | ISBN
    9780870711138 (ebook)
Subjects: LCSH: Law—Oregon. | Law—United States.
Classification: LCC KF213.S338 S38 2021 | DDC 347.795/03334 $a B—dc23
LC record available at https://lccn.loc.gov/2021018398

♾ This paper meets the requirements of ANSI/NISO Z39.48-1992
(Permanence of Paper).

First published in 2021 by Oregon State University Press, in cooperation with the
Wayne Morse Center for Law and Politics, University of Oregon
Printed in the United States of America

Oregon State University Press
121 The Valley Library
Corvallis OR 97331-4501
541-737-3166 • fax 541-737-3170
www.osupress.oregonstate.edu

for Rebecca and Ben

Contents

PART 1: A VOICE FOR JUSTICE
with an introduction by Sharon Schuman

PART 2: THE PATH NOT TAKEN
with an introduction by Sharon Schuman

PART 3: IN TRANSITION: FROM LITERATURE TO LAW
with an introduction by Sharon Schuman

PART 4: WRITING AND SPEAKING ABOUT LAW
with an introduction by Margie Paris

PART 5: ON THE BENCH
with an introduction by Alycia Sykora

PART 6: SPEECHES AND TRIBUTES
with an introduction by Sharon Schuman

EPILOGUE : LEGACY

Foreword

MARGARET HALLOCK, FOUNDING DIRECTOR, WAYNE MORSE
CENTER FOR LAW AND POLITICS, UNIVERSITY OF OREGON

David Schuman was a loyal friend and supporter of the Wayne Morse Center for Law and Politics. We were treated to his deep intelligence, compassion, and political savvy through his participation and advice on numerous fronts. He served on our advisory board, and he consistently took time to interview candidates for the Wayne Morse Law Fellowship. We were struck by his empathy and compassion for law students—he understood their struggles and achievements. He was also a voice of reason on policy issues that we debated. And he was a touchstone—the person one spoke to before moving forward.

The Wayne Morse Center is honored to co-publish this book, an astonishingly broad collection of writings. Sharon Schuman displays her own brilliance in curating this collection that highlights Judge Schuman's humanism as well as his deep legal thinking.

In the summer of 2021, the Wayne Morse Center is launching the David Schuman Legal Justice Fellowship for law students who want to follow in his footsteps. Recipients will receive financial support and undertake legal work and research. All proceeds from this book will go to that project. We are also soliciting contributions at waynemorsecenter. uoregon.edu, and we hope readers will consider supporting this fellowship in order to further Judge Schuman's legacy for generations to come.

Introduction

GARRETT EPPS

In the twelfth chapter of the Book of Deuteronomy, the God of Abraham and Isaac—who has led the Hebrew nation through the desert, a cloud by day and a pillar of fire by night—instructs them to appoint "magistrates and officials" to govern the promised land. To those officials, God then says, "You shall not judge unfairly: you shall show no partiality; you shall not take bribes, for bribes blind the eyes of the discerning and upset the plea of the just. Justice, justice shall you pursue, that you may thrive and occupy the land that the lord your God is giving you."

In 2020, the world learned in grief that the words, "Justice, justice shall you pursue," had been inscribed on a plaque in the chambers of Justice Ruth Bader Ginsburg, who died at age eighty-seven in September. But they are inscribed in other places as well, and most particularly in the hearts of at least some of the "magistrates and officials" who preside over the legal system of the United States.

David Schuman—who died only months before Justice Ginsburg— lived by those words during his years as a judge of the Oregon Court of Appeals. Indeed, the entire seventy-five years of Judge Schuman's life could be seen as a pilgrimage toward the ideal of "justice, justice"—or perhaps more properly, the ideal of becoming one of those too-rare but essential humans in whose hearts justice lives and through whose actions it makes its way, however uncertainly, into the world.

David Schuman was by temperament and function a judge for years before he ascended to a place on the Oregon Court of Appeals. As for so many of us, only at the end of his life did it become clear what his life's goal had been; as for too few of us, it became obvious as well that, in his years on the bench, he had attained it.

This book is a record of that pilgrimage in full—of the slow (but in retrospect inevitable) metamorphosis of a rebellious Chicago teenager into a mature jurist who left an indelible mark on the law of his adopted state.

That transformation proceeded by stages—first, a grounding as a man of letters; then emergence as a lawyer in the old-fashioned humanistic sense of that term; and finally, as a public servant who could not only pursue justice but also, on occasions, attain it. It's a record worth studying both for its scope and for the grace its author embodied at every stage.

David Schuman's life story began (as it ended) in a passion, and a gift, for athletic pursuits. A champion speed skater in his native Chicago, he passed up the chance to try out for the 1964 Olympics to enter Stanford. There he studied psychology, along the way picking up a command of Italian ("corrente, non fluente," he insisted), and met Sharon Johnson, to whom he remained married and devoted for fifty-one years. He graduated in 1966 with a degree in psychology, then switched to literature as a graduate student at San Francisco State. Teaching posts drew him and Sharon to Deep Springs College, a small but prestigious young men's college on a ranch near Bishop, California, at the mountainous eastern hinge of the Golden State. There he taught literature and learned to butcher a cow, though not to rope or ride.

At the age of forty, he graduated from the University of Oregon School of Law, and remained in or near Eugene for the rest of his life, raising a family there and becoming, by turns, an Oregon Justice Department lawyer, a professor at the Law School, the deputy attorney general of the state, and finally a judge.

Beginning as an undergraduate, he wrote elegant stories marked by an unusual wisdom. "Cold Turkey" and "Show Business" are in a sense fictional self-portraits, imagined images of the young adult he could have become had he made different choices in life. "The Winner," written when he was on the faculty of Deep Springs College, is a moving and wry portrait of the death struggle (visible to no one but the two contestants and God) between two sedate-seeming Holocaust survivors who have separately found refuge in the California desert. His essay "Education and Solipsism" introduces a theme that underlay much of his writing, legal and humanistic—the tension between the American invention, "individualism," and the need of a healthy community for full membership by all individuals within it. That duty to the community, and the distinctly mixed satisfaction of knowing that one has met it, is a theme of most of his writing in every genre. It can be found in its full, conflicted form in his 1984 essay, "The Political Community, The Individual, and Control of Public School Curriculum" (available at avoiceforjustice.

com), written as a law student, which ponders the enduring question of when it is appropriate for a community to insist that those within it not only consent to its values but agree to be shaped—and to let their children be shaped—by the collective will rather than their own.

After law school, he had the formative experience of an apprenticeship as the clerk of the late Justice Hans Linde of the Oregon Supreme Court. Linde's mentorship would follow him all the days of his life; indeed, the two men died only a few months apart, Schuman at seventy-five and Linde at ninety-six. Linde's contribution to Schuman's sense of community was profound: the elder jurist had an austere but intensely creative philosophy of judging. Linde's "first things first" philosophy required a judge to determine, to the extent possible, what a legal provision meant within state law and as measured against the state constitution, and only then to apply federal constitutional rules to it; for if it was not valid under state law, the issue of validity under the US Constitution was irrelevant. This philosophy was enunciated most fully in a 1980 lecture published in the University of Baltimore Law Review, and it entered the scholarly and judicial dialogue at precisely the time that the federal judiciary had begun to turn its back on expanding and elaborating the rights of individuals against power of the states and the national government. "First things first" was not, as too many visions of what judges call "our federalism" were then and are now, an excuse for localism as set against the values of the nation, but rather an explanation of the ways in which individual states and their legal system could illuminate and expand the rights of citizens and the means by which they sought, through state and local self-government, to realize those aims of the Constitution's Preamble that lie within a state's purview: justice, liberty, tranquility, security, and "the general welfare."

The Linde-Schuman vision of the Oregon Constitution as a primary source of rights and concepts informs the scholarly writings about its history found in part 4—and they inform the judicial opinions in part 5. In both of his legal incarnations (scholar and judge) Schuman's work was precise, and not, to use a word he disliked, "individualistic." As a judge, Schuman never lost sight of the fact that the law was not a stage on which judges and lawyers could preen, but a field for the pursuit of "justice, justice" for the ordinary people caught within its toils. Privately, he could be scathing in comments on judges who styled themselves as the stars of the courtroom. He himself never ridiculed litigants, though an occasional flash of dry humor makes its way into his judicial prose. His former clerk Margarita Molina points us to the discussion, in State v. McBean, of Oregon's criminal prosecution of a man who, by stamping on a fire, had spread it—even though, he insisted in court, he had intended to extinguish it. Reversing a conviction for reckless burning, Schuman could not resist implicitly rebuking the prosecution for its strained theory that anyone should have known that stomping on the fire would surely spread it: "On the scale of what is and is not common knowledge, the tendency of stomping on a fire to extinguish it lies, we believe, somewhere between 'the rising of the sun' and 'the fable of the frozen snake.'"

Perhaps the fullest mature expression of his own creed emerges from the commencement address, reprinted in part 1, titled "Lawyers in Hell," which relates the ethical duties of lawyers both to Socratic ethics and the poetry of the Divine Comedy. There is little humor indeed when Schuman instructs the law school graduates that a "person with a well-ordered soul, with what we today would reductively call 'the right priorities,' is immune from the only kind of evil that matters, which is corruption and perversion." He sent a generation of law students into practice with that advice in their ears.

It might, perhaps, be fitting to end a summary of David Schuman's career with that vatic pronouncement; but a career is more than its credo, and a human being—son, husband, father, colleague, friend—is more than a career. And however passionately David Schuman did believe in the ideals of "Lawyers in Hell," he maintained always a wry and skeptical view of how much he, or any other human, could embody them. The true voice of the man I admired, and the friend on whose practical wisdom I relied implicitly, is heard most fully in the story "Cold Turkey," written while he was still a literature professor. The seemingly autobiographical narrator looks back at his own folly as a fifteen-year-old and the perverse delight he took in sharing it with his mischievous grandfather, now many years dead. The final words of the story, addressed to the departed grandfather, are not just funny and warm, but they are in a way (the way that Robert Frost defined as with "inner seriousness" and thus necessarily with "outer humor") a moving apologia (one mixing true humility with the faintest touch of justified satisfaction) for David Schuman's life:

Since your death, I've been a fraternity boy, a fraternity drop-out, a history major, an intellectual, a war-protester, a draft-resister, a dope-dabbler, and an assistant professor. I think that at one point I may have had a small nervous breakdown. All that was before I was twenty-seven and believe it or not it was all considered normal. Now I have one profession, one wife, two children, two cars and three degrees. I try to work hard without being fanatic, and resist quackery without being rigid. I try to be spontaneous without being a psychopath, and to have self-esteem without being a narcissist. I try to be decent and open, even if that means sometimes being a fool and sucker. These endeavors give me some pleasure, yet I am frequently anxiety-ridden, overcome by a desire to atone, to apologize, without really knowing what for. In 1971 I gave up smoking. Cold turkey, Grandpa. Honest.

Acknowledgments

This book would not have been possible without the help of friends and colleagues of David Schuman. As a non-lawyer, I am ill-equipped to choose among 672 appellate opinions a handful to represent David's jurisprudence. I turned to his law clerks: Alix Wicks, Margarita Molina, Lindsay Kandra, Melissa Aubin, Erin Donald, Andy Lopata, Rachel Martin, Dave Munsey, Mardell Ployhar, Megan Thompson, Danielle Lordi, David Blasher, Sarah Einowski, Rebekah Murphy, Lauren Blessing, and Eamon McCleery. A special thank you to Alix Wicks, Rita Molina, Melissa Aubin, Sara Einowski, and Eamon McCleery, for selecting, shortening, or writing introductions to judicial opinions. Thank you also Justice Jack Landau, for selecting, trimming, and introducing dissents, and to Judge Alycia Sykora for introducing part 5, "On the Bench."

I am also ill-equipped to choose among David's law review articles. Thank you, Margie Paris, UO Law School emeritus dean, for making the final selections and editing them down, with the help of Melissa Aubin. I am also extremely grateful to Garrett Epps, who is the most qualified person I know to write an introduction to David's diverse writings. Thank you also, Margaret Hallock, for writing the foreword on behalf of the Wayne Morse Center for Law and Politics at the University of Oregon, and to the Morse Center itself for co-publishing this book.

I would also like to thank the contributors to the epilogue: Chief Judge James Egan of the Oregon Court of Appeals, Justice Jack Landau of the Oregon Supreme Court, Chief Justice Martha Walters, Oregon Attorney General Ellen Rosenblum, UO Assistant Professor of Law Kristen Bell, and WSU Emeritus Professor of Political Science Nick Lovrich—all willing to take time to speak about David's legacy. In particular, David Linde, son of Oregon Supreme Court Justice Hans Linde, arranged for Judge Rex Armstrong of the Oregon Court of Appeals and Judge Henry Breithaupt of the Oregon Tax Court to interview Justice Linde and record his thoughts about David.

The short story "Saturday Night" would have been impossible to locate without the help of an anonymous librarian in the Stanford University archives. Stewart Brand, founder of *CoEvolution Quarterly*, gave permission to republish "Education and Solipsism"; the *Oregon Law Review* gave permission to republish "The Creation of the Oregon Constitution," as well as David's tribute to Dave Frohnmayer; the *American Law Review* at Georgetown University gave permission to republish "Taking Law Seriously: Communitarian Search and Seizure"; The *Register Guard* gave permission to republish two op-eds and an interview with David from when he was deputy attorney general; the *Appellate Almanac* gave permission to reprint David's dedication to Hans Linde.

I would also like to thank Kim Hogeland and Marty Brown, acquisitions editor and marketing manager, respectively, at Oregon State University Press, who have guided me with patience and confidence through a daunting process, as well as copy editor Susan Campbell, whose encouraging yet meticulous editing made the book better, and LeeAnn Agost, who, in creating the website for this book, avoiceforjustice.com, created a home for everything that had to be left out and much more. University of Oregon photographer Jack Liu contributed photos. Shiwanni Johnson, a third-year UO law student and fellow of the Wayne Morse Center, has been invaluable, digitizing documents, keeping track of permissions, editing texts, and creating an index to David's judicial opinions for the website.

Throughout this process, three brilliant and committed women—Rebecca Dinwoodie Flynn, Margaret Hallock, and Margie Paris—have been my champions. Finally, I want to thank the friends and family who have helped me through a difficult year, especially my sister-in-law Sarah Dietzel, and my children, Rebecca and Ben, without whom this project, and so much more, would never have come to pass.

Sharon Schuman, February 4, 2021

PART 1

A Voice for Justice

The speech, opinion editorials, and interview presented here introduce readers to David Schuman in his own voice, advocating for justice. Whether he was speaking to law students and their families at graduation, addressing readers of a local newspaper, or explaining what the Oregon attorney general does for the people of Oregon, he used his intellect, wit, and moral compass to help promote the public conversation that sustains democracy.

—Sharon Schuman

David Schuman delivering "Lawyers in Hell," UO Law School Commencement 2013 (Courtesy of Jack Liu)

Lawyers in Hell:
A Law School Commencement Sermon (1989)

This speech was the Commencement Charge to graduates at the University of Oregon Law School, when David Schuman was assistant professor and commencement marshal there. It was reprinted in Old Oregon, *University of Oregon (Autumn 1989).*

The commencement charge is traditionally an occasion for sententious and gratuitous advice of a moralistic cast, phrased in stately cadences and lofty diction, and studded with profound quotations from the classics of antiquity. It is traditionally an opportunity to deliver a speech of high seriousness and moral purpose aspiring to, and sometimes actually achieving, self-righteousness, pomposity, and poor taste.

This afternoon, I hope to follow in that tradition.

I do this despite the fact that some of you who will remain nameless have advised me to "be funny." For the past two weeks I have been grading exams, and if there's anything less likely than taking exams to put you in a humorous frame of mind, it's grading them. The tragic muse is the more appropriate. How funny is it, for example, that one of you who is about to be inflicted upon the legal profession wrote this sentence?

> This legislation is necessary because the drug problem in America has risen to academic proportions.

Or this one, from an earlier semester?

> A statute implicating a suspect class must further a compelling state interest and be narrowly circumcised.

If it's "funny" you want, there's a man who hangs out in front of the bookstore selling what he claims is The Greatest Joke Book Ever Written. I suggest you buy it. I plan to deliver a sermon.

And like many sermons, mine this afternoon will explicate a text. Ever mindful of the "wall of separation" which the Constitution erects between church and state, I have not chosen my text from the Bible, but from the next best thing: from Dante, in particular from the thirty-fourth Canto of his *Inferno*, the last Canto before Dante and Virgil emerge from the horrors of Hell into the dawn of Purgatory—that is, from the region where the ordeals only inflict pain, into the region where the ordeals also serve to prepare the sinners for redemption and glory. I presume that I need not belabor the obvious relevance of this text to the occasion of your last official act in law school before you emerge into preparation for the bar.

The thirty-fourth Canto depicts the ninth and deepest circle of Hell, where Satan himself dwells, chewing on the eternally tortured bodies of history's greatest traitors—the circle farthest from the grace and harmony and enlightenment of God's grandeur and of the human community. Due to what must have been an oversight on Dante's part, there are no lawyers in the Ninth Circle. The place commands our attention this afternoon anyway, because two of its features make it relevant to modern practitioners of the legal profession: its demographics and its climate.

The Ninth Circle is noteworthy first for the character of its population. Dwelling elsewhere are the slaves of greed or lust, the mass murderers, the false prophets, the barrators, the pedophiles, the drunks, and the thieves. The lowest level is reserved for a particular breed of pervert—namely, for those like Satan himself, who before the fall was the most glorious and gifted of angels and sat at the very side of the Lord. It is reserved for those who have taken great and empowering gifts, which in Dante's mind moved naturally toward the good, and perverted them to the service of evil.

In the Ninth Circle dwell those who have abused the gift of great power. As future attorneys you must attend to the warning that inheres in this literary image.

Many people, perhaps you among them, come to law school because they correctly perceive that attorneys have a state-granted monopoly on access to the force that can move the system and make it do good things. Law school is where we come to obtain the power to promote our values.

But during our three years of legal education, as we become more and more adept in the mysteries of power, too often a strange metamorphosis takes place. Power corrupts—or, in any event, something happens to the altruism even as the empowerment proceeds.

I do not refer now to the champions of environmental causes who suddenly begin showing up in a three-piece suit for on-campus interviews with law firms whose major clients have names like Consolidated Clear-Cut Incorporated; nor to the crusader for peace who takes a job with a firm that represents the Acme Cruise Missile Company; nor to the defender of family values and law and order who takes a job with a three-person firm in Drain, Oregon, and devotes her talents to the defense of drunk drivers and spouse abusers.

I refer more generally to all of us as we begin to confuse what is legal for what is right, what we can lawfully do for what we should do, as though any action, no matter how obstructionist, captious, obnoxious, dishonorable, deranged, demented, or cruel that is not literally prohibited by some rule of positive law therefore has an ethical seal of approval.

Meanwhile, as the altruism pales, the empowerment continues apace. By the end of the third year, on the threshold of membership in the profession, as you take these diplomas from Mrs. Ackerman, you receive not only a piece of parchment, but the keys to the city as well. Once you are fully accepted into the profession, you not only will have exclusive access to the levers that move the system—the forms and rituals of transaction, administration, and litigation—you will also have a quantity of power that can only be called magical and terrifying.

If you were a member of a different culture and you had this power an anthropologist would call you a witch, a wizard, a voodoo doctor, or a prophet, and you would be either venerated or ostracized, but in either case you would be feared. For you are soon to acquire the power to utter a few special words of hocus pocus, or make a few marks on paper, or punch a few buttons on a telephone and by those actions alone inflict pain, humiliation, and perhaps ruinous financial expense on your clients' enemies or your own. By those actions alone you will be able to call down upon your enemies the official machinery of the judicial system, knowing that this machinery itself, with you now licensed to operate it, can cripple all who are involuntarily drawn into its range even as it officially vindicates them. For this reason, you will have the power to make enemies wake up at 3:30 a.m. in a cold sweat.

True, you can exercise this power to serve the virtuous and the downtrodden, but, as we have all seen too many times, only your good faith or your grace prevents you from exercising your power this way in the service of evil.

I want to clarify what I am and am not asking you to do about this. I am not asking you to wear sackcloth and ashes or to don the hair shirt of suffering or take vows of poverty—especially those of you who are single parents, or who have long-neglected family obligations, or who have amassed a student loan, payments on which would devour the discretionary income of a legal aid attorney or deputy public defender well into the twenty-first century. You need not serve the disadvantaged to do good, nor is serving them a guarantee that you are not perverting your power. Surely by now we all know that the poor as well as the rich can be corrupt and evil bullies, as can those of all political persuasions—even, alas, our own.

Nor am I asking you to serve only the virtuous—I am too well-schooled in the apologetics of the adversary system to make the mistake of imputing the moral character of the client to the advocate.

I am saying that as an attorney you can pervert your power not only by promoting evil causes or clients, but by falling into evil ways. The legal route has a high road and a low road. They are both legal, but one of them is perverse. If as an attorney you file a suit or an appeal for its nuisance or harassment value, or take unnecessary delays, or inflate your billable hours, or turn in shoddy work because that's all the client can afford, or conduct trial by press conference, you are perverting power and doing evil of the most obvious sort, even if your client is a pure saint and you have violated no law or disciplinary rule. At times like this you are probably coming perilously close to the perversion of your gift that will earn you a place in the Ninth Circle.

In addition to the character of its inhabitants, the Ninth Circle is also noteworthy for its climate. Modern readers of Dante are frequently surprised to discover that this remotest circle of Hell does not broil in flames; rather it is frozen over with ice. Something in our collective unconscious seems automatically to link "ice" to "hatred." That is not the association that drove Dante to make ice the motif of deepest Hell, for Dante and the scholastics, like Dostoevsky and the existentialists, drew a distinction between hatred, on the one hand, and failure to make basic human connection, to empathize, to love, on the other; ice symbolizes the latter of these defects: failure to connect. Hatred at least involves passion. Failure to connect, to empathize, on the other hand, involves a freezing up of the emotions and a perversion of the teleological tendency of humans to be drawn to each other. The sinners at the center of the Ninth Circle, unlike those in Upper Hell, are not tormented by passion; they are each frozen into complete isolation. The worst sinners in Hell are those who on Earth failed to cultivate human connections, who severed themselves from their community and their God. Tocqueville noted, in a purely secular context, that this failure to connect with others "originates as much in deficiencies of mind as in perversity of heart."

What does this excursion into the taxonomy of sin have to do with law school graduation? Tocqueville also noticed something about legal education. He said, "People who have made a special study of the laws derive from this occupation certain habits of order, a taste for formalities, and a kind of instinctive regard for the regular connection of ideas, which naturally render them very hostile to the . . . passions."

I think Tocqueville had in mind something more significant than work habits and dress codes. He meant that legal study and practice attract and reinforce certain personality traits—a tendency to see abstract general rules instead of the real people who occupy them, to regard others as instruments that can help you achieve your goal, or impediments that can hinder you. This cast of mind noted by Tocqueville is the natural and inevitable outcome of a training in legal analysis that rewards you precisely to the extent you can refine out of every situation all of those motley and unpredictable elements like personality, sentiment, and compassion—the elements we commonly associate not with ice but with warmth—and deal instead with pure cold abstractions, and with people only as tokens or counters to be subjected to impersonal mechanical and neutral formulas.

I am not standing here today asking you to replace your training with vague, gushy sympathy toward the world in general—what Saul Bellow calls "potato love." I am not, in other words, asking you to reject your legal, analytical training and conduct yourself professionally like a fool and a sucker. But I am reminding you, in the words of the prophet, to do justice and love mercy, to let your devotion to the rule of law remain open always to the heart's way of knowing. When you read about an oil spill or a freeway pileup and the first thing you think about is proximate cause or strict liability, instead of the victims' fear and pain; when you hear of a racist or sexist or anti-Semitic or homophobic practice or policy or remark and the first thing that comes to your mind is the equal protection clause or Section 1983 or strict scrutiny instead of the victims' rage and humiliation—then you have over-learned your law school lessons and taken one step closer to the icy realm of the Ninth Circle.

Coldness of heart and perversion of power—these are among the dangers that you confront in your new profession. But I would be unfaithful to this occasion and to Dante if I sounded this warning and then fell silent. Neither my purpose nor Dante's is to terrorize, but to educate and to inoculate, to expose you to the sins of others so that you may know them and avoid them.

This is where it gets pompous and pretentious.

Because you are not children who need me to tell you how to cope with the perils of real life. You are cops, contractors, construction workers, probation officers, car repair shop proprietors, tree planters, nurses, opera singers, candy store owners, high state officials, jewelry makers, accountants, mothers, legal secretaries, mathematics teachers, waiters, writers, fathers, and newlyweds. One of you has even been—of all things—an English professor. Your average age is thirty. (Since some of you are pushing sixty, incidentally, I figure that means that at least three of you must be under twelve.) So if I can help inoculate you at all, it is only by way of suggestion.

Here is that suggestion. It will be on the final. Remember that Dante did not try to move through Hell and Purgatory to Heaven by himself. Dante was not an "individualist." In fact, the word "individualist" didn't even exist when Dante wrote and wouldn't be invented for another five and a half centuries. Dante knew only the sin of egoism, and would have regarded self-reliance and self-fulfillment as at best foolish and misguided. Dante proceeded through Hell and Purgatory to Heaven accompanied by his teacher, Virgil, and by the image of his beloved, Beatrice. Virgil taught him something about the perversion of power, and Beatrice helped him avoid succumbing to coldness of heart.

Dante did not call Virgil his teacher. He used an older word, a word that has fallen into some disrespect: authority. To Dante an authority was not someone who constrained his freedom, but rather someone whose example enlightened and enabled, and in that sense authored or created. I suggest that in your professional life you assemble in your mind a panel of authorities to whose example you look for inspiration and guidance.

You need not look far. As an authority in courage you might draft Ron LeMay, for whom climbing the stairs and walking across this stage were acts of pure physical valor; or Darlene Szumko, for whom standing before you this afternoon must have been a graceful victory over the terror of stage fright. As an authority on persistence in the face of adversity you might want to draft any one of your classmates who is a single parent, or who lost a parent during law school, or who is black or Hispanic or Asian or gay or lesbian or Native American and succeeded in law school despite being the object of prejudice and stereotype.

But your most important panel, and probably the most active in your new profession, is your panel of authorities on integrity, on not perverting power, on how to do what is right instead of what is expedient. For this panel you couldn't find better members than two men in whose sphere you have been living for these last three years: I refer to Paul Olum and Hans Linde. And if any of us on this platform today appear on your panel, we have attained the highest honor available to those of our vocation.

These people, whoever they are, might serve as your authorities, your Virgils, guiding you past the propensity to pervert your power. But how do you avoid that other evil of the Ninth Circle and the legal profession, coldness of heart? Who will be your Beatrice? To the extent that Beatrice represents a romantic love object, I cannot suggest one for you without violating the canons of common sense, good taste, and several sections of the Oregon Criminal Code. But Beatrice is not only the object of Dante's romantic affection; in a way she represents his transcendence of self, his connection with the human community.

I have already suggested that there is a logical relationship between legal training and analysis, isolation, failure to connect, and coldness of heart. Our training focuses our attention on conflict and competition between individuals, either real or corporate. The unstated message on every page of our casebooks is that truth and justice emerge from the form of intellectual warfare known as litigation, in which rational maximizers of their own self-interest do battle for superiority.

Our commitment to this form of activity cannot be contained within our professional style or method. Our lives do not consist of hermetically sealed compartments. You may already have noticed that law students, law professors, and lawyers tend to adopt cross-examination as a form of casual and domestic conversation. So maybe, in order to promote a life that is personally connected to others, we should attend to some of the more subtle, benevolent, and convivial aspects of our training and profession.

Because we are not only certified pit bulls, hired guns, or sharks, to use a few of the more colorful and less obscene descriptions of our co-professionals. We are also specially qualified to participate in the public life of the community. As thoughtful commentators from Plato to Wayne Morse have realized, law is much more than litigation. Socrates from his cell calls the laws of Athens, even as they are poised to kill him, his mother and his father—that which gave him his identity and his roles, which bound him to others in a web of support and obligation, and in so doing made it possible for him to be a human animal.

Most of us before we came to law school believed that "law" was the sinew of the community, the community's values made manifest, the fruit of public discussion and debate about what constitutes or promotes a life of virtue—and not what some judge said about the mailbox rule. We must try to be "lawyers" in this larger sense of "law" as well, to use our access to the machinery of the system not only to promote the private interests of litigants but to forge a public life worth living. If we devote at least part of our professional lives to this endeavor, we enlarge our sphere of concern so that it includes not only argument in the service of private wealth, but debate in the service of our shared lives. This opening up of ourselves to our fellows, I suggest, is our Beatrice, our inoculation against coldness of heart, our insurance against the Ninth Circle.

Socrates tells us that no evil can ever befall a good person. Socrates was no fool and neither am I and neither are you. We all know that a good person is as likely as a bad one to get hit by a truck. What Socrates meant was something like this: A person with a well-ordered soul, with what we today would reductively call "the right priorities," is immune from the only kind of evil that matters, which is corruption and perversion. To what extent you are good people in this sense remains to be seen. Some would say that your three years in law school have reduced your chances. I disagree. I believe that if you attend to your authorities and open yourself to your fellows, you will be able to say that, like Dante's, your journey has strengthened and braced you so that you might emerge at last into your own redemption and glory of principled power and abundance of heart.

Deputy Attorney General Weighs Initiatives (2000)

David Schuman served for six years as deputy attorney general to Hardy Myers, a position that he relished. Four years into his term, he was interviewed by David Steves for the Eugene Register-Guard *(August 21), largely about the initiative process.*

David Schuman traded his position as constitutional scholar and associate dean at the University of Oregon law school to serve as deputy to Attorney General Hardy Myers when he took office in 1997. Although he had planned to stay only two years, Schuman remains in the position nearly four years later. As the Department of Justice's top appointed attorney, Schuman oversees all the legal matters dealt with by what is, in effect, the state of Oregon's law firm.

Q: It's an interesting transition you made from legal scholar to deputy attorney general. What kind of perspective does that allow you to bring to your job?
A: In many ways I feel like I moved from the grandstands to the playing field. As a professor and a scholar, I was much more of a critic who occasionally hoped that something I screamed out might somehow get the attention of one of the players. As the deputy attorney general, I'm a player, and it's much more interesting in many ways and it's much more exciting.

I think coming from an academic background gave me a certain kind of theoretical framework that people who go from law school into practice don't have. So I spent a lot of time thinking about how a constitution should be interpreted. What a constitution is. What the function of a constitution is in a polity. That sort of thing. I call that a theoretical perspective as opposed to a partisan perspective. That gives me a kind of mooring when I approach a particular problem.

Q: How much of your job deals with constitutional issues versus more routine legal issues?

A: It's probably fifty-fifty, but that's because in Oregon the initiative and referendum are in the constitution. An enormous amount of my time and the time of other assistant attorneys general, not to mention the Oregon Supreme Court, is spent dealing with, in one way or another, the initiative process—everything from drafting ballot titles, which is something the attorney general's office has to do by statute, to defending our draft of ballot titles against challengers, to interpreting sometimes ambiguous measures after they've been passed, or sometimes before they've been passed in the form of an attorney general's opinion, to defending them if they do pass. That takes up a huge amount of time.

If you're referring to more traditional constitutional things like free speech cases, separation of powers cases, equal protection cases, that's a much smaller area, although it's a much bigger area of my particular practice than it is in the rest of the department because I'm interested in it and I get to choose what I do.

Q: Given the enormous workload created by initiatives, such as you've just described, how would you reinvent the initiative system?

A: I would reduce the workload in the ballot title area by not having the attorney general and the Oregon Supreme Court involved in drafting, defending, and judging ballot titles for measures that never reach the ballot. We had 166 proposed measures during this last election cycle, and 26 of them made the ballot.

And yet all 166 had to have attorney general–drafted ballot titles. They had to stay open for a week to allow people to comment on them and object. Many of them were challenged in court. The whole process occupied an enormous amount of time, and it turned out to be wheel-spinning, because these didn't make the ballot in any event. So it seems to me that one simple and fairly straightforward reform would be to reduce the amount of work that both the attorney general's office and the Oregon Supreme Court do on measures that don't make the ballot.

Q: Without a ballot title when initiatives are being circulated for signatures, wouldn't this make more difficult the job of explaining what the measure does?

A: For some measures, for short measures, signature-gatherers could simply have the text itself. But for those initiatives that are complicated or long enough that they would need a ballot title, you could have ballot titles drafted by some sort of committee, a nonpolitical group. For example, two people chosen by the proponents, two people chosen by opponents, and one person chosen by the other four. They could draft a ballot title that would be adequate, that would be sufficient for the purpose of gathering signatures.

The real fight over ballot titles seems to be over minutiae: Where does a comma go? Are you going to use this word or that word because of the connotation? That sort of thing can influence an election, because people see the ballot title and that's usually all they see. But in terms of whether you're going to sign a petition or not, I don't think that kind of technical distinction makes that big of a difference.

Q: *A lot of initiative sponsors do what's called "title shopping." Could you explain this?*

A: That's one sort of abuse of the current system. If someone has a fairly complex measure, they'll submit it in three or four or five slightly different forms. It's like a menu, and they ultimately get to choose their favorite one. Meanwhile, we're out there drafting five or six ballot titles, and everyone knows that only one is going anywhere, if that.

Another abuse is that people will challenge ballot titles in order to run out the legal process so that there's less time for the signature-gathering process. This process can't begin until the Oregon Supreme Court has certified a ballot title. With their docket the way it is, especially being clogged up by ballot-title challenges, sometimes that reduces by months the amount of time people have to gather signatures.

Q: *What about the wording of these measures, which are often written by nonlawyers? When they pass they are almost always challenged, and often they're tossed because they've got legal or constitutional problems.*

A: One thing would be to encourage people who are going to draft and submit constitutional amendments or other initiatives to run them by legislative counsel before they turn them in. They already can do that. Legislative counsel will look at proposed initiatives and render informal advice, completely voluntary. No one has to take this advice.

Unfortunately, people who tend to avail themselves of the initiative process have such a deep-seated distrust of government that they often fail to take advantage of this. I don't know if there would be some way to compel them to do that by statute. That would probably be politically difficult. Another thing that could be done, and I'm not saying this would be a particularly good idea, would be to change the constitution so that the courts could pass judgment on the constitutionality of proposed measures before they're enacted. Currently, under the constitution the way it's written, you can't do that because the case is not a real case; it's hypothetical.

Q: One of the measures on the ballot was sponsored by Bill Sizemore's Oregon Taxpayers United to prevent the legislature from doing anything to the initiative system. What do you think of this?

A: I think it's probably unnecessary because the legislature is already so nervous about changing the initiative system. They're reluctant to do it in any event. If you look back over the last few biennia, you can see that there really have been no significant legislative changes to the initiative process. So I think people who are in politics in the state of Oregon understand that the initiative system is off-limits to tinkering.

Women Deserve Yes on Measure 89 (2014)

This opinion editorial was published in the Eugene Register-Guard, *October 16, 2014, shortly after David Schuman retired from the bench.*

Opponents of Measure 89, which would add to the Oregon Constitution an amendment prohibiting discrimination on the basis of sex, argue that our constitution already prohibits such discrimination. They also note that our state constitution—the longest in the nation—already is cluttered with unnecessary provisions, and an Equal Rights Amendment would just make things worse.

I agree with those arguments. I'm going to vote for Measure 89 anyway. Here's why.

Article I, section 20, of the Oregon Constitution provides that when state or local governments provide individuals or classes of individuals "privileges or immunities," those benefits must be made available "on the same terms," equally, to all citizens. When first enacted along with the rest of the Oregon Constitution in 1859, the Privileges and Immunities Clause was not intended to prohibit discrimination against minority groups; we know that, because the voters who ratified it also voted to prohibit African-Americans from living in Oregon, and statutes (fortunately never enforced) called for whipping those who refused to leave.

The clause probably was designed to prohibit the legislature from granting special economic favors to insiders or cronies.

However, for at least the past thirty-three years, the Oregon Supreme Court has held that Article I, section 20, is this state's version of the Equal Protection Clause in the US Constitution, prohibiting invidious discrimination based on race, religion, gender, and other traits unrelated to merit. In fact, the court has held that the Privileges and Immunities Clause provides even stronger protections against gender discrimination than its federal counterpart.

That is why I agree that Measure 89 would duplicate existing state constitutional bans on gender discrimination.

However, what the Oregon Supreme Court gives, it can also take away. There is no guarantee that future Oregon Supreme Court justices will refrain from reinterpreting Article I, section 20, in such a way as to diminish protections against gender discrimination.

The possibility of reinterpretation is not limited to some doomsday takeover by partisan fanatics. The current court—all of whose members, I hasten to add, are my friends in whose fairness, intelligence, and freedom from bias I have complete confidence—has, nonetheless, shown a conspicuous willingness to overrule precedent, particularly when doing so is, in their eyes, compelled by "original intent" and "plain text"—both of which could excuse rolling back the protections against invidious discrimination that for decades have inhered in Article I, section 20.

In most of the cases where the court has overruled precedent, it has been urged to do so by lawyers for the Oregon Department of Justice. That is so because the cases usually involve the enforcement of criminal laws; the person claiming that law enforcement violated his or her constitutional rights is usually a criminal defendant seeking the suppression of unconstitutionally seized evidence or the invalidation of an allegedly discriminatory statute.

Ominously, for purposes of gender equality, the Department of Justice recently submitted a brief to the court urging it to disavow the long-standing interpretation of Article I, section 20, and to hold instead that the Privileges and Immunities Clause prohibits only what it was intended to prohibit 155 years ago, when slavery was still flourishing in much of the country and women couldn't hold property, enter into contracts, or vote.

The court rejected that argument—for now. I hope and believe that current and future lawyers in the Department of Justice will avoid such arguments, which may serve legitimate purposes in individual criminal cases but poorly serve the majority of citizens who are not involved in crime. If such arguments are advanced, I hope that future Oregon Supreme Courts will continue to reject them.

If they don't, one might ask, wouldn't women still have the protection against invidious discrimination afforded by the Equal Protection Clause? The answer is that they will—but that such protection is weaker than what's currently available under Article I, section 20, and the current United States Supreme Court has not been, to put it mildly, friendly to gender equality claims. In other words, if in the future Department of

Justice lawyers continue to urge the court to reinterpret Article I, section 20, and the court ultimately complies, women's claims for equal treatment will be substantially weakened.

I hope that doesn't happen. But women in this state deserve more than hopes. They deserve Measure 89.

Travel Ban Rulings Based on Law (2017)

This opinion editorial was published in the Eugene Register-Guard *on February 22, 2017. Appearing almost four years prior to the assault on the US Capitol on January 6, 2021, it now carries an eerie prescience.*

In her February 19 guest viewpoint, "Progressive Judges Overstep Their Authority," Eugene attorney Laura Cooper asserts that the federal trial and appellate judges who temporarily stayed enforcement of President Trump's travel ban were driven by their progressive political biases and overreached their constitutional authority. As a retired judge and a long-time professor of constitutional law, I find much in the article that merits response. I will limit myself to three issues.

First, there is no evidence to support the charge that the judges acted to further a progressive political agenda. In fact, all of the evidence is to the contrary. Nothing in the judicial or extra-judicial writings of any of the well-regarded judges—the trial court judge or the three judges on the appellate panel—indicates an ideological bias, much less a progressive one. In fact, two of the four were appointed to the bench by a conservative Republican president.

Second, the author asserts that federal judges who exercise judicial review of a presidential executive order "tread on dangerous constitutional ground." That assertion, not to mince words, is dead wrong.

Since our nation's founding, federal judges have had authority to decide whether actions by either of the other two branches of government conform to the Constitution, and to invalidate actions that do not. The power of judicial review applies even to executive orders imposing restrictions on ethnic groups, issued for the asserted objective of protecting national security.

Korematsu v. United States is the most obvious example. In that case, the Supreme Court heard a challenge to the constitutionality of statutes issued pursuant to President Franklin D. Roosevelt's Executive Order 9066 ordering the internment of Japanese and Japanese-Americans during World War II. Although the outcome of that case has been universally discredited, the Supreme Court's constitutional authority to hear and decide it was and is unquestioned.

Third, and most distressing, the author's suggestion that the president could refuse to obey a court order because judges have "neither armies nor squads of police to enforce their decision," is unoriginal, unwise, and unpatriotic. A well-known myth has it that when President Jackson learned of a Supreme Court decision that he disliked, he remarked that Chief Justice John Marshall "has made his decision; now let him enforce it." In reality, neither Jackson nor any other president has decided to defy a final judicial order—not even Richard Nixon, who obeyed a Supreme Court decision ordering him to release Watergate-related tapes that he knew would doom his presidency.

Why? Because serious people understand that, despite our constitutional system under which each branch can "check" the others, it remains the case that each branch has the raw power to hobble, and even destroy, the others.

For example, Congress, while it cannot reduce the compensation of federal judges during a term of office, nonetheless, in exercising its "power of the purse," has the raw power to pass such a paltry judicial budget that courts would be unable to perform their core functions. Many reputable scholars believe that Congress has the raw power to so limit the jurisdiction of federal courts as to render them irrelevant.

The courts, for their part, can declare statutes passed by Congress to be unconstitutional and dismiss cases in which those statutes are invoked. The judicial branch has the raw power to refuse to administer the oath of office to a newly elected president. The president, in turn, can simply decide to order executive agencies under his or her control to not spend money that Congress has appropriated for legislative programs that the president does not support.

Members of each branch, however, understand that the survival of our constitutional democracy, the delicate experiment that has endured for longer than any other constitutional democracy in history, depends on conformity to certain prudential constraints on the exercise of raw power, because the exercise of raw power leads to constitutional crisis. One of these constraints is that final judicial judgments must be obeyed, even if the judicial branch has "neither armies nor squads of police" to enforce them.

Ultimately, there is one point on which Cooper and I agree. Nobody wants the constitutional crisis that would certainly ensue if the president decided to abandon constraint and defy a final court order. We can only hope that, in Cooper's words, "both sides behave like adults." I am confident that members of the judicial branch will continue to do so.

PART 2

The Path Not Taken

Until he went to law school, David Schuman was an English professor and writer of fiction. The precision, passion, and intellect in his appellate opinions are at least in part a consequence of this earlier life. The five stories and one essay included here reflect an empathetic mind and express persistent themes that were to occupy David as a judge: personal responsibility, individualism, and injustice related to age, gender, ethnicity, and economic need. Four of these stories were published, three during law school. The essay, "Education and Solipsism," which first appeared in *CoEvolution Quarterly,* is a trenchant critique of higher education in America and a description of a unique alternative college. The teaching experience described here created a foundation for communitarian aspects of David's legal thinking.

—Sharon Schuman

Saturday Night (1965)

This story first appeared in Stanford University's undergraduate literary magazine, Workshop.

Seated at his desk, Norman had been staring at a mimeographed page of numbers and graphs for more than a half hour. Finally, he took a clean sheet of notebook paper from the drawer. "Patient 1-A's persistent pattern of avoidance," he wrote carefully, "coupled with his refusal to place his token next to that of the experimenter, indicates that the patient manifests, to an abnormal degree, symptoms of intro-punitive guilt and shallow affect." He skipped a line, printed "1-B" neatly in the left margin, leaned back his chair and lit a cigarette. There were "1-"s through "l-M", and the families of "2-" through "15-" were equally large. At this rate, he thought, I should finish next Monday's assignment sometime in August, assuming I work straight through. He was calculating when he would finish if he allowed five hours per day for eating and sleeping when a quarter-inch ash fell into his lap and shattered his concentration.

Norman was taking Professor Barnard's Measurement of Personality seminar. The subject matter of the course was mostly analysis of Professor Barnard's Personality Device, a three-foot-by-three-foot piece of plywood, painted light green, upon which the patient and the tester each moved his token, a red plastic checker with black linear facial features. A second experimenter recorded the patient's moves and later classified them into such categories as "intimate," "hostile," or "withdrawing." The page before Norman contained the records of two hundred psychotic adolescents. His assignment was to write a "one-sentence personality sketch" of each. From the given data, Norman could deduce exactly nothing about the patients; "Intro-punitive guilt" and "shallow affect" were two of Professor Bernard's favorite psychopathologies; Norman therefore attributed them to 1-A.

Norman stood up and brushed the ash off his pants. There were two ashtrays in his three-room apartment, and they were both overflowing.

Norman emptied one into the wastebasket and, noticing how stale it smelled, carried it into the bathroom and held it under a stream of hot water. Slowly at first, then all at once, the caked-on carbon gave way to reveal the plump face and blue plaid bonnet of a prepubescent farm girl. Surrounding her face was the inscription, everything's better with blue bonnet on it—it tastes just like the 70¢ spread. She looks like Barbara, thought Norman as he dried the ashtray. Then he took it back to his desk and confronted Patient 1-B.

Now Norman remembered that Professor Bernard also taught a graduate seminar, Psychoanalysis and Literature. Next to "1-B" he wrote, "Patient 1-B is Captain Ahab." Without consulting the data, he moved on to "1-C": "Patient 1-C," he wrote, "is either Shakespeare or Ben Jonson cleverly disguised as Shakespeare." He took a long last pull on his cigarette and crushed it into the dimpled face of the Blue Bonnet girl. She doesn't really look like Barbara, he thought. Just the hair. He turned off the desk lamp and got up and stood looking out the window. It was dusk. I will call Barbara, he thought, and talk to her and laugh and see how she's been. I'll call her as soon as they turn on the streetlights. Barbara: black boots and blond hair, he thought, smiling. In a blue bonnet. On cobbled back streets. Beautiful Barbara, the barbaric bewitching belle of—. The street lamps interrupted him. He sat by the telephone and dialed her number.

Two rings. Then, "Hullo?" Norman recognized Joan, Barbara's roommate.

"Hello Joan. Barb there?"

"Yeah. Who's this?"

"This," said Norman in his best Everett Dirksen voice, "is the ghost of Christmas Past." He heard the receiver being set down and muffled voices in the background, and after a few seconds Barbara said, "Hello?"

"Hello. This is not, in fact, the ghost of Christmas Past. It's Norman."

"I would never have guessed. How are you? What've you been doing? I never see you anymore."

"Yeah, well, I've been working pretty hard—as a matter of fact I've been working like a madman—you see, I've got this thing due Monday, and . . ."

"I just turned in a paper today," she said. "It's really good to have it done. Did I tell you about it?"

"No," said Norman. He leaned back in the chair and kicked off his shoes. "What was it about?"

"Alienation in Shakespeare."

"I see. 'Macbeth: A Middle-Aged Holden Caulfield?' Crazy."

"You don't have to be so sarcastic all the time. I thought it was a good topic."

"Well, it probably is, but the whole idea just sort of underwhelms me."

"There you go again! I don't think you can say two damn sentences without . . ."

"Woah! Hold on! Allow me to beg the hell out of your pardon," he said. "No really, I'm sorry. It's just that, you know, work gets so—hell, I dunno, so stupid. You know what I mean?"

"No," she said. "I just love my classes. But I guess I do know what you mean. I had this history course and we just had so much reading—at least a hundred pages every night . . ."

"That's not what I mean," said Norman. "I don't mind a lot of work. It's just all this numbers graphs monkeys rats reinforcement conditioning shit that we got . . ."

"Must you swear so much?"

"Sorry. Once again I beg the hell out of your pardon. But listen, do you see what I mean?"

"Yes," she said, "I guess so."

"I dunno. I just don't know. I mean, hell, . . ."

"Norman I think you oughta see a psychiatrist." She said it fast, trying to sneak it in.

"What?!" said Norman laughing, running his free hand through his hair. "I do!"

"Norman, I'm being serious. Very serious."

"So'm I. Every Monday. Nine till eleven-fifty. Dr. Bernard, over at the psych department. We play checkers."

"Are you serious? Really?"

"Yes."

"God. I didn't know that. How long have you been going?"

"Since the start of the semester."

"Really? Checkers? That's a little unusual, isn't it?"

"You said it," said Norman. "He's very progressive."

"I see. Sort of like Play Therapy, huh?"

"Yeah, sort of. But listen, I didn't call to discuss my mental health. I just thought that if you weren't doing anything we could get together later and have some coffee or something and talk. I mean, hell, I haven't seen you in so long."

"Aww," she said, sounding almost sad. "I'd like to—I really would, and it's sweet of you to ask—but I can't."

Norman had a rule with Barbara: Never Ask Why Not. He broke it. "Why not?"

"Why not! What the hell do you mean 'why not'! I'm not deformed or anything, or a nun! God! At least a month I haven't seen him then out of the blue—and on a Saturday night at seven o'clock no less—he calls up and says . . ."

"Oh Christ! If that's it—I mean if I've offended your goddam pride by calling at the last minute—well, may the good Lord slap my wrist."

"Norman, I've got a date."

"Well why the hell didn't you just say so? If you'da just said, 'Norman, I've got a date,' that woulda been, . . . I mean, hell, you know how I hate this pride crap."

"Well what do you want me to do?"

"I just told you, for Christ's sake! All you gotta do is . . ."

"I know. But you'da still been mad. Last time I said . . ."

"Last time," said Norman, "you gave me some bullshit about your hair. You had to wash your goddam hair."

"Norman, will you please watch your language?"

"Some nights I just can't seem to do anything right."

"I think you oughta get some rest tonight, Norman. You oughta just stay home and watch TV and go to bed early."

"I'd really like to, Barbara, but I have to wash my hair."

"Norman! Why do you say things like that? Why do you have to be this way? You used to be funny. I used to really enjoy talking to you."

"That was when you had dirty hair."

"You see? You see what I mean?"

Norman sighed. "Yeah. I guess you're right. In the future I promise to do my best to do my duty to God and my country and to obey the scout law. You see? I can't help it! I just open my mouth and Thor, the Samoan God of Sarcasm, descends unto my larynx and behold! he interjecteth his vile product—sarcasm—yea verily and unto the fourth generation was it so!"

"God, Norman. You're nuts. You're crazy!"

"Yes," said Norman, "I'm a victim of intro-punitive guilt and shallow affect."

"Is that what Dr. Barnyard says?"

"Barnard. Yes, that's all he ever says."

"Well," said Barb, "I really have to fly. It's getting late and I got to get dressed."

"OK."

"Get some sleep, Norman."

"OK."

"And keep in touch, y'hear?"

"OK," said Norman, and he hung up. I should have told her, he thought. I should have told her what a bitch she is. I should have told her what a stupid worthless turd she is and the stupid worthless things I do just because she's a God damn woman.

The ringing phone startled him. If that's her, he thought, I'll tell her.

"Hello?"

"Norm? This is Mike. What's shakin'?" Mike only called when he wanted something. Last time it had been Norm's Economics notebook. Mike's was behind, could he just come over and look at Norman's and he'd do the same for Norm someday after all what are friends for.

"Nothing much, Mike. How you been?"

"Mellow, baby, strictly mellow. Workin' my ass off, of course, but keepin' my head above water. Barely. You know how it is."

"Yeah, I know how it is. I've got a lot of work myself. As a matter of fact, I've got this thing due Monday I'm working on now, and . . ."

"Right. I won't keep you long. It's just that I've got this date tonight with your old girlfriend, and I thought . . ."

"Who?" said Norman, controlling his voice but straightening slightly. "Helen?"

"No man, that sleazy hag? No, you know, that blond I used to see you with at the library all the time."

"Barbara."

"Yeah, Barbara. Anyhow, I was just wondering, y'know, what does she like to do? I mean, the house is having this party tonight, and sometimes they get out of hand. D'you hear about last week? Man! Happy and T. J. got just out-of-sight blasted, I mean just bombed—the two of 'em finished a whole damn fifth of Southern Comfort—anyhow, they were just so . . ."

"I heard."

"Oh," said Mike. He sounded deprived. "Anyhow, we're having another one tonight and I wondered if maybe I shouldn't bring old what's-her-name."

"Barbara."

"I mean, first date and everything, some chicks . . ."

"She'll love it."

"Yeah? Really? Christ, she had me fooled. No lie? She'll love it? Hey! Listen! She doesn't—she's not—I mean, you know, I don't suppose . . ."

"Like a bunny," said Norman softly, carefully. Then, "By the way, Mike, did you know that everything's better with Blue Bonnet on it? You can't tell it from the seventy-cent spread. And I mean that from the bottom of my heart, Mike baby."

"What? Norm? Hey, man, I think you best be getting' some sleep. I think you're goin' nuts! Anyhow, thanks for the info. I just . . ."

Norman hung up. Ah yes, he thought, I am going out of my mind. He got up and walked into the kitchen, lit a cigarette, and turned on the radio. Johnny Cash was singing:

Love is a burning thing.

And it makes a fiery ring.

"Pardon me, Mr. Cash," said Norman aloud, "I'm from the American Opinion Poll, and I'm taking a survey. In your opinion, is Norman Hansen in or out of his mind?"

I fell into, into the burning ring of fire;

I fell down, down, down, and the flames, they rose higher.

Norman tapped an ash onto the floor. Sing, Johnny, he thought. Sing your head off.

Cold Turkey: To Sam and Nancy (1977–1978)

*Written over a two-month period between October and November of
1977, when David and his family were in Fairfax, California, on vaca-
tion from Deep Springs College, this story was revised in August of 1978.
Sam was David's older brother, Nancy his brother's wife. Of the five
stories presented here, this is the only one unpublished until now.*

In early September, 1960, I was fifteen, and I'd just completed my first
real summer job: my father had pulled a few strings and gotten me on
a crew of construction plumbers. After work I used to go to Ricky's
delicatessen wearing my ostentatiously grimy work clothes and a hard
hat; I'd sit there over a cherry phosphate and fries, smoking a Kool and
feeling superior to the other patrons, most of whom were well-tanned
high school students who had spent the day swimming at Tower Road
Beach, or playing tennis at Lake Shore Country Club. Being a "construction worker" made me something of an exotic to my friends, who didn't
know that my co-workers referred to me as either "Junior," shortened
from "Junior Executive" because I lived in Winnetka, or "kike," and that
my duties on this construction job consisted of fetching coffee and sweet
rolls for the real plumbers and scouring out recently installed fixtures
before they were inspected by the general contractor. So while everybody
imagined that I spent my days hefting steel pipes while balancing on an
I-beam thirty-five stories above the Loop, in fact I hefted steel wool and
Ajax, on my knees, in every bathroom of a nearly completed luxury hotel
on North Michigan Avenue. The only uses to which I put my hard hat
were to appease the city building inspector and to keep water off my hair
when I forgot to flip the spout from "shower" to "bath" before rinsing out
a tub. One of my co-workers, Vic, was an eighteen-year-old apprentice
from Cicero who lived with his mother and spent his money and affect
on an old customized Ford. "It's a clean deuce, Junior—you know what a
deuce is? '32, right? Chopped and channeled, tuck and roll, radical rake,
full lakers, T-bird mill, bored and stroked, ported and polished, Offy

cam. You know what that means, Junior? Watchoo drive, some kind of
Jew canoe with balloon tires and Dyna-slush transmission? Huh?" Vic,
when he found out I lived on the North Shore, used to pester me to
steal car parts for him from all the Jew canoes by which he imagined I
was surrounded, because while it was true they were clumsy leviathans,
they nonetheless had huge engines, several components of which were
in great demand among local hot-rodders. Vic's particular fetish was the
enormous Weber four-barrel carburetor that came stock on every late
model Oldsmobile equipped with the optional J2 engine.

Now, our family's neighbor in Winnetka, Mr. Cann, happened to own
just such a car. He also happened to own a loud, vicious, and deranged
German shepherd named Lady who had been terrorizing me for years
and had once actually taken a chunk out of my upper left thigh as I tried
to deliver Cann's newspaper.

Here I was, then, on the last weekend before my sophomore year in
high school. I wanted to show my friend Andrew McKing that a summer of "construction work" had taught me a thing or two about the
world south of Evanston; I wanted, at the same time, to show Vic that
his evaluation of me and my suburban monde ("you ain't got a hair on
your ass, none of you") was inaccurate; and I wanted to show Cann that
people who harbor dangerous and demented dogs will be subject, in the
flowering of time, to an anonymous but inexorable revenge. So McKing
and I, armed only with a pair of socket wrenches, a long screwdriver,
and a well-studied Oldsmobile shop manual, loitered around my room,
which overlooked Cann's driveway, until we saw him and Lady going
out for their habitual late-night stroll. We knew that they were heading
for the train station to buy an early edition of the morning paper—no
newsboy in his right mind would go near that house. So as soon as they
were out of sight, we climbed the fence and popped the hood latch on
his Olds. Within fifteen seconds I'd loosened the wing nut and removed
the air filter—remember, this was in the days before a parts thief's job
was complicated by a lot of clumsy pollution control equipment. Four
nuts unfastened the carb from the manifold, one screw freed the throttle
linkage, one clamp disconnected the fuel line. We lifted out the carburetor, set the air cleaner upside down on the block, eased down the hood,
and made our getaway. Total elapsed time, portal to portal: less than
five minutes. We put the carburetor in the trunk of McKing's car, to be
delivered next day to Vic in Cicero ("Oh, by the way, Vic, here's a little

something my buddy and I picked up the other night. Know what this is?") and washed the grease and oil off our hands in the kitchen sink. From the next room emerged the familiar sounds of my grandfather in the grips of a coughing spasm.

He had once been a prosperous salesman of refrigerators, with a large Victorian house on Sheridan Road and a gold seventeen-jewel pocket watch with the initials JCF engraved on the back in elaborate script letters: Julius Caesar Freidman. "Caesar" was his own addition. The Depression ruined his business; I have his watch now, and when you hold it upside down under a bright lamp and tilt it, you can see very small five-digit numbers precisely etched around the monogram by cautious pawnbrokers on guard against fraudulent claims. In 1932, after my mother was married, Grandpa moved to the city and got a job at the old Sherman Hotel as a maitre d'. I found out a couple of years ago that he'd actually worked there as a bartender, but even if I'd known the difference as a child, it would not have mattered; he obviously had an exotic job, unlike my father, a mere lawyer. Grandpa, when my mother took me to visit him at work, would hoist me onto a high bar stool, fix me a Coke in a glass with miniature ice cubes and a slice of lemon, and solemnly introduce me to the impressive-looking men he was always talking to. Once, one of these men turned out to be Ray Scalley, former shortstop for the Cubs. I was dazzled. Did it matter to me at that minute that Scalley's lifetime average was well under .275, and that he'd been one of the league's most notorious chokes? That he'd never been able to move to his right? That as an infielder and a hitter, he was a ludicrous gangly parody of my hero, Nellie Fox, the Sox second baseman after whom I'd modelled my own punchy batting style, my unorthodox sidearm flip to first, and my wad of Dubble Bubble tucked in one cheek, adolescent homage to Nellie's chaw of Red Man tobacco? None of this mattered, believe me, as I stood there shaking the hand of a one-time major leaguer—the hand that had tagged out Musial and Robinson and Campanella. Never mind that the same hand had frequently bobbled routine ground balls, or come off the pivot with a throw into the lower box seats. It doesn't matter even now, as I look back on the scene and realize that the whole encounter was a setup. Scalley just happened to be in the bar when my mother and I came in? He just happened to have with him an official National League baseball, autographed by him and his old Cub teammates? Come on! And, as I picture it now, is that a wink Grandpa and my mother exchange as I stand there speechless and awestricken? And is there cash in that white envelope Grandpa slips Scalley after we've left? Say it ain't so, Ray!

But so what if it is? This still beats an afternoon visiting my father's office at Kixhugh, Farr, and Morse, where the big thrills were a fresh comic book (one of the innocuous ones approved by Parents' Magazine), an elevator ride, a few words with a South Side slumlord real-estate-nik, and a chance to watch the water cooler tank belch basso bubbles as the spout spit an icy stream into my small folded paper cup. No sir—give me the dim, leathery Sherman Hotel Bar, with its seven-inch black-and-white TV set behind the counter tuned to the Cubs game or the fights, and my grandfather laughing softly with his cronies, all of whom smoked cigars, most of whom were fat, and some of whom, I infer in retrospect, must have been bookies or ward heelers.

When he retired and moved in with us in Winnetka, Grandpa was still fat and a cigar smoker. He still wore dark three-piece suits with a heavy gold watch chain across the vest. I still played baseball—I was on the freshman team at high school, but I never got into a game unless we had a huge lead, or were hopelessly behind. During his two years with us my interest in baseball got smaller and smaller. Grandpa got more and more withered until even the interior contours of his mouth shrunk, and his dentures no longer fit, so that he had trouble eating, and midway through every meal he'd gag on his loose teeth, making terrible wet retching sounds, spitting chewed food onto his plate as he tried to get up and shuffle feebly to the bathroom. There, within easy earshot of the table, he'd retch for another couple of minutes, then emerge, pale and chagrined. "Sorry, kids," he'd say, and we'd all pretend nothing had happened. Once, when I had a friend over for dinner, Grandpa's gagging got so bad that he couldn't even manage to stand up. He turned red and gestured jerkily, fighting for air. I thought he was going to die. My father finally pried open his mouth with one hand, and with the index finger of the other, reached in and flipped out the dentures. They clattered down and lay there, pink and saliva coated, among the uneaten peas and car-rots. Grandpa slowly caught his breath and I wished that one of us, pref-erable him, were dead. For two years, this dapper pink bald fat man had been sitting in my family's spare room coughing and coughing, and each cough seemed to deflate him a little until his dark vested suits fit him like drop cloths, and he stopped dressing and spent all day shuffling around the house in his slippers and an old purple wool robe, and his skin didn't fit so he looked more and more shriveled and hollow until finally one Sunday afternoon in October he coughed himself to death. I'll get to that.

I was awakened by Cann's starter motor whining away under my window. Normally I liked to sleep late on weekends, but I figured this vignette would be too good to miss, so I got up and watched. After a few minutes of fruitless cranking Cann decided to investigate. He opened the hood and poked his head around for a couple of minutes. Then, in spite of the fact that his loose air filter was staring him in the face, upside down, his throttle linkage wasn't linked to anything, and his fuel line was dripping gasoline all over his shiny loafers, he slammed his hood and started to crank some more. I laughed to myself and wrote off Cann as the typical suburban moron who probably thinks that when you unscrew a light bulb, electricity flows out the socket.

At that point I got a whiff of gasoline fumes and noticed that there was smoke coming from under the hood. I opened the window and yelled, but Cann couldn't hear me over his grinding starter. So before I could even stop to calculate the consequences, I was downstairs in our basement rummaging for the fire extinguisher, then outside and over the fence. By then the smoke was thick and black. I deftly threw open the hood—much too deftly, if anybody had known to notice—and flames shot out. Cann ran for cover, as I doused his entire engine. In the process, the air filter slid off and I saw that the fuel line was hanging right over the badly corroded distributor cap. When Cann had cranked the engine, gasoline must have dripped onto his arcing points. I gave the whole car another spray for good measure. Then I sprayed down Cann's dog, who had taken it upon himself to snarl and bark at me. Meanwhile, a small crowd had gathered: Cann, my father, my mother, Mrs. Cann, and the postman.

"What's going on?" asked my father.

"My God damn car blew up, that's what."

"I heard him trying to get started, and then I smelled something funny. By the time I got to the window, I could see smoke," I said.

"I think you saved my life."

"Well, I don't know about that . . ."

"Look," said the postman, leaning under the hood. "The carburetor's gone."

"Really?" said Cann. "Are you sure?"

"Isn't it that big loose thing over there?" I asked, pointing at the air filter.

Everybody assured me that it was not.

A distant siren was getting closer and louder. "Who called the police?" I asked.

"That's probably the fire department," said my mother. "I did."

A hook-and-ladder truck and a police car arrived, and despite the fact that the fire was quite dead, they insisted on thoroughly drenching the entire car, upholstery and all. Then they hosed down the driveway until there was no trace of gasoline, while a policeman interviewed Cann and me. It turned out, the officer informed us, that Cann's car was one of many that had been stripped of their carburetors in recent months. "West Side punks," he said. "They use them on their hot rods. If I were you, Mr. Kahn, I'd get me a dog."

"Cann," said Cann.

"He has one," I said.

"And he didn't bark last night?"

"She. No, Officer, not a sound."

"I didn't hear anything either," I volunteered.

"Some dog," said Cann.

I excused myself from the conversation and made a quick call to McKing. Within a half hour he'd called back to let me know that not only the carburetor, but also the wrenches, the screwdriver, the oil rag, the shop manual, and the shirt he'd worn last night were in a weighted burlap sack on the bottom of Lake Michigan, ten or fifteen feet off the end of the Glencoe pier, where, to the best of my knowledge, they reside to this day. As I hung up I heard Grandpa gagging over his breakfast.

Late one Friday night about a month later, I walked in the back door of our house after an evening spent with McKing and a couple of other friends driving around smoking cigarettes and drinking beer, dumping garbage on the lawn in front of the Winnetka Police Station, rotating street signs, shining flashlights on the make-outs in Gillson Park, pissing in planters, putting condoms over the exhaust pipes of parked cars, igniting beer farts, harassing the latest ex-con counterman at the Hubbard Woods Toddle House, blowing up mailboxes with cherry bombs, and mooning the crowds coming out of Beth El. I sat down at the table in the dark kitchen, slightly drunk from the beer and from the heady excitement of another typical date-less teen-age rich-kid Friday night of the pre-dope era. I was eating a dill pickle, so that when I checked in with my parents—at least one of whom I had to awaken whenever I came home "no matter how late, just so we know you're safe"—so that when I said "I'm home" they could not smell hops, malt, or tobacco, but pure wholesome garlic. Suddenly the overhead light came on. Standing by the switch, blinking, in his old ratty robe and pajamas, barefoot, was my grandfather.

"Hi, Grandpa. You're up late."

"Your clever friends," he said. As I was walking from the car to the house, they'd burned rubber down about fifteen feet of our driveway.

"Sorry."

"I couldn't sleep anyway. I've become a very light sleeper."

He sat down across from me and I found myself hoping he wouldn't try to eat anything. Then I noticed that his teeth were out so it didn't matter. My mood immediately improved.

"My friends were trying to be funny."

"Your friends are punks. You're a punk, too, but I'm hoping you'll grow out of it."

To me the word "punk" always sounded like it belonged in a Paul Harvey newscast or a Tribune editorial; it brought to mind images of James Dean and Elvis Presley. Vic was a punk. My friends and I considered ourselves different. More refined. We wore Ivy League button-down shirts, chinos, poplin windbreakers, and scuffed penny loafers.

"That's right, Grandpa, and I've just come home from a big rumble. Protecting my turf. Luckily only two of my gang got snuffed, man, but we got six of them Highland Park Jesters."

"It ain't funny, McGee," he said. "You've probably been up to some kind of no-good." He thought about that for a moment, looking down at the table. "Myself, I used to turn over outhouses," he said. Then he looked up and focused on me. "Got a smoke?"

Since both my grandfather and I passed ourselves off as nonsmokers, the question took me by surprise, and I didn't know quite how to respond. My father hated tobacco, and I went to great lengths to hide my indulgence. I gargled Listerine four or five times a day. I munched on Sen-Sen and Clorets. I alternated smoking hands to avoid collecting nicotine stains. Before entering the house I always concealed the pack I was carrying, not in a pocket, where the rectangular bulge could give me away, but stuffed in my underpants; when I got to my room, I would then hide it carefully in the back of my socks drawer. Grandpa, for his part, had been commanded after his latest chest X-ray, which I suspect looked like the aftermath of an ink war, to stop smoking immediately. Everyone thought he had complied. He'd gone "cold turkey" and as a result felt like a "spring chicken"—his own little extended metaphor, not bad, he allowed, for an immigrant ("It's a play on words, Bobby. A fowl play, you might say"). He became an evangelical nonsmoker, trying to convert my mother, who consumed three packs a day, by ceaselessly testifying to his own improved condition: "I can smell the air, Joan. I can taste food. I'm ahead five bucks a week."

"But you still cough. Your clothes still smell like an ashtray."

"You expect miracles overnight? I smoked for fifty years!"

Anyway, when he asked me for a cigarette, I was stunned.

"I thought you quit. Dr. Eisner's orders."

"I quit cigars. As for cigarettes," he said, "what Dr. Eisner and your mother don't know won't hurt them. Do you have one or not?"

"As a matter of fact," I said, standing up and reaching into my briefs, "I do seem to recall having some Kools around here somewhere. Ah," I said, extracting the package, "here they are. Imagine that." I pushed the pack across the table.

"Oy," he said. He gingerly took one out, lit it, and leaned back, inhaling lightly as he shook out the match.

"Keep the pack," I told him. "How did you know I smoked?"

"Bobby," he said, "for years your mother has smoked twenty packs a week. Two cartons. For the past few months, her stockpile in the linen closet has been shrinking at the rate of two-and-a-half cartons a week. Somebody's been filching four, five packs and I'm only responsible for two of them. I was not born yesterday." He smoked in silence for a couple of minutes. "It's a rotten habit and I hope someday you'll give it up." He looked past my shoulder into the darkened kitchen and paused. "Myself, I started on corn silk rolled in newspaper."

"Tell me about these outhouses you used to turn over."

"Well," he said, "there's nothing much to tell. We'd wait until right around bedtime, when folks were likely to be making a deposit, if you know what I mean. Then we'd hide behind a fence, and when we saw somebody go in an outhouse we'd hesitate about thirty seconds to be sure he was in the act, then we'd tiptoe up behind and turn it over. Mostly they were nothing but tall shacks, sitting over a hole in the ground. We'd turn it over and run like hell. Nobody ever caught us, because we were careful, and also because it's damned hard to run with your trousers around your ankles." He took a final pull on his cigarette, crushed it out, and smiled down at the table. "Boys will be boys." He took another cigarette from the pack and lit up, this time inhaling deeply.

"What else did you do?"

"Oh, I don't know, Bobby. Nothing much. We didn't have much time, and we didn't have cars. And then there was the war." He smoked quietly. I was dying for a smoke myself but afraid of getting caught.

"Gimme a puff, Grandpa?"

He handed me the cigarette. I took a drag and gave it what would have been considered an impressive treatment by the crowd in the second-floor boys' room at New Trier High School: I opened my lips a crack, extended my jaw, and snorted vigorously, sucking the escaping smoke up through my nostrils: your classical French Inhale, as exotic and darkly attractive as a French Kiss or a French Tickler. Or a French Laundry, which I probably thought was one where they washed your shirts by tongue. Then instead of exhaling straightforwardly, I ejected a rapid-fire series of flawless smoke rings, a talent I had cultivated by hours of assiduous practice in front of various mirrors.

As each ring got farther from my mouth it increased in size and decreased in velocity, until it hung in one spot, shimmering. Then its successor would pass through it, until it too stopped. Et cetera. Out there over the kitchen table my smoke rings were putting on an air show that made the Goodyear Blimp look erratic. Grandpa didn't notice.

"Actually," he said, "we did all sorts of things. We filched vegetables. We snuck onto the streetcar. Mostly we snuck into the ballpark. We had a hundred ways into the ballpark and none of them cost a penny."

If he had a hundred ways I'd already heard them all, and I was in no mood to hear any of them again. The one puff I'd taken was too big; I felt slightly sick. I had the start of a beer hangover.

"We did a lot of mischief," he went on, "but never anything malicious. We never hurt anybody, and we never stole."

"You just said you filched vegetables."

"Filching is one thing. You filch vegetables from somebody's back yard. You filch cigarettes or change from your parents. Stealing is something else. You steal from stores. You steal things people need. You steal," he said, taking an enormous puff of smoke, "carburetors."

He literally choked on the word. Before the first syllable was out he began sputtering and by the last he was in a full-scale coughing jag. I got up to fix him a glass of water, because he always wanted a drink when a fit ended. But this fit didn't end; it got worse. He wheezed, choked, and gasped. He grabbed at his throat with both hands. In a panic, I ran upstairs and roused my father.

"Grandpa's choking! In the kitchen!"

He was still at it when we got there.

My father yelled in his ear, "Raise your arms, Dad," and began to slap him firmly on the back with the flat of his hand. The coughing diminished and stopped. Grandpa, his face pale and covered with sweat, tried to drink some water. That started him off again, but only briefly.

"OK now, Dad?"

"Yeah, fine, Sam. Thanks."

"Can I help you to bed?"

"No, thank you, Sam. I'll be OK." He stood up and began to shuffle toward his room.

"What's going on here?" My mother, awakened by the noise, stood in the kitchen doorway in her oversize white terrycloth bathrobe. "Are you all right, Dad?"

"Nothing at all. I'm fine. Me and Bobby here were having a small chat and I got to coughing."

At that moment I remembered the half-empty pack of Kools lying on the table, directly under the hanging lamp. The pack suddenly seemed not only oversize and shiny but situated in such a way as to demand attention. All the perspective lines in the room converged on it, and on the ashtray next to it, complete with ostentatiously smouldering butt. The entire kitchen was like a clumsy quattrocento cartoon, designed to emphasize to the dullest imaginable viewer that in a room populated by one person too old to smoke and one too young, somebody, nonetheless, was smoking. My mother was a slow awakener, but not so slow as to miss this.

"And to whom might these belong?" Her syntax always turned British when she was angry. Now she was pointing at the cigarettes as though they were pornographic.

"They might belong to the Sheik of Araby," Grandpa said. "They might belong to Fibber McGee. But in actual fact, Joan, they belong to me." He winked at her with exaggerated charm.

"Dad, you know what Dr. Eisner said."

"I know what he said, Joan, and I don't want to discuss it. I'm going to bed."

"Well," said my mother, who found it hard to sustain moral outrage at smoking, "just don't think I'm anybody's fool. You've been smoking my cigarettes since you quit cigars, to the tune of four, five packs a week." She gave him a wistful smile and he winked again.

"You weren't born yesterday, Joan."

"I'm going to bed," said my father.

"Me too," I said.

The actual death was about as undramatic as a death can be. A couple of weeks into October he caught the flu and stopped coming to meals. My feelings about this were mixed. The flu turned into pneumonia, and he stopped getting out of bed at all. Once or twice a day I was ushered into his room to kiss him on the cheek and ask him how he felt, but by this time he was rarely awake except to cough. His face was thin and bristly. My mother gave me to understand that he was in diapers. Then one Sunday afternoon when my brother and I were shooting baskets in the driveway, my father called us inside and sat us down around the kitchen table.

"Grandpa just died," he said.

"In there?" I asked, for no reason that I have ever been able to discern.

"About an hour ago. Dr. Eisner's here now."

"What should we do?" I was hoping we wouldn't have to pay some sort of last respects, or stick around while they did whatever it was they did to dead people.

"Well," said my father, "some men will come in an ambulance. Stay out of their way. You can go finish your game at the park."

"Will Mom and Grandma mind?" Somehow the idea of playing one-on-one or "ghost" while a bunch of strangers hustled away what was left of my grandfather didn't seem right.

"It's OK."

So we played basketball until dark, then came home, ate delicatessen, and watched TV. We tried to be quiet and inconspicuous. When my mother came in to kiss me good-night—something she hadn't done in years—she sat on the edge of the bed for a while, crying quietly. I felt tired and embarrassed, but I didn't feel like crying. My own lack of emotion came to me with a mixture of chagrin, surprise, and relief.

The memorial service was three days later. Afterward, we sat shiva. Aunt Rose and my mother got drunk. Aunt Jo and Grandma sat together in a corner looking at old photograph albums. My father kept busy refilling drinks and trays. Toward evening, when people began to leave, I found myself standing by the buffet with Rose, Jo, and my mother, eating leftover sliced turkey, potato salad dregs, soggy lettuce leaves, and brackish pitted black olives.

"You know, Joan," said Rose, "it's too bad Julie couldn't have lived to see Bobby grown up. He always told me he wanted to stay alive long enough to have great-grandchildren."

"Bullshit, Rose, if you'll pardon my French," said Jo. "He told me he just wanted to stay alive long enough to see the Cubs in the World Series again."

At this they all had a good laugh-cry.

"He loved his Cubbies," said my mother. "When I was a girl and he went to the ballpark he'd always keep a score card. That man could look at it a week later and tell you everything that happened. And I don't mean just who did what, I mean what the count was on Hank Sauer when he was decked by an inside curveball that didn't break."

"I think he went to his grave convinced that the Cubs would be first division next year, and that the year after they'd win the pennant," said Rose. "Is that right?"

She was asking me. Grandpa and I had had a standing bet on every Cubs and Sox game, so I was apparently known as his baseball confidant.

"That's right," I said. I was suddenly uncomfortable. My necktie was chafing. I excused myself and went out to shoot baskets in the dusk.

After it got too dark to see, I snuck into the garage and took a cigarette from the package my mother always kept on the ledge over the glove compartment. Sitting in the front seat of our Pontiac station wagon, I lit up and inhaled deeply. One breath was insufficient to expel all the smoke, but I immediately inhaled again anyway. Over and over I did this. I took in smoke every breath. The coal burned bright red, and the car filled with fumes. I had to shut my eyes, but they still stung. When the cigarette was about half gone, I became dizzy and nauseated. Then I started to sweat and cough. Finally, hot tears flowed. I jerked open the door and after a few minutes of breathing in the cold fresh air, I went back in the house, still shaky. My mother and father were sitting at the kitchen table.

"You look awful," said my mother.

"I feel terrible."

As I climbed the stairs I heard my mother say, "He's been crying, Sam. He went outside to cry."

Well, Grandpa, here are a couple of things I want to pass along.

The Cubs, although they still play on real grass, in real daylight, in a real baseball park, rarely play anything resembling real baseball after July: they're still strictly second division. Sorry.

Since your death, I've been a fraternity boy, a fraternity drop-out, a history major, an intellectual, a war-protester, a draft-resister, a dope-dabbler, and an assistant professor. I think that at one point I may have had a small nervous breakdown. All that was before I was twenty-seven and believe it or not it was all considered normal. Now I have one profession, one wife, two children, two cars, and three degrees. I try to work hard without being fanatic, and resist quackery without being rigid. I try to be spontaneous without being a psychopath, and to have self-esteem without being a narcissist. I try to be decent and open, even if that means sometimes being a fool and sucker. These endeavors give me some pleasure, yet I am frequently anxiety-ridden, overcome by a desire to atone, to apologize, without really knowing what for. In 1971 I gave up smoking. Cold turkey, Grandpa. Honest.

Show Business (1981)

This story first appeared in the Webster Review 6.

By the time Thomas Jefferson was my age he was already a Founding Father. Shakespeare at thirty-five had polished off a dozen plays, including *Julius Caesar.* Caesar himself, by the way, was a relatively late bloomer: at my age he was only governor of Hither Spain. Napoleon was made first consul of France at thirty-one, and four years later became emperor. By the time Christ was my age, of course, he'd been God for two years.

And me? I'm still a junior partner—still on salary. My major miracle so far in life was giving up cigarettes. That plus a six-year hitch at Foxx and Tuttle, defending subcontractors whose drywall isn't up to code and plea-bargaining for the prodigal offspring of corporate clients, constitute my time on the cross. OK—it's true that I have a lovely wife and a healthy two-year-old, as well as a sufficient income. But it's also true that while these accomplishments rank me just above Willy Loman on the scale of Middle Class Achievement, I'm still trailing Ozzie Nelson.

Enough! Forgive me this self-pity. It comes in a package with my delusions of grandeur. Hang in there. The sex and violence are coming right up.

"Robert," said my grandmother when she telephoned me last week, "come and have supper with us on Friday. Come early. Your cousin is going to be on Merv Griffin!" This invitation should have put me on my guard at once. I'd been burned in a similar incident six years ago, when I accompanied my grandparents to San Francisco for the opening of Debbie's first film. For the twenty months prior to that night, during the whole time the picture was in production, amidst all the prerelease publicity, my grandparents had been in the immigrants' equivalent of heaven: their granddaughter, only two generations from the sweatshops, a Hollywood Movie Star! The movie she starred in, alas, turned out to be pompous and turgid—except for the sex scenes. Not just your "full frontal nudity," as they say in the industry, and none of your simulated lovemaking, either. No siree, when Debbie Pearl (born Perlstein) breaks into the skin trade, it's not smut, it's "courageous," and it's in a "serious" film with a multi-million-dollar budget, directed by a Cannes winner and filmed on two continents. None of which diminished in the least my desire to crawl under my seat and evaporate when, sitting next to my octogenarian grandparents, I had to watch their Little Debbie, the Movie Star, flesh of their flesh, perform on a twenty-nine-year-old ex-busboy from Jersey City what is still euphemistically called in many jurisdictions a "crime against nature."

And what were my grandparents' reactions to this? Did they have the simultaneous coronaries I feared? Did they rush from the theater and jump off the Golden Gate Bridge? None of the above, folks. As far as I could tell, they weren't even embarrassed. My grandfather, I'm convinced, managed to persuade himself that Debbie was performing some sort of elaborate first aid—some exotic variation of mouth-to-mouth resuscitation. Grandma's only comment afterward when an enterprising stringer for Herb Caen asked her what she thought of the film was this: "I liked some parts better than others." Meanwhile, the constant barrage of Debbie information to which I am subjected every time I visit my grandparents has never slackened. "Bob, did I tell you? Debbie's going to be interviewed in the *Examiner.*" I fail to find an adequate response, and grunt instead. "Robert, I'm so excited! Debbie's been invited to the Warsaw Festival!" Grunt. "Debbie's been offered another film!" "Oh? *Guess Who's Coming at Dinner*? *Citizen Chain*? *Spring on the Virgin*? *The African Drag Queen*? *The 400 Blows*?" Instead of this display of cynicism—I grunt.

So, my grandmother's invitation promised an evening of listening to second-hand press releases and Hollywood gossip, and fighting down sarcasm, in the company of my grandparents, one of whom has been aggressively senile for three years and who inevitably propels me into severe depressions. It will come as no surprise to anybody knowledgeable in the pathology of family dynamics that I therefore accepted the invitation at once.

My grandmother meets us at the door to warn us that Grandpa is having one of his "bad days." This means he's been up moaning since dawn, carrying on about a lawyer who supposedly swindled him out of $25,000 in 1957. When my grandmother tries to reason with him, he accuses her of lying. "Do you know what he said to me?" she whispers to my wife, evidently afraid that our son will be contaminated by such hysteria. "He yelled, 'Rose, get out of here. I can't stand to look at your face!'"

Inside, my grandfather's sitting in his wheelchair with an afghan over his shoulders and a heating pad on his thighs. He seems to be in pain, as usual. Seven years ago they stuck in a pacemaker so that his heart could keep ticking away as regular as clockwork while the rest of his body atrophied into so much rubbish. He has prostate and gum trouble, as well as shingles. Sitting there, his skin fitting him a full size too large, he reminds me of one of the desiccated, shriveled pieces of fruit that I usually find under the back seat of the car when I finally get around to cleaning it out. From just behind the point of his chin, twin veins drape like chains on a swag lamp and disappear into his turtleneck. I have the sudden perception that without the collar to hold them in, these veins would suddenly swing free into his lap like unplugged cords. He's staring through unevenly perched bifocals at the TV, which is off. Merv Griffin isn't scheduled to come on for another two hours, but my grandfather is so eager that he can't look away to acknowledge our arrival. Grandma puts her mouth near his ear and says, "Herman, the kids are here."

"Oh," he says, continuing to look at the blank TV. Susan and Grandma retire to the kitchen to finish the lunch dishes, leaving me and my son with the old man. After a few minutes of silence he says, "Turn on the TV. Mike Douglas, number five. Louder, Bobby, I don't hear so good anymore." One of Mike's guests happens to be black. "Look," Grandpa says, "let me explain you something. The blacks, they get a salary from the government. Free land, too. Some of them are very rich, Bobby. It isn't fair." All of a sudden, a concern for fairness! From a man who made his fortune on property depreciation schemes and capital-gains loopholes! Whose idea of "developing" real estate is to chop all the stately old oak trees off of a lovely hill, then level it and put up a condominium called "Oak Hill." My impulse at this point is to trot out my irony—against a senile eighty-eight-year-old who never went past the seventh grade! To marshal my rhetorical forces, summon my command of the facts—in short, to argue as though I were in court! Instead, I grunt and fume. Finally he wheels himself away and stares at the TV.

And there he sits, unable to distinguish between the shows and the commercials. One minute he's watching Tony Bennett, and the next he's riveted to a grocery store ad featuring a lady who's so delighted with the produce that she starts fondling a green pepper and doing a little two-step with the box boy. "What's she saying?" Grandpa asks me. While I'm still fumbling for an explanation, he directs me to wheel him into his office, where he hands me the telephone directory and says, "Look up Dorfman, Samuel K." As I thumb through the book he informs me that Debbie is going to be on TV. "I think she's on Ed Sullivan. That's some girl, your cousin."

"Grandpa, Ed Sullivan's been off the air for years. It's only Merv Griffin."

"That's right. Ed Sullivan."

"Grandpa!" I start, but then I catch myself. Why argue? I find Dorfman's number and yell it into Grandpa's ear.

"Dial it, will you please? I can't see the numbers anymore."

"Mr. Dorfman, please," I say into the phone, and Grandpa holds out his bony hand for the receiver.

"Dorfman?" he says after a moment. Suddenly he's animated and vital; he leans forward in his wheelchair and looks straight across his desk, as though it's Dorfman and not me standing there next to the antique brass lamp. "Listen, you thief. You're a crooked, lying shyster. Do you hear me? A crooked bastard. You're a regular *dreck.*" He's shouting into the phone and spitting furiously, all the way to my shirt front. "Listen, *gonif.* This is Herman Fried. I don't give a damn about the twenty-five thousand. I got plenty more where that came from. I got a granddaughter on Ed Sullivan, too. But you—I hope you get a cancer on your lips. I hope you have to crap through your *pupick* into a bag! I hope your granddaughter marries a *shvartze!* Did you hear that?"

"Herman!" says my grandmother, who's run in from the kitchen, "I've begged you to stop this." She snatches the phone and says, "Sam, this is Rose. I'm sorry. Yes, I know. I will. Thank you, Sam."

"That *dreck* crook stole my money," he says when she's hung up. "I trusted him and he robbed me blind." Grandma gives him a look and a shrug and starts to wheel him back to the TV. "And you," he shouts, trying to look back at her over his shoulder, "you still play canasta with his wife!" Then he looks straight at me, desperate for an ally. "Bobby, she plays canasta with that bastard's wife!"

"It's OK, sweetheart," Grandma says to Gabriel, who's standing in the doorway crying. "Your Bumpa was upset, but now he's all better."

The Merv Griffin show this afternoon is a panel discussion of cocaine. The guests are a medical researcher, a government official, and Debbie.

The doctor begins with a history of cocaine through the ages, then sum-marizes its pharmacological properties. The official outlines its effects and dangers, and the extent of its abuse. After nearly a half hour of this drivel, during which Debbie sits quietly with a slight smirk on her face, Merv brings her into the conversation by asking her if her own impres-sions agree with the experts. Her answers are delivered in such a way as to indicate that while these clowns had their noses in law books and test tubes, hers was at the business end of a straw. Clearly, Merv has asked her to be on his show as the voice of extensive firsthand experience with a dangerous and illegal drug. Yet to view my grandparents during all this, you'd think it was a 4-H Jamboree and Debbie was dilating on the finer points of putting up apricot preserves. "There she is, Rose, that's her!" Grandpa says every time Debbie's on camera—and every time a female appears in a commercial. Meanwhile, Merv's handing her little pieces of cocaine paraphernalia, and she's explaining to the American public what they're for. "This is a fancy razor blade. It's used to pulverize the cocaine into a fine dust and cut it into a straight line for snorting. This little spoon is solid gold, and you use it to hold the cocaine up to your nostril. This is a mirror with straight grooves etched in it . . ." And on she goes, as lovely, articulate, and ingenuous as ever, until Merv interrupts for a commercial. "Well," says Grandma, "I think she's conducting herself very well. Those men are so stuffy!" "Grandma!" I want to yell. "This isn't a script she's reading! This is real! She really takes dope! Up her nose, for God's sake! The same nose that cost your daughter and son-in-law so much to get fixed!"

When they return to the air, Merv asks Debbie, who by now is begin-ning to relish her role as the Cocaine Maven of Southern California, to describe the effects of the drug on the user. Her account seems to be a testimonial, comparing cocaine favorably with heroin, angel dust, and assorted pills that she refers to only by color, as though every sentient human being on earth knew the difference between a Red and a Green. "The only bad thing," she says, "is that it's a fascist drug. You keep taking it and getting into a more and more aggressive space." Here, the experts disagree with her. They tell her that there is no survey research to show evidence of a link between cocaine use and overt violent behavior, that native cultures of astounding passivity have been ingesting the coca plant for years— "Wait a minute," Debbie breaks in. "Have either of you ever taken cocaine?" They both confess that they have not. "Then let me tell you something about how it is. There are people in LA who can stick a finger in one nostril and out the other. There are people who tell you they have the sniffles every day of the year. I know people who wake up every morning and have a toot before they hit the freeway. If that's their trip, fine. That's the space they're in. But I also have friends whose old men do a lot of cocaine and then beat them up. That happens quite a bit."

"You know of this personally?" the official asks.

"Yes," she says, shooting Merv a look, "and so does everybody else in show business."

"We'll be right back," Merv says, "after this brief message." Again, no visible reaction from my grandparents. The apple of their collective eye has just confessed to several million viewers that she's on intimate terms with forms of behavior that every culture known to man has considered taboo since the beginning of time. My grandmother's comment? "Robert, don't you think Debbie's too thin?" Of course she's thin, Grandma! There's no calories in dope! My God!

For the rest of the show, Merv conspicuously ignores her. Afterwards, while Grandma and Susan set the table and conduct a postmortem on Debbie's appearance, Grandpa corners me and launches into an encomium. "That's some cousin, Bobby, isn't it?" Grunt. "Do you know how much she got for that last movie? Two million dollars. Imagine that!" In his dotage, Grandpa's once-sharp mind has begun to misplace decimal points. Instead of disabusing him, I nod. And grunt.

This euphoria lasts through the evening news and well into dinner. Finally, between the meat and the noodle pudding, he has an arthritis attack. "Rose, I got pain, get me a Darvon. Oooo!" Before dessert, he's been taken to bed, a beaten man, leaving behind as his totem a half-chewed veal chop. We contemplate our ice cream in silence.

Suddenly Grandpa calls to me from his bed. "Bobby! Baaahbeee! Come here!" Between sobs he confides his hope that the Angel of Death will come and carry him away before morning. I have heard this wish before; I can neither agree nor disagree without seeming cruel. So instead, I look down at his withered figure under the comforter; I breathe in the mingled odors of hair oil, stale urine, and Ben-Gay; I wrench from myself, for the hundredth time at least, the decision to love him, the free verdict of my heart; and I give him a perfunctory kiss on the forehead.

On the way home, just as we get to Lake Shore Drive, with Gabriel finally asleep and traffic thinning out, a startling thought occurs to me:

what does my grandmother say to Debbie about me? The grandson with no TV shows, no movies, no festivals? Who's never been in *People*? "Oh, Debbie, it's so exciting! Your cousin Robert copped a plea for Brauer the roofer's son and got him off with three months' probation! Would you believe it? That cousin of yours has been married for *twelve years*! To the same woman, no less! What stability! What reliability! What *prudence*!" Even stipulating the most generous and creative description, I still come off sounding like a boiled potato in the feast of life.

And what have I done to earn this role? According to what bizarre system of justice and retribution is this fate being visited on me? OK, sure, I didn't have to watch the Cossacks bayonet my parents for sport. I didn't ride steerage to New York when I was six. I never knew a Nazi. I wouldn't know a push-cart from a go-kart, a sweatshop from a sweet-shop. I never had to scheme and slave my way through the coat-and-suit business into real estate until I finally got my Cadillac and my house with a turn-around driveway on Sheridan Road. Still, aren't I possessed by the same demons? Don't I work hard? Look: I get up before dawn five days a week and put my nose to the typewriter, cranking out my latest brief, whatever it may be. I eat a high-fiber, low-calorie breakfast. At the office, I don't fool around with the secretaries or the Xerox machine. I bill diligently. I eat lunch from a paper bag—and save the bag. An hour a day I donate *pro bono publico*. I jog. I hug my kid daily. I help with the dishes and do my share of the diapers. Before bed I read the reports and neaten up the house. My wife and I have sex at least twice a week and she always has at least one orgasm per session. I make no kinky demands, honest. I recycle glass and garbage. I'm a member of the Sierra Club. I wear a seat belt and drive fifty-five. I look both ways before crossing. I clean my plate. I never put coins in my mouth. God damn it, I'm the little piggy who built his house out of bricks! I'm the rabbit who steered clear of Mr. McGregor's garden! I'm the tortoise, as opposed to the hare! I'm doing everything right! So why am I still a junior partner? Why do I feel like I'm on a year-to-year contract with the cosmos? Hey, God! Hey, Merv! Hey, Grandpa! I'm your legitimate heir, you thief! You bastard! You traitor! I'm the one who loves you!

Tracy (1981)

This story first appeared in Four Quarters *30, with this note from the editors: "Tracy" is David Schuman's first acceptance; we are sure it won't be his last. He teaches English and is an assistant dean at Deep Springs College, a 'cattle and alfalfa ranch in the high desert of Eastern California."*

As Tracy pulled into Bishop, the setting sun was backlighting snow banners on the Sierra crest. He parked by the Safeway and phoned LA from the booth across the street. He had to deal with two secretaries before he finally got through to Lane.

"Tracy Houston, Mr. Lane," he said, rubbing his hand back and forth across his three-day growth of whiskers. "Up in Bishop."

"Of course, Tracy. What can I do for you?"

"Nothing. I'm fine. I wanted you to know that I got the Case going, but the backhoe needs a fuel pump."

"Can you work around it?"

Sure, Tracy thought. I can scrape with my hands. I can dig with my fingernails. I can move rocks with my goddamn teeth. "No sir," he said. "I thought I'd check with you before I ordered a new one."

"OK, Tracy. Go ahead. Whatever you need."

There was a short silence.

"What else can I do for you, Tracy?"

"Well," he said, looking out of the booth toward the east, where the Inyo Mountains glowed pink in the dusk, "it'll take the better part of a week to get the fuel pump. I figured I'd wait around here till it comes, then take it on up and put it in. By then it'll be too cold to do much of anything else, so I'll just close down for the winter. Silver Peak and Mollie Gibson both."

"Tell you what, Tracy. Order the fuel pump, and while you're waiting, go on up and close Mollie Gibson. Then come back down, and by that time the pump will be in and you can take it up and close down Silver Peak. That'll save me a week's time."

"The trouble is, Mr. Lane, is that makes a couple hundred miles extra driving for me."

"I understand that, Tracy, but I don't pay you for sitting around Bishop. I'd be contributing to the delinquency of a miner. An old miner."

Tracy could hear Lane chuckling at his own joke.

"Call me when they're both closed." Lane said. "I think I can see my way clear to another bonus this year."

"Yes sir," he said. He thought: fifty goddamn dollars.

"Then in the spring, we'll see how you're feeling, and what my needs are. You'll be spending the winter with Herman?"

"Herman died, Mr. Lane. Last April. I got a trailer out on the reservation." Across the street, kids were writing WASH ME in the grime on Tracy's old green Ford pickup. Dust, he thought. He'd emptied a half pint of Old Crow on the way down, and it was making him reflective. You leave anything outside long enough around here and before long it's dust. A dead cow turns into a rotting carcass, white bones, pebbles, dust in the wind. Paint chips and flakes and blows away. Tracy once again rubbed his bristly face. Even skin dries up, and after a lifetime you feel like a lizard with whiskers. "Last April the tenth."

"I'm sorry to hear that."

"He was fifteen years younger than me."

"Well, Tracy, you'll outlive all of us."

I'll sure as hell outlive you, you flatlander son of a bitch, he thought. I'll be working Mollie Gibson and Silver Peak, Lida and Bristlecone Copper, too, when you're a goddamn stiff in some cemetery on a road with a number instead of a name. "I'm seventy-three now, Mr. Lane. My father died at a hundred and eight."

"That's wonderful, Tracy. I have to make some calls now."

"It ain't wonderful for me." He jammed a fist into his pocket. There was an area on his lower forearm where most of the skin had fused to the nylon jacket he'd had on in the fire after the accident. When they'd finally found a hospital that would admit him, and the doctor pulled away the jacket after all those hours, the skin came too, and the raw spot still hurt whenever it rubbed against rough fabric. So he pulled out his hand. "As a matter of fact, Mr. Lane, I'm not sure I'll be working for you in the spring, even if I'm still fit for it. I may be coming into some money."

"One of your prospects?"

"No sir. My lawsuit. From the accident. My lawyer in Vegas is suing the hospital that sent me away. For a hundred grand."

"You told me about that, Tracy. Now I really must hang up. Call me when you get everything closed down, and we'll let spring take care of itself."

"I don't think so, Mr. Lane."

"You don't think so? What does that mean, Tracy?"

Tracy said nothing.

"Have you been drinking, Tracy?"

His ankle was beginning to throb seriously so he shifted his weight off it, carrying himself on one leg and propping himself against the corner of the booth.

"I don't care what you do on your own time, Tracy, but—"

"Mr. Lane," he cut in, "what time I got left is all my own."

"Not when you're on a job for me, it isn't."

Tracy's weight-bearing leg was stiffening up, but his ankle still hurt when he tried to shift back to it. Outside, a man in a pickup, wearing a cowboy hat and a down vest, was arguing over a parking space with a Mercedes owner in double-knits. The last pink light faded on White Mountain Peak, and the long valley twilight began. Tracy took a deep breath. "In that case, Mr. Lane," he said, "I quit."

In the Safeway he bought a bag of corn chips, two pork chops, a package of frozen carrots, Twinkies, a fifth of Old Crow, and a paper. The checkout girl remembered him from when she was seven and he was a crossing guard at the grade school.

He set the grocery bag on the little counter next to the sink, and even before he lit the pilot on the furnace he got out his reading glasses and went through his mail until he found the letter he'd been waiting for: from the lawyer in Vegas. Although the letter was less than a page long, it took Tracy about five minutes to read it through the first time. He lit the pilot and turned on the heat. Then he read the letter a second time, faster. There were some words and phrases he wasn't sure he understood—*continuance, litigation, obstreperous*—but the gist was clear: they had shunted the case off on some new kid named Fleming, and this Fleming was reporting that the best offer he could get out of the Nevada hospital was fifteen hundred dollars, just what Tracy's stay in the Bishop hospital had cost him when they finally got him there. Tracy could, of course, press the lawsuit—but Fleming did not recommend that course of action because of the expense, the lengthy delays, and the odds against him recovering anything: the evidence showed that the Nevada hospital had reasonable cause to think that Tracy was not injured but drunk.

Fifteen hundred dollars, he thought. Seven hours pinned under that goddamn pickup, freezing and burnt and bleeding, and three more while they bat me around from hospital to hospital like a hot potato. And who's this Fleming bastard? What happened to old man Foxx and his talk about a hundred grand?

He put away his groceries, except for the bourbon, and poured himself half a glass. The trailer was beginning to warm up, so he took off his wool jacket and hung it on a hook in the narrow closet. Taped to the inside of the door was a snapshot: Tracy, grinning, wearing his Tony Lama boots, a cowboy shirt with pearl buttons, and a turquoise slide tie. His thin black hair was slicked across his forehead and his glasses were perched cockeyed on his long straight nose. He had each arm around a daughter: June, the younger, pregnant; Joanelle, already a mother twice, hair piled on her head, plump and acting coy for the camera. Behind them was a stand of cottonwoods, sheltering a ranch house made of timbers and random rock. Herman's house. Herman's camera, too.

The doorbell sounded. It was Roy Montes, telling him he had a phone call. "It's your daughter. She's been calling for about a week."

Roy's house was painted light green. In the almost-faded daylight Tracy could make out a couple of gutted cars set up on cinder blocks in the front lawn, hollow sockets where the headlights had been, hoods and trunks raised. They looked like heifers that had eaten too-rich feed, rolled over, and died of bloat. The phone was on the table by the front door.

"Hello, June," Tracy said.

"It's Joanelle, Daddy."

"Ah!" Joanelle lived in Los Angeles. Tracy hadn't seen her since Herman's funeral. "How are you? How're the kids?"

"We're all fine. How are you? Done for the winter?"

"Yes," he said. "I'm done."

"Listen, Daddy, I want to talk to you about Christmas. Did you get the tickets?"

"What tickets?"

"June and Richard are sending you an airplane ticket to Cleveland for Christmas. So you can visit them."

"Well," Tracy said, "that's very nice." Tracy had never been to Cleveland. Richard and June came to Bishop every summer for Richard's research; whenever he visited he always asked Tracy to talk into a tape recorder about the old days.

"We were wondering how long you'll be staying with us down here. Can we count on you for a week around New Year's?"

"Well, Jo, if the ticket's to Cleveland, I don't see how I could do that."

"Daddy, it's by way of LA. We thought you'd spend some time with us on your way home. The kids are counting on it."

Tracy turned his back toward the dining room where the Montes family was eating. He hunched up his shoulders and lowered his voice. "Joanelle, honey, if this ticket is a present from June and Richard, I can't go and use it to visit you folks."

"I don't know what June wrote," said Joanelle, her voice taking on an edge, "but she made me and Joey pay for half of that ticket. It's from us, too, take my word for it."

"I do."

"So?"

"So," said Tracy.

"So you'll spend some time with us?"

"Maybe on my way out," Tracy said. "If I'm going all the way to Cleveland I may as well stay awhile. I may decide to winter with them."

"Daddy," said Joanelle, "June said to make sure you came here after Christmas. On your way home. She and Richard are going to Jamaica on the twenty-eighth and you have to be gone by then."

"I see."

"So we'll count on you."

"Well," said Tracy, "I guess so."

They chatted for a few minutes. Then he talked to his grandchildren and finally hung up. Back home, he poured himself another drink. He turned off the light and looked out the window. The moon was up, so bright it cast sharp shadows. The snowy Sierra peaks looked one-dimensional in the thin light. Tracy remembered the time he'd found the body up on Bishop Pass. He'd been hunting with Herman in Dusy Basin, behind the Palisades where they went every deer season, when an early blizzard came blowing in from the coast. They'd sat it out in a Forest

Service cabin—enjoyed it, in fact, with a good fire, canned food, and whiskey until it ran out, snow piling up over the windows, an occasional flake finding its way through a chink in the logs, settling on the earth floor, and slowly melting. When the weather cleared, they packed up and headed out on snowshoes, and just over the pass, above Saddlebag Lake, they came on the body: a man about forty, a deer hunter from his clothes, but a flatlander, too, with smooth pale skin. He'd huddled up by a boulder and frozen stiff. They tried to pack him out but they couldn't even get him uncurled, so they climbed down and found a ranger and took a sled to bring back the body. Solid as a tree trunk, Tracy remembered, looking out toward the Sierra. We had to lash him on like a buck.

He drained his drink and went to Montes's to phone June in Cleveland. He thanked her for the tickets, and he told her that he couldn't make it for Christmas. He had to stay in Bishop because of his lawsuit. "They're real hopeful," he told her when she seemed dubious. "They got half a dozen lawyers on the case. It'll be worth my while to see this through."

June warned him about lawyers and their pie-in-the-sky promises. She begged him to reconsider, but he was adamant.

"When it's all over, in the spring, I'll take me a trip and visit you and Joanelle both. Or maybe what I'll do is send you all tickets to come out here. We'll have a reunion. I believe that's what I'll do," he said.

"Now Daddy. Don't go counting your chickens."

"I'm not," he said. "But I'm not leaving here this winter, either."

"Well, let us know if you change your mind."

"I'll do that."

"And be careful with the lawyers."

"I'll do that too," he said, and hung up.

The gravel road cut through the desert and ended abruptly at a clearing some five miles east of the four-lane. Tracy left his pickup with several others and, in the moonlight, found the path that zigzagged through the creosote and rabbitbrush. Soon he could smell smoke. He walked steadily in spite of his throbbing ankle.

The sweathouse was a low hut—old horse blankets, burlap sacks, and flour bags draped over a frame of branches held together with baling wire, and standing in willows by a shallow culvert next to a creek. In front, before a parting that served as doorway, was a fire pit with large basalt stones heating up on a bed of coals. Tracy slowly undressed, stacking his clothing in a pile next to the others': crouching, naked except for his glasses, he entered the hut. Sweat popped onto his forehead at once. His glasses steamed up, so he took them off and held them in his hand.

The only light came from the fire outside, and it gave everything a red-bronze tinge. Shadows jumped and shimmered as a light wind played over the coals and made the fire momentarily brighter. Tracy found an empty space on the ground near the entrance and sat down. In the back, deep in shadows, were two men he couldn't make out. Closer to him there were five or six he recognized. Near the center old Paul Moose sat on a cut-down yard chair with his son Louis at his feet. Louis was tending the rocks: every few minutes he'd scoop water from a small drum and pour it over the hot basalt he'd carried from the fire outside with a shovel. Steam would explode in a hiss, filling the hut. Tracy folded his legs, delicately finding a position that didn't hurt his ankle, and breathed deeply. Soon sweat streamed down his face and flowed down his torso from neck and armpits. He kept his eyes closed, heard Louis take out a stone and bring in a fresh one, kept breathing slowly. Images crowded into his mind: Lane, June, deer on the highway, Nevada Hospital, his trailer, Silver Peak, Deadman Summit, Herman, Tule Springs, the Sierra in moonlight. His wife, dead now fifteen years. They passed in review for a long time and he let them enter and exit as they pleased. After five or six rocks had cooled, the images slowed down and finally the image he saw was the inside of the sweat, Louis Moose scooping water onto the basalt: so he opened his eyes. Nobody had moved. He noticed that some of the others were chanting. He closed his eyes again and his thoughts turned to the sounds of others' breathing and chanting, the hiss of steam, the feel of sweat, the sweat and the steam themselves: water from the Sierra snowpack melting into Rock Creek and flowing down the shoulder of the mountain in a thin vein, past aspen and lodgepole, over a fall, then fanning out and slowing down, to wind through the sage and the willow shoots in this culvert where Louis Moose harvested it and turned it into steam, into air for breath. In and out, over and over, eyes closed. In his mind they were breathing the mountain, bathing in the vapor they shared with it and with each other and with all who had sat in the sweathouse.

He woke up the next morning just at first light. The sun was not yet over the Inyo crest, and Tracy was quite cold under his blanket. He'd slept in his clothes.

For breakfast he finished last night's dinner: half a cold pork chop, some Fritos, and reheated coffee. He washed the dishes, made the bed, threw away the mail. As an afterthought, he went through it in the wastebasket until he found the letter from the lawyer; that, he tore neatly in half.

There were no lights at the Montes house, so Tracy drove to the booth near Safeway. He got Lane's home phone from information, but the line was busy, so he walked down the block to the NAPA store and ordered a fuel pump for the backhoe. When he phoned again, he got right through.

"Hello, Mr. Lane? Tracy Houston, up in Bishop?"

"Yes, Tracy."

"I got your Case going, but I think the backhoe's going to need a fuel pump. I wanted to get your OK before I went ahead and ordered it."

"Tracy," said Lane, "you told me all that yesterday."

"I did?"

"You did."

"To tell you the truth," said Tracy, "I don't remember too much of yesterday. My ankle was hurting so I had a couple drinks when I got down. I called you?"

"You did. I told you to order the fuel pump for the backhoe and while you were waiting for it to close down Mollie Gibson."

"I'll be damned."

"Can you do that?"

"Yes sir. I'll get right on it. I'll call you when I have everything buttoned up."

"OK, Tracy. If you can't get me at the office, leave a message with Carol. The secretary."

"Will do."

Tracy had coffee at the grill and then drove down the valley toward Big Pine. The jagged, snowy Sierra loomed to the west, and to the east, in Nevada, were the arid and rolling Inyos. A cold wind was blowing tumbleweed across the four-lane. Tracy remembered the valley before LA stole the water—rich alfalfa fields and tall cottonwoods had dotted the desert. There'd been deer, bighorn sheep, and tule elk. He'd worked on the aqueduct—helped build it during the day, and helped blow it up at night. Everybody had. But it finally went through anyway, as everybody knew it would, and now, thought Tracy, as he faced an unbroken line of cars and motor homes headed north, all we got here is tourists from LA. And coyotes, to eat their garbage. The deer and the bighorn sheep and the tule elk—driven up into the mountains, where they freeze. Or get so hungry they wander down to the highway and jump in front of headlights. And me, Tracy thought, I've been shooting deer for years, and eating them, too—I swerve to miss one and end up under the pickup in a ditch by the road all night.

At the Big Pine General Store, he bought a fifth and some frozen beef, then headed east on the county highway toward Joshua Pass and the Inyos. The sun was over the ridge. The air was cold and bright; it made his lungs feel brittle. Overhead the sky deepened to a dark blue. White Mountain Peak, up behind Mollie Gibson, seemed to throb in the morning sky. It was the only peak in the Inyos with snow. God damn, thought Tracy, if it don't look cold and clean. He took a deep breath. God damn if it don't look close enough to reach out and kiss.

The Winner (1983)

This story first appeared in Four Quarters *32, with this note from the editor: "Since his story 'Tracy' was published here in summer 1981, David Schuman has 'moved from the desert to the rain forest' (Eugene, Oregon) and 'from one side of the podium to the other' (he is now a second-year law student instead of a professor and assistant dean). He continues 'to harbor ambitions to write fiction, although of late my most creative piece of work was an appellate brief in defense of a farmer who had inadvertently trespassed onto his neighbor's blackberry patch.'"*

Every three or four months, Mrs. Steindorf would work up a short piano recital for the hard core of retired music-lovers from Los Angeles, as well as the local professional set and an occasional cultivated cowboy's wife. They all sat in her living room in concentric semicircles around a nine-foot Bechstein, fashioned for Mrs. Steindorf's father by Otto Bechstein himself in 1903, and the only relic from her first life in Germany. The programs ran to Brahms and Chopin—after all, Bishop was a cattle-and-alfalfa town where the old men chewed toothpicks and at night you still heard coyotes in the foothills—but nonetheless she threw in an occasional dose of Hindemith, and they would even sit still for some early Bartók. They arrived early and they did not cough or clap between movements.

These same people also attended the recitals of Mrs. Hargy, who lived fifty miles to the south in the town of Independence and had performed similar programs on the first Thursday of every month for a decade. It was suspected that the two pianists did not get along; thus a rustle went through Mrs. Steindorf's audience one Sunday in late February when, during the second movement of a Beethoven sonata, Mrs. Hargy made an entrance.

Both women were nearly eighty, and both were refugees: there the resemblance ended. Mrs. Steindorf had studied in Leipzig with "the great Schnabel," as she invariably called him. She was tiny and bird-like, and still spoke with a heavy accent. Mrs. Hargy, a Hungarian, was a former pupil

60

of Bartók. She'd learned her manners and her English from a nanny and spoke like a BBC newscaster. She had bright white hair and great bearing. She entered Mrs. Steindorf's living room as though it were empty, and sat near the door. When the piece ended, the two women acknowledged each other with a nod. At intermission, instead of mingling with the audience, Mrs. Steindorf retreated to her bedroom while Mrs. Hargy held court. When asked, she paid Mrs. Steindorf small compliments: "She's quite . . . expressive, isn't she?" She spent some minutes in conversation with Lydia Mangin, Mrs. Steindorf's star pupil, a shy twelve-year-old whose parents had conservatory ambitions for her.

When the program resumed, Mrs. Steindorf played Bartók. Afterwards Mrs. Hargy went to congratulate her, and the crowd around Mrs. Steindorf parted like the Red Sea. The women kissed cheeks. The burghers beamed. "I enjoyed the program immensely," Mrs. Hargy said. She was perhaps ten inches taller than Mrs. Steindorf.

"Ah, but I felt very nervous, especially with the Bartók. I felt like I was poaching."

"Nonsense," said Mrs. Hargy.

"I'm looking forward to your program next week, if I can get a ride. Eight-thirty?"

"Eight o'clock. As usual."

"Righto," said Mrs. Steindorf, who used slang to neutralize her accent. "On the nose. I won't be late and make an interruption."

Lydia Mangin was Mrs. Steindorf's principal joy. Only music could explain the bond between this withered and wary survivor, this daughter of Leipzig's Jewish elite, raised to evenings at the Gewandhaus, lessons with the Great Schnabel, dinner parties for the Duke's brother, walks through the university where her father, the Rector and a famous Egyptologist, presided like a prince—between Mrs. Steindorf, victim of terror and displacement, and Lydia Mangin, twelve, blonde, daughter of an optometrist, child of the open range, companion to cattle and alfalfa. In a strange way they communicated like members of the same family. Lydia would arrive for her lesson and plunk her books on Mrs. Steindorf's table, squirm out of her jacket, and play through the piece she was working on. Conversation was formal: good afternoon Miss Mangin, good afternoon Mrs. Steindorf, how are you today, fine thank you. Mrs. Steindorf stood looking over her pupil's shoulder. Lydia chewed on her lower lip as she played. At the end of the lesson Mrs. Steindorf would bring out four small oatmeal cookies with orange-rind, a family recipe, on a hand-painted Dresden plate, and they would each have two while Mrs. Steindorf critiqued Lydia's progress and sipped tea. "The adagio is pure kitsch, Lydia," she'd say, tracing arcs in front of her face with liver-spotted and arthritic hands. "You know what it is, kitsch?"

"Not exactly."

"Pretension. Tail fins. Windows with shutters that don't close."

Lydia nodded again, still in the dark.

For the parents, Mrs. Steindorf felt pure contempt. "These drayhorses have produced a thoroughbred," she thought to herself as she watched Lydia drive off with the optometrist, bouncing on the seat of his pristine pickup. She had once tried to explain Lydia's talent to them. "She can sense the personality of the music. Do you understand? She has all of the right instincts. She plays Strauss as though she grew up in Vienna and Bach as though she were in church."

"Wasn't Bach a Catholic?" the optometrist asked with suspicion.

"You better believe it," Mrs. Steindorf said, and changed the subject forever.

One day shortly after the recital, Lydia was late for her lesson. After fifteen minutes Mrs. Steindorf's irritation gave way to fear—ambulances, masked men—so she phoned the parents. Mrs. Mangin explained that Lydia was sick.

"Next time, please call to cancel. Now if I can speak to her, I'll give her some exercises for next week."

"She's sleeping just now," Mrs. Mangin said after a short silence.

Three days later a note arrived in the mail. It was typed on flowery stationery, from the optometrist's wife, informing Mrs. Steindorf that Lydia would no longer be studying piano with her. Enclosed was a check covering three months' lessons in advance.

Never before had Mrs. Steindorf lost a student in this way—one she liked, one who had promise. She brewed a cup of tea and reread the note. She had a palpable urge, located, she was surprised to notice, just below her throat, to telephone the Mangins and demand an explanation. Instead she returned the check in a plain envelope and went about her business. Still, during the next weeks, she discovered how much Lydia's lessons had sustained her. Mrs. Steindorf's life was precise and regular.

There were few peaks: the weekly shopping trip in the senior citizen's minivan, random telephone calls from her children, a monthly haircut, recitals. Lydia's lessons had been her weekends; they'd marked passing time; the weeks rose toward them and fell away. Now, she found herself feeling flat. She tired easily and snapped at her students. When the last one left at the end of the day, she'd sit at the piano and watch the sun set behind Mount Tom, and vow to be milder. Formerly a fastidious eater and a consumer of literature in three languages, she now began to improvise dinner—a can of tuna, a frozen entree, a couple of slices of bread with butter and sugar—and eat it watching TV. Frequently she fell asleep in front of the set, only to wake up in the middle of the night, stumble out of her clothes and into bed, and then lie awake until dawn. Lydia's lessons lurked in her mind like a lost lover.

Finally she telephoned. She identified herself to the mother and with no preliminaries said, "I honestly believe you're making a big mistake. Your daughter has a gift and she was developing it rapidly. I don't say this for the money. I have more students than I can handle."

Lydia's mother put the optometrist on. He mumbled something about "second opinions."

"Did she want to quit? She always seemed delighted to be here."

"It's nothing personal," he said. "We were very happy with her progress."

"So?"

"We just thought it might be time for a change. We felt Mrs. Hargy might have something to teach her, too, and we can't afford two teachers."

"She's taking lessons from Mrs. Hargy?"

"That's right."

"But Mrs. Hargy is not a musician! She's a corpse! There's no life in her playing! She's a . . . robot! And you—you're a kidnapper!" She slammed down the receiver, and as it hummed faintly into the evening she stared out at the mountains.

Several weeks passed. At night she imagined confrontations—with the parents, with Mrs. Hargy, with Lydia. In these she was always forceful but calm. She maintained her dignity. She prevailed, and when she did, and the optometrist was apologizing, she was gracious but distant. She drove a hard bargain.

But none of this ever happened, and finally Mrs. Steindorf made a decision. Reviewing her life, she decided that she had too often merely survived where she should have struggled; she had hoped and begged and fled where she should have schemed and fought. She took out her finest notepaper and had a cup of tea to steady her hand and wrote a letter to Mrs. Hargy. She overpraised the April recital; expressed hope that two people with such similar backgrounds, and practically neighbors, might cultivate more of a relationship; and suggested that by way of a start they get together soon for some four-hand. Mrs. Steindorf volunteered to make the trip to Independence. She closed with a long Teutonic formality: "With great esteem, sincerely, your most devoted admirer, Mrs. Hilda Steindorf."

There was no answer.

She waited a week and then another; finally she telephoned. For two days nobody answered, and Mrs. Steindorf found herself suspecting that the Hungarian, notoriously frail and much operated upon, had died. She confronted this possibility with mixed emotions: to die alone, to lie undiscovered and rotting, was one of Mrs. Steindorf's greatest fears. She wished it on nobody. But the thought of inheriting Lydia tempered her dread.

On the third day, just as she was going to make her final try before alerting the police, Mrs. Hargy called her. "I've been in hospital," she explained. "I haven't had time to answer my mail."

"Nothing serious, I hope."

"Ulcers," Mrs. Hargy said. "I'm afraid we'll have to delay our four-hand."

"I'll take a rain check." Mrs. Steindorf hoped the expression evened the score for Mrs. Hargy's flawless inflections. "Should we wait a couple of weeks?"

"At least."

"OK then, how about two weeks from Sunday? As you can see, I'm determined. We can't wait forever, at our age."

After a brief silence, Mrs. Hargy said, "I'm not certain I'll be ready to travel by then."

"Then I'll come to Independence." When she said this, Mrs. Steindorf actually had to squeeze her eyes shut, as if in pain. "Unless you're otherwise tied up."

"No, of course not. I was about to suggest it myself. Shall we say three-thirty?"

"I'll be there," Mrs. Steindorf said. "On the nose."

She had no strategy. She had no ideas. She had only the powerful urge to talk to Mrs. Hargy about Lydia—to explain, to confess, to gossip. To confess what? she thought, riding down to Independence on the bus. Confess like some Catholic? Although it was a warm afternoon in the valley, there was fresh snow in the mountains and the bus was slowed by a steady traffic of skiers heading back to LA after the weekend at Mammoth. Mrs. Steindorf sat on the west side and watched the Sierra. The highway followed the aqueduct, next to the old narrow-gauge right-of-way. Just north of town was a campground and an historical site: the mass grave of victims from the 1872 earthquake. Mass graves made Mrs. Steindorf think in German.

She climbed down in front of the Whitney Vista Motel and walked three blocks to Mrs. Hargy's house, a white cottage on a corner lot. The lawn was green and there were jonquils in the flowerbed. Lilacs were in bloom. Mrs. Hargy answered the door and the two women kissed at each other's cheeks. "Your garden is beautiful," Mrs. Steindorf said, pulling off her white gloves. "In Bishop nothing is up yet. It blows like crazy for weeks. The apple trees blossomed one day and that night it was twenty-three degrees Fahrenheit. How are you feeling?"

"I'm well, thank you," Mrs. Hargy replied. In fact she looked pale and ancient. "Let me take your coat. Shall we play first and have tea later?"

"Fine." Mrs. Steindorf rubbed her hands together and the women slid onto the bench. "Could we raise this a little?"

"I'm afraid that would be too high for me. I'll get you a phone book." But the Eastern Sierra directory was only a half-inch thick, so Mrs. Steindorf sat on an old English-Hungarian dictionary. The piano was a Steinway, a nine-foot concert grand; it filled the half of the room nearest the window. Late afternoon sun filtered through the curtains; for a second Mrs. Steindorf imagined a scene in similar light, from her first life: twelve years old, on the bench with the Great Schnabel, nervous but at the same time at home, cared for. In the next room, hunched over a papyrus, her father, the Rector.

They began with a Mozart concerto. Mrs. Steindorf had practiced it and she played well. The Steinway was stiffer than her Bechstein, but a piano is still a piano. Mrs. Hargy made technical mistakes and lacked her usual precision. As Mrs. Steindorf realized this, she began to pick up the tempo. At the end of the first movement, Mrs. Hargy lit a cigarette, and set it on an ashtray next to the music rest. "Let's take this adagio," she said.

Mrs. Steindorf sang a few measures in a croaking soprano.

"I think that's too fast. We don't want to lose anything here." Mrs. Steindorf fanned cigarette smoke away from her face and capitulated. Midway through the movement Mrs. Hargy missed an entrance and stopped. "I'm terribly sorry," she said, taking a puff on her cigarette.

"Three measures after G," Mrs. Steindorf said, and they began again.

As the afternoon waned, Mrs. Hargy seemed to regain her facility at the same time that fatigue robbed her of its benefits. She played beautifully but made stupid mistakes. Between each movement she lit a cigarette, which burned to an ashen cylinder as she played. Once she tilted it carelessly on the edge of the ashtray; in the middle of a scherzo it burned past its fulcrum and tumbled onto the carpet. Mrs. Steindorf stopped at once but Mrs. Hargy kept playing until she came to a rest and then scooped it up without missing a beat.

When there was no longer enough window light to see the music, Mrs. Hargy suggested a break. "I have trouble at dusk," she said. "I must take my glaucoma drops."

"My eyes," Mrs. Steindorf said, "are as good as ever. The rest of me is falling apart."

"You seem quite strong."

"Knock wood," she said, tapping the piano bench.

Mrs. Hargy served tea and cake. "This is my special almond torte," she said. "I can't eat it but I enjoy making it."

"You must give me the recipe," Mrs. Steindorf said automatically.

"That I can't do, and I'll tell you why." She set down her teacup and pivoted toward Mrs. Steindorf. "There was a cafe in Budapest that was famous throughout Central Europe for its pastries. Even in Vienna it was spoken of with respect. The most famous item of all was this chocolate-almond torte. Winston Churchill, before the war, used to have it flown to him in London." She paused to sip tea. "The proprietors of this cafe had a daughter, and since they were rich and had aspirations, and this was

Budapest, they assumed she would be a talented pianist. They sent her to Bartók, and he passed her to me."

"Like a hot potato," Mrs. Steindorf said, slicing herself another small wedge of the torte.

"Just so. The girl was not hopeless and after three years she played creditably. When she became engaged to a magistrate's son, her parents decided she'd charmed him with an afternoon of Chopin, and out of gratitude they gave me the recipe to their famous torte. I was sworn to secrecy. I had to sign an oath."

"I eat mostly from cans and TV dinners," Mrs. Steindorf said. "I never learned to cook."

"One secret I will reveal: it hasn't a speck of flour in it."

"Tell me," Mrs. Steindorf said, "I had an uncle in Budapest who was a very well-known physician: Dr. Kleiner."

Mrs. Hargy set down her cup. "The Dr. Kleiner?"

"The bone doctor."

"Of course I knew him. Everybody knew him. I went to him once myself. I'd caught my little finger in a door and all the other doctors were talking about amputations. They were debating about whether to cut at the first or second joint. Their favorite word was 'gangrene.' I went to your uncle finally and when I mentioned amputation, he said— I'll never forget it—'those butchers would probably have it ground into their sausage!'"

Mrs. Steindorf cackled and clapped her hands one time.

"He set the bone and I was playing within the month. He was guest of honor at my next recital."

"He was a great music lover," Mrs. Steindorf said, "and a wonderful doctor. In the family he was also known as something of a louse."

"A louse?"

"He got a divorce, which was a disgrace to the whole family, and we were forbidden to mention his name. *Persona non grata.*"

"What a pity. He was such a gentleman with me. Of course I was only ten or eleven."

"And then," Mrs. Steindorf said, "very early we heard he was taken in a concentration camp."

"Ah," Mrs. Hargy said. "I'm so sorry."

Mrs. Steindorf drained her cup and set it down on her saucer.

"Another slice of cake?"

"No, I'm full," she said, leaning back. "When I left Germany in 1938 the first place I went was Milan. My Italian was not so good. When I ate in restaurants and couldn't finish I'd tell the waiter I was full—'*sono piena*.' Immediately they would begin to dote on me and offer me congratulations. Finally I found out that I'd really been saying, 'I'm pregnant.'"

Mrs. Hargy lifted an eyebrow.

"'Full' and 'pregnant' are the same in Italian slang."

"How long were you in Italy?"

"I went there to wait for my husband. He'd stayed in Leipzig to finish closing up his business. He was going to meet me in Lugano after two weeks and then we were going to England." Mrs. Steindorf hesitated, and looked out the window into the dusk. "He was one of those people who never really believed in the Nazis. He'd been decorated in the First War. Big deal: an Iron Cross First Class, and the Hohenzollern with Crown and Swords for nine air victories. The medals were inscribed, 'The gratitude of your Fatherland is assured you.' After two months of waiting for him my visa expired and I had to leave. It was three years before I found out what happened to him."

"He was captured?"

"Rounded up," Mrs. Steindorf said. "Along with my father. The Rector and the war hero. To the Nazis just a couple of Jews."

Mrs. Hargy poured herself more tea and lit a cigarette. Her hand was not steady.

"Luckily my boys were with me and not him," Mrs. Steindorf said.

"Your children?"

"Franz and Nicholas."

There was a short silence. Mrs. Hargy stood up to clear away the tea service.

"Lydia Mangin," Mrs. Steindorf said, and paused, not knowing how to finish the sentence. "Lydia Mangin is progressing, I hope?"

Mrs. Hargy spoke from the kitchen. "She is indeed. I'm concentrating on her technique and her self-discipline. She could become an extraordinary pianist."

"She's terrific, but she's only eleven," Mrs. Steindorf said with a trace of heat. "How much self-discipline can we expect?"

Mrs. Hargy reentered the living room, wiping her hands on a dish towel. "I expect a great deal," she said. "Shall we play another piece?"

"She has a natural touch. I wouldn't tamper with it."

"No," Mrs. Hargy said. "I suppose not."

"She doesn't tire you out?"

"Not at all." She leafed through a pile of sheet music. "Shall we try some Brahms?"

Mrs. Steindorf glanced at her watch. "Holy Toledo! It's five-forty! I must catch my bus."

"You have twenty minutes," Mrs. Hargy said. "I'll get your coat."

At the door they shook hands formally. "I hope we can do this again soon," Mrs. Hargy said. Mrs. Steindorf nodded in silence.

All the way to Bishop, she stared at the Sierra and reviewed the conversation. Finally she blushed at her lie. Her husband, Franz, had not been "rounded up"; under cover of chaos, after Mrs. Steindorf had fled to Italy, he'd eloped to Sweden with his secretary. He'd died there, of old age, in 1978. The shame! Mrs. Steindorf cowered in her seat and cried.

A week later Lydia returned. Her mother called to ask if Mrs. Steindorf could "make room"; she offered more money. "You know my rates," Mrs. Steindorf said. "I make no exceptions, up or down. My concern is that I don't think Lydia should be changing teachers all the time. Learning the piano is not like a smorgasbord. If I take her on, I want it understood that I am her only piano teacher."

"That's our understanding."

"OK. It's a deal. Tell her the usual time."

And so the lessons resumed. Mrs. Steindorf conceded to herself that Lydia's playing had profited from Mrs. Hargy; her phrasing was cleaner, more positive. The girl herself was unchanged; she remained polite and reserved, a proper tourist in Mrs. Steindorf's old world. Mrs. Hargy was not discussed.

Every Wednesday, Mrs. Steindorf availed herself of the County Senior's Door-to-Door Mini-Bus to go to the Safeway for her shopping, and it was on one of these excursions shortly after Lydia's return that she discovered from snatches of an overheard conversation that Mrs. Hargy was back in the hospital. When she got downtown, Mrs. Steindorf immediately splurged on a taxi—her first since moving to Bishop—and made it to Mrs. Hargy's bedside in time for the end of visiting hours.

The Hungarian was the only occupant of a double room. She looked pained and pale, and it took her a few seconds to recognize Mrs.

Steindorf. "Hilda," she said. "How thoughtful of you to come." For a moment it looked as though she were trying to stand up and be gracious.

Mrs. Steindorf, fighting off a rush of nausea, gave Mrs. Hargy a quick peck on the cheek.

"Once more into the breach," Mrs. Hargy said.

"What is it this time?"

"The usual."

"And what's the usual? Since when do they operate more than once on an ulcer? Iren," Mrs. Steindorf said, "Lydia Mangin has resumed her lessons with me. For that I have you to thank. She . . ." Here Mrs. Steindorf did not know how to proceed. She had planned to say, "she will cheer up what's left of my life," or "she gives me something to look forward to," but these phrases, at the last minute, would not pass. "She learned a lot about playing the piano from you."

"She's very talented," Mrs. Hargy said.

"When do they operate?"

"Tomorrow."

"Well," Mrs. Steindorf said, "I wanted to come by and look in on you." She stepped briskly across the room and the two women kissed cheeks again. "God Bless," she said, and left. As she hurried down the hall past the nurses' station, she thought to herself, "Kaput, that one." She was on the verge of tears. In spite of history's most systematic teachers, she had not learned to deal with death.

A week passed, and then one morning Mrs. Steindorf got an early phone call from Father Torrens, the priest at St. Anthony's and one of the local music-lovers. "Hilda," he said, "Iren died last night."

"Ach," she said. "Cancer?"

"Cancer."

"Of what?"

"I don't know, Hilda. Of everything, pretty much." After a pause he added, "Listen, Hilda, I know you and Iren had your differences . . . "

"But we were friends," Mrs. Steindorf interrupted.

"So Iren told me."

"She did?"

"Hilda, she asked me to see if you'd play something at her funeral."

"In the church? This was her idea? Are such things allowed?"

"I was somewhat surprised," Father Torrens said. "It's a bit irregular, but I told her it was OK with me. She assured me you'd do it."

"Of course," she said. "Of course I'll do it."

Mrs. Steindorf was not comfortable in church under any circumstances, and the day of the funeral was worse than usual. She was confused: was she a mourner or a performer? a friend or a hired hand?

Too, she imagined that people resented her, suspected her of feigning Christianity. If there had been a separate section conspicuously marked for visitors and Jews . . . Instead she was front and center, surrounded by people who knew when to kneel, cross themselves, pray. She sat tense and silent, looking out past the alfalfa fields to the mountains. She began to think about the Italian Alps. She had spent a month at Lake Como, waiting for her husband, and it was there, on the terrace of her hotel, sipping caffe latte and watching her boys at their sailing lessons, that she had received the letter from him in Sweden. She could still not think of that moment without a small but persistent part of her mind honestly believing that there had been some mistake, or that it was all a cruel joke.

She shifted in her seat and folded her hands on her lap. Lydia was sitting between her parents near the exit. The father, a plump scrubbed man with a fastidious little beard, was wearing a powder-blue blazer. To a funeral! thought Mrs. Steindorf. Contempt rose in her throat like bile. Then she noticed the priest was cuing her.

She adjusted the seat and sat for a few moments to compose herself, staring at the crest and logo: Steinway. The familiar name was a comfort. She struck the first chord and at once she knew she would play better than she had since Leipzig. She could hear every note and phrase before she played them, hear them shape themselves into song; her fingers, liberated and supple as though she were twenty-one, were drawn through the music by momentum. Phrases flowed from her fingers through the instrument and filled the room like heat. They spilled out of the church toward meadow and mountain. Mrs. Steindorf was shocked at her own intensity. "Not dead yet," she muttered to herself, and thought, *Listen to this, optometrists, kidnappers, Christians. I'm not the dead one after all. I'm the winner.*

Education and Solipsism (1981)

This article first appeared in CoEvolution Quarterly 29. *It was reprinted in* DSC 100 *(2018), a volume that commemorates the one-hundredth anniversary of the founding of Deep Springs College.*

sol•ip•sism (sŏl´ĭp-sĭz´əm, sō´lĭp) n. The theory that the self is the only reality. [L *sōlus*, alone + *ipse*, self + -ISM.] —sol'ip•sist n. —sol'ip•sis'tic adj
—*American Heritage Dictionary*

I recently had cause to look through the catalog of a fully accredited institution of higher learning called John F. Kennedy University of Orinda, California. The courses there fell into two categories: on the one hand, there was a graduate program in parapsychology, English offerings such as "Literature of the Mystic Quest" and "The Energy of Communication," a two-year sequence called "The Tapestry of Knowledge," something on "Varieties of Mind-Body Therapies"—in other words, the sort of psychojunk you expect to see advertised on the bulletin board at your local frozen yogurt parlor. On the other hand were courses of straight no-nonsense training: Police Science, Personnel Management, Business Administration, and Accounting. I couldn't help wondering how the Primal Scream majors got along with the pre-cops when they happened to meet up in the cafeteria.

I was about to dismiss the school as just so much institutionalized Bay Area weirdness when it occurred to me that John F. Kennedy University was on to something. Not only were the touchy-feely courses and the career training united by the dynamic of egoism and narcissism masquerading as "potential"; too, the university was responding in predictable and understandable fashion to real shortcomings in our conventional colleges. All over the nation, people are beginning to see that the increase in college enrollments has not led to a decrease in misery, small-mindedness, or social pathology; people are beginning to call for education that is integrative, value-oriented, and humane—at the same time that they demand practicality and cost-effectiveness. Universities respond to this conflicting message with such token reforms as refurbished core curricula and affinity-group housing, all the while coming more and more into the power of the marketing specialists, the Management by Objective seminarians, and the bottom-line boys. John F. Kennedy University is unique only in that it takes both routes at the same time.

There are better responses, and I will describe one in some detail. But first, it is necessary to recognize that in crucial ways our colleges are structured to produce not citizens and compassionate people, but self-serving egomaniacs.

The normal college performs several functions quite well: students with discipline and curiosity can emerge with impressive verbal and quantitative skills, a sufficient familiarity with the Western tradition of thought, and thorough knowledge of an academic field. In four years of more or less independent living they can establish goals and identities outside the influence of the home. I do not mean to belittle these accomplishments.

Yet it seems to me that all too frequently they take place in an environment that isolates and fragments the individual. During his first week in a normal college the student, no matter what courses he chooses, learns that the next few years consist of a series of obstacles—classes, distribution requirements, exams, theses—leading finally to graduation. The defining characteristic of these tasks, and what makes them almost unique in human endeavor, is that they are faced by the individual alone, and that success or failure in them has consequences to the individual alone. As a result, one of the undeniable and pervasive fictions colleges teach every day is that life's problems present themselves to individuals, are solved or not solved by individuals, with repercussions that do not extend beyond individuals. Thus, when we see people in later life deserting their families, exploiting their employees, cheating their bosses, befouling their environment, and otherwise indulging themselves, all the while blithely assuring everybody that while they might not be acting well, it's OK because they are "taking responsibility for their actions," these people are repeating the lesson they learned, among other places, in college, where they could flunk a test, cut a class, or skip an assignment without visibly affecting anybody but themselves. College is where we are confirmed in our delusion that the source and outer frontier of all significant action is the self.

And if this weren't bad enough, the concept of "self" that conventional colleges promote is preposterously distorted. I am not the first to point out that in spite of all the rhetoric to the contrary, our system of higher education produces cerebrating machines by intention, and emotional, ethical, and physical people only as an afterthought. At most universities, certain elements of the human character are identified over and over, in the classroom, as crucial to the survival of the race: sympathy and compassion, the ability to make responsible judgments, the ability to live together in harmony. Yet the situation in which these abilities are lauded is one where competition and caginess determine success, and important decisions are the exclusive reserve of the teacher. When it comes to actually cultivating the desirable human traits, or even to providing a milieu in which they might be nurtured, the academy either begs off entirely or else establishes an ill-financed and ineptly staffed Office of Student Services—whose principal duties are likely to consist of cafeteria policy and Greek residence coordination.

Why can't college education—or at least part of it—take place in an environment that not only allows but that demands moral, ethical, and emotional growth? An environment where values must be discovered and tested as part of everyday life? An environment that combines freedom with serious obligation, exposing thoughtlessness and self-indulgence, providing students the rare and difficult opportunity to find out what it means to make decisions and to live with their consequences—in other words, what it means to try to live virtuously?

Nothing in my first fifteen years as a student and teacher in some of the finest universities in the country led me to believe that such an environment was even contemplated, much less accomplished. Then I discovered a little-known institution called Deep Springs College, and although I now work there, I think I am objective when I say that it proves higher education need not be solipsistic.

Deep Springs looks like one of those settlements in the high desert of Nevada that sits there, a mile or so off a minor highway, nothing more than a few weathered ranch buildings, a scattered collection of semi-defunct rusted-out vehicles with their hoods perpetually raised, some cows, and a stand of cottonwoods. It appears to be just another of the small-scale beef-and-alfalfa operations scattered throughout the lunar expanse of sand, sagebrush, and abrupt rocky hills of the Great Basin, where the principal industry is nuclear waste disposal. No food, no gas, no lodging.

Next service, eighty-five miles. In fact, Deep Springs is one of the nation's most unusual colleges, and has been since it was founded in 1917.

Radical even by modern standards, it must have seemed truly bizarre then. In deeding the land to the college, the founder, an industrialist named L. L. Nunn, specified that the enrollment should be held below twenty-six students, all of whom, in addition to their studies, would participate in a program of self-government and work at least half time on the cattle ranch that is the college campus. The students were designated as the beneficial owners of the property, legally held by a board of trustees mandated to "ascertain, consider and comply with, the desires of the student body." One of these trustees, according to the deed, was always to be an elected student. No fees whatsoever were to be charged.

None of this has changed since the founding. The student body is still responsible for the conduct of its own members. All students work twenty hours per week—not in payment for their education, but as an integral part of it. There is no core curriculum and no degrees are awarded. After two or three years at Deep Springs, students transfer to conventional colleges as juniors.

These innovative features are bound together by a strong thread of traditionalism—some would say conservatism. At present, because of a clause in the original deed of trust, Deep Springs still has an all-male student body.[1] The admissions policy is extremely selective: SAT scores average around 700 verbal and 700 math, and qualities of character and motivation are equally high. Although the classes are small (averaging three or four students) and often student-initiated, they are, by common consent, rigorously academic in their form and content, with reading assignments, papers, exams, and grades. The teachers are almost all PhDs from places like Harvard, the University of Chicago, Yale, Cornell, Berkeley, and MIT—the same colleges to which many of the students transfer. Students affirm and maintain two "ground rules": nobody may use non-medicinal drugs, and nobody may leave the fifty-square-mile valley in which the college is located. Over the years, the alumni have tended toward the professions, academia, and government. There are a few novelists, composers, and painters. One or two are journalists. There are two university presidents, a federal judge, an ambassador. There is also a blacksmith, a riverboat pilot, and a member of the Weather

---

1 Deep Springs College became coeducational in 2018.—S.S.

Underground. There have been, since 1917, only about 450 alumni, and on the whole they have fulfilled the founder's hopes that they would become responsible, altruistic, and idealistic citizens—not the "hirelings of the avaricious" that "our educational institutions too often prepare." Almost to a man, they live modestly, serve prodigiously, and look back on Deep Springs as the pivotal experience of their lives.

That experience, in fact as well as theory, little resembles what we usually think of as college life. Most of the students are up well before dawn, putting on overalls and boots to trudge through the dark to the chores. Some go off to milk the cows, some to feed the stock, some to set the tables for breakfast. At 7:30, when the old railroad bell rings to announce the meal, faculty, staff, families, and students drift to the boarding house from their nearby dorms and homes. Breakfast consists of milk less than two hours old, served from steel pitchers; home-churned butter; eggs from the henhouse; and perhaps sausage from a pig that was raised and slaughtered by the students.

The morning is taken up with classes—normal undergraduate courses like Freshman English, French 2, Calculus, Introduction to Philosophy, and Shakespeare. The pace is rapid, and the discussions are animated. Frequently, when class is over, the discussion will spill out onto the lawn or into the boarding house, where it may continue for hours.

Classes end at lunchtime. The afternoon is devoted to ranch work. Students raise hay and cattle for sale, and have a dairy herd, bees, pigs, and a garden for domestic use. They also work in the office, library, bookstore, and dining hall. In essence, they staff the entire operation, with limited professional help. Faculty spend the afternoons preparing classes. On the rare occasions when they have a spare hour or two, they are free to join in the labor. The work ends with dinner, and once again the whole community gathers to eat. During the meal someone taps a pitcher and begins the announcements: the student admissions committee will meet at eight to continue its review of applicants for next year's class; madrigal group at seven-thirty; volleyball between dinner and meetings; volunteers are needed to clean the chicken coop.

These activities wind down by nine or nine-thirty, and serious study begins (it is also carried on during the morning between classes, and at all odd hours). For a break, a student might wander to the boarding house, where the coffee urn is always on, there to find other students, perhaps a teacher or two, and endless talk. Lights burn late. The library never closes.

As the last student is going to bed, perhaps having put the finishing touches on a term paper, the first is getting up for morning milking.

How does a life like this—anachronistic and contrived as it is—provide an education for the real world? If one starts from the premise that the world needs people who are not only schooled in the usual academic sense but are also responsible and compassionate, then three features of the Deep Springs program emerge as essential—features that could easily be reproduced elsewhere: the intensity that derives from smallness and isolation; the distribution of powers; and the integrated programs of study, labor, and self-government.

The conventional college is structured around the motif of escape. Students escape the "real world" of work and accountability on campus. They escape the campus by going into town for entertainment. Socially, jocks escape nerds, fraternity men escape intellectuals, blacks escape whites, Young Americans for Freedom escape Students for a Democratic Society, faculty escape students. Everybody escapes thinking about curricular matters through chemical stupefaction and through the greatest escape of all: sleep. I think it is significant that the drugs of choice on college campuses have always been soporific (alcohol) or isolationist (marijuana), and the activity of choice has always been some form of escapism, frequently epitomized either by leaving or passing out.

With its population of about forty-five, Deep Springs is the only settlement in its valley. The nearest town is an hour away, on the other side of a magnificent but torturous 7,000-foot mountain pass. As a result, the community is socially self-contained. While mail comes in daily, and five or six times a semester there are visitors (family, guest speakers, applicants), the system remains emotionally sealed.

From this simple fact flow enormous consequences. People who, on the normal campus, would dismiss each other immediately, often become as close as brothers at Deep Springs. They eat, study, work, and govern together. Late at night, any two of them are likely to find themselves the only people within a twenty-five-mile radius who are awake. They will decide to have some coffee together and might end up sitting in the deserted boarding house until dawn. When this happens, and it happens frequently, superficial qualities retreat into insignificance, and human ones emerge. While real difficulties between people may remain, the judgments that are formed tend to be generous. Disliking someone at Deep Springs comes to be seen as a luxury and, like most luxuries, a waste.

Thus, easy judgments are discouraged. So too is that easiest of all judgments: the refusal to judge. Every year, two or three students arrive professing that whatever an individual does is his business, so long as nobody else is harmed, and that to judge him is a mistake if not a downright sin. I sometimes think that one of the only lessons high schools teach is that a "value judgment" is a morally reprehensible act tantamount to child molestation. In any case, in small communities, two facts quickly become evident: one is that those actions which are "harmless to others" are rare indeed. If a student sleeps through morning dairy, and the cows don't get milked, they get mastitis, and when that happens nobody has milk. When there are only three students in a class and one of them is unprepared, the discussion suffers in ways that are immediately obvious. In a place like Deep Springs the consequences of all actions are conspicuous. A second lesson is that judgments get made, one way or another. A sick cow, an empty milk pitcher, a turgid class are objectively and unambiguously bad. In such cases, committing a value judgment is a creative and constructive act. It places blame where it belongs, thus liberating the innocent, and it helps prevent future errors, thus aiding in the education of the guilty. It sets boundaries on the retribution, and it affirms that the community has identifiable values. If the judgment is executed in the spirit of generosity— and it usually is, not only because its maker and its receiver will probably have to face each other over breakfast the next morning, but also, given the circumstances, because the roles may soon be reversed—then the most valuable lesson of all occurs: the student finds that failure is not fatal, but human. Only at that point can he profit from it.

And who, exactly, does the final judging? To whom are students, teachers, and staff finally accountable? In other words, where does the real power lie?

Many colleges deal with this question in ways that no political theorist has seriously entertained since Aristotle distinguished the household from the state in Book I of the *Politics*. In the last couple of decades, the concept of in loco parentis has disappeared only in the sense that it was synonymous with paternalism. The university still operates like a family. Now, it is merely a "progressive" family instead of a despotic one. It is no longer accurate to say that all of the power is concentrated in a few fatherly administrators. But it remains a fact that when a question of rights, privileges, or jurisdiction arises, the contending factions square off like a couple of twelve-year-olds at recess. The atmosphere is permissive, but it is important to remember that "permissive" is a term from the lexicon of child psychology, not education or politics.

When colleges are overtly political, and use political terms, it is a politics of conflicting interest groups and of inherent inequality that is invoked. Nowhere do members of what we cynically call the university community talk or act as though there were, in fact, a community in the university. The ideas of mutual restraint, obligation, participation, and agreement on major goals and basic philosophy that mark the discourse of true communities appear, at the conventional college, only in the textbooks of political theory classes. It is no coincidence, of course, that these classes themselves are more and more forced into extinction, to be replaced by ones that use the "clean" and "value free" terminology of social science, survey research, and bureaucracy: the language that is itself appropriate to the political structure of the liberal multiversity. That this is the structure of the political world, writ small, does not justify the situation. If colleges are the DNA of society, then we don't have far to look to discover how we might restore to the world that sense of community it needs.

One way might be to introduce young people to authority structures which are neither authoritarian nor flaccid, but political—in the Greek sense, where politics meant constant public participation in the ongoing effort to arrive at a good and just civic life. Smallness is a necessary quality for such a structure (Aristotle limited the size of the polis to those who could gather within hearing of a single orator), but it is not sufficient. A reasonably egalitarian and flexible distribution of power is also necessary.

For example, at Deep Springs, the board of trustees has de jure authority to act for the college. The chairman's signature appears on contracts and IRS forms. But the board is obligated by the founding document, the deed of trust, to respect and comply with student sentiment and to that end a student is a full voting member. Also, the adult trustees live far from the college and convene there only twice a year, and thus could not interfere in the day-to-day operations if they wanted to—which they don't. In their absence, the chief administrator is the director,[2] but his powers are nowhere spelled out. The deed of trust specifically gives the student

---

2 The title "director" has been replaced by "president," but the duties remain the same. The first female president was installed in 2020.—S.S.

body responsibility for "the conduct of its own members," but what does that mean? Academic evaluation, power to sell the cattle, admissions and expulsions? Or quiet hours, dress codes, and films committee? Lurking in the background to confuse the issue even further is the alumni association, a powerful force in matters of institutional policy, and the faculty, traditionally preeminent in curriculum and academic affairs.

As a result of this nebulous power structure, nobody can arbitrarily pronounce on a public matter, and then justify himself by invoking some etched-in-marble constitution. This fact affects both the content of the decisions made and the method of reaching them. Suddenly, considerations like mutual benefit, fairness, ethical content, even tradition, enter the picture where formerly chapter and verse would have sufficed. When the students vote to exercise their rights by adopting a stray dog, and then that dog bites a faculty member's infant daughter, they have learned an important distinction between power and justice. A teacher who offers a class that nobody is interested in, merely because teachers have that right, and then finds himself with an empty classroom, has learned the same distinction. Very quickly, everybody learns that the only effective way to act is after exhaustive public debate, with all parties having the opportunity to formulate and present their point of view.

I do not mean either to describe or advocate a system where nobody is in charge. In fact, real authority exists, but not merely by virtue of status or prerogative; it stems from reason, and devolves on an individual or group that (to paraphrase Hannah Arendt) can show itself to be right, or that has been right so often in the past that its advice cannot be safely ignored.

This notion frequently turns up in an interdisciplinary seminar called "Problems in Community and Authority." The course demonstrates the most unusual and valuable of Deep Springs' features: the interdependence of the academics, the labor, and the self-government. Being bright and thoughtful young people, the students come into the seminar (usually offered as part of the orientation semester) with some well-entrenched theories. There are for example the high school Emersonians, repulsed by years of petty regulations, uninspiring teachers, and lowest-common-denominator curriculum. They come to college hoping to find Transcendental Heaven, where the individual's unfettered expressions of freedom magically coalesce into utopia. They enter the seminar believing that the government which governs least is best; that the ideal human condition is absolute liberty.

Then there are the high school Nietzscheans. Unchallenged, frustrated by a system that has failed to provide them structures for the development of their potential, disgusted with current trends of permissiveness and lack of standards, resentful of their high school's leveling tendency, they come to college hoping to find an environment that will provide them with discipline, channel their energy, and surround them with equals. They enter the seminar thinking that human progress will occur only in a context of control and dedication.

As the course moves from Plato and Aristotle through Thoreau and Mill, picking up Marx, Locke, Shakespeare, Orwell, Tocqueville, Melville, and others along the way, the students are alternately challenged and reinforced in their beliefs. Meanwhile, the Emersonian will notice that his liberty to drink fresh milk depends on his roommate's lack of liberty to sleep past 4:30; a Nietzschean may be elected to the position of labor commissioner and discover that order and discipline involve telling a friend he has to spend all day Sunday castrating calves; in fact order and discipline may involve spending Sunday that way himself. In any case, he frequently finds himself being arbitrary and insensitive.

By the end of the course, everybody's ideas about liberty and society are sophisticated indeed; the students still have theories, no doubt, but they are true to experience, as that experience has been sensitized and refined by the best that has been thought and written on the subject. Locke believes that one acquires a right to property by mixing one's labor with it. A student mixes his labor with the alfalfa field all afternoon—poisoning gophers. Does he therefore own it? Marx says that alienation in labor is the result of the worker's relationship to the means of production. A student gets up early in the morning to slaughter a steer. He uses his own knife, he is the beneficial owner of the animal, and it will end up on his plate with nobody deriving a profit from it along the way. Yet, when he slips the knife into the animal's throat and gropes for the jugular, does he feel at one with himself and his work? A student believes that the past is nothing but an encumbrance that each individual must cast off in order to create his own relevant world, unfettered by tradition and outmoded ideology. Fine. But when the toilet in the guest cottage springs a leak, he discovers that scrapping the old system to put in a new one is simply not possible, because the plumbing is an extensive and delicate network; it's tied in to the boiler, which has an electric thermostat run by the generator, and if the generator fails the irrigation lines stop sprinkling, and the alfalfa dies . . . and . . . So he learns to work within the context of what he has inherited. He discovers that many of the modern parts he can use are shabby when compared to the old ones he is replacing. And he learns that the generations of student maintenance men who over the decades have compiled a plumbing system manual—by now grease-stained and dog-eared—these dead hands of the past are not his stale oppressors, but the very agents of his liberation. A student condemns Goneril and Regan when they mistreat old Lear. Age has its prerogatives; "reason not the need." But where is this magnanimity when the cooks, a retired couple from Nevada, insist that the students wear shirts and shoes in the boarding house? Over and over, daily, the Deep Springs student must test his theory against the world that he inhabits and that his theories help to shape. He soon discovers that while any fool can have an ideal, it takes character to live up to one. He learns that to be of value, an ideal must bear some relation to behavior, without losing its defining essence of impossibility.

In the normal college, idealism too often serves as the handmaiden of despair. Lofty goals like the cure for cancer, the end of racism and poverty, the Great American Novel, all prove not only elusive, but totally out of range. All too frequently, the next step is a retreat into cynicism, hedonism, careerism, or narcissism. In a community where the student confronts as part of his daily life imperatives that cannot be abandoned, such a retreat is impossible. The leaking toilet must be fixed, the hay must be put up before first snow, the composition must be written, even when these tasks are "impossible." The student who sits in philosophy class expounding the theory of the Übermensch, then spends two hours trying to overcome a mule's desire to remain unharnessed, has learned an undeniable lesson about aspiring toward the godhead: he must do it, of course, but he must bring to the task some qualities of humility, commitment, dedication, and resilience.

I do not mean to propose Deep Springs as a utopia, or as a solution to the problems of education and society. The college's refusal to admit women is a serious shortcoming. Given the world of the 1980s, an all-male college that claims to value ethical development and to produce leaders is not just an anachronism, but an affront. Too, the school pays its faculty and staff poorly, and its elitism offends our democratic impulses.

But these problems are peculiar to this one institution; they are not of its essence, and similar schools could be structured so as to avoid them.[3] Other problems, however, are inherent in just those qualities that make the school successful, and anyone who contemplates such a venture should be willing to accept them. At a certain point, intensity becomes frustration, accountability and openness become exhibitionism, and community becomes a pain in the neck. The small and isolated setting soon begins to give events a bizarre warp. Tiny irritations assume huge proportions: everything is a crisis, from a broken ditto machine to a fallen cake. Petty personal disputes can escalate quickly into feuds. Xenophobia and philosophical inbreeding are constant dangers.

On a more profound level, failure can become tragic. The stakes are high. At a normal college, failure is defined as a late paper, a dull class, a slanderous editorial in the school paper. At Deep Springs, failure is cruelty, insensitivity, arrogance, or irresponsibility. It involves real pain and suffering. It is unusual to live in such a place for any length of time without coming to believe that life presents one trial after another.

Yet it is equally unusual to emerge without coming to the belief that with discipline, patience, and cooperation, humans are capable of prevailing, and that the struggle is itself an education. Two years in a small, intense, isolated, self-governing community—no matter how rigorous the academic offerings—is not enough education for anybody. But it is enough so that when the student moves on to the more conventional academy, he does so with a new vision of himself and the world. What he sees is not just self, status and salary, mortgages and Mercedes, but a set of living obligations and possibilities.

---

3 In the twenty-first century, several new colleges have been founded on the Deep Springs model: among them, the Arete Project (https://areteproject.org/mission/); Outer Coast College (http://outercoast.org/about.html); and Thoreau College (https://www.thoreaucollege.org/mission-2).—S.S.

PART 3

In Transition: From Literature to Law

David Schuman's law school paper on the LA aqueduct, excerpted here, reveals a writer in transition. With a novelist's eye, he describes the impact of the aqueduct on the natural world of the Owens Valley. Excerpts from his paper about *The Merchant of Venice* reflect a former English professor's emerging legal mind. Because of space limitations, we have not included his first legal publication, as a third-year law student ("The Political Community, the Individual, and Control of Public School Curriculum," *Oregon Law Review* 63, no. 2, 1984), in which he combines legal analysis with his interest in education, as well as the political theory orientation he gained team-teaching at Deep Springs College. He later advocated for this approach in several other law review articles, including "Taking Law Seriously: Communitarian Search and Seizure," featured in part 4. All of David Schuman's law review articles can be found complete at avoiceforjustice.com.

—Sharon Schuman

from "A Legal History of the Los Angeles Aqueduct" (1982)

Included here are excerpts from a paper David Schuman submitted in 1982, as a student at the University of Oregon School of Law. This paper describes the same landscape featured in the short stories "Tracy" and "The Winner" in part 2 (the complete paper can be found at avoiceforjustice.com).

INTRODUCTION

Several times each spring, the Owens Valley, a narrow and semiarid gorge between the Sierra Nevada and the Inyo-White Mountain ranges in eastern California,[1] is visited by strong southerly winds. On those occasions, a motorist passing down the length of the valley, returning, say, from a ski weekend at Mammoth to his home in Los Angeles, will travel through what appears to be a dense, dry fog. He will be unable to see the 10,000' escarpments rising to Mount Whitney on the west and White Mountain Peak on the east; he will miss the small alfalfa ranches, the basaltic outcroppings, the extinct volcanic cones, the sage and rabbitbrush; he will pass by the county road leading to the world's oldest living things[2] and America's oldest experimental college;[3] in towns with names like Bishop, Lone Pine, and Independence he will see many of the residents, natives as well as Southern California transplants who have migrated in search of clean air, breathing through bandanas or surgical masks. Finally, as he reaches the southern end of the valley, the air will

---

1 Owens Valley proper extends from Owens Lake on the south to Crowley Lake on the north, a distance of seventy-five miles. The next geographical unit is Mono Basin, which extends north another twenty-five miles. In water disputes, these two regions are often treated as one.

2 Bristlecone pines grow in the White Mountains twenty-three miles northeast of Big Pine, California. Several are more than four thousand years old; G. Schumacher, *Deepest Valley* 52 (1969).

3 Deep Springs College, founded 1917. See D. Schuman, "Education and Solipsism," *CoEvolution Quarterly* 94 (1981).

suddenly clear, and a few miles down the road, if he stops to look back, he will discover the source of this hundred-mile fog: he has just passed what was once Owens Lake, and from its now-dry bottom, driven by the wind, rises a tower of alkaline dust that engulfs the entire Owens Valley.

If the hypothetical tourist continues his trip south; if he notices the aqueduct that parallels the highway into Los Angeles; and if, when he arrives home, he turns on the tap water, swims in his pool, washes his car, or hoses the leaves off his lawn, he will have witnessed and participated in a legal battle that reaches back at least to 1880,[4] and that shows in microcosm some of the major trends in American legal history. For Owens Lake was not always dry. Less than a century ago, two steamboats carried silver from the mines at one end to the railhead at the other.[5] Since that time, under the rubric of "public benefit," with the blessing of courts and legislatures, the water that once flowed into Owens Lake has been diverted to Los Angeles reservoirs.

CONCLUSION

The fate of the world does not depend on whether the Supreme Court of California decides to preserve a suitable environment for brine shrimp. Compared to the threat of nuclear war, the threat of a desiccated Mono Lake and a parched Owens Valley seem trivial. The disputes that have surrounded California water law and the Los Angeles Aqueduct are meaningful not because they have shaped history but because they have reflected it. If that reflection is not warped, then the last two centuries have witnessed one profound transformation in the legal conception of property, while the next century may witness another. As America changed from a rural, agricultural nation to one consecrated to the gospel of urban, capital-intensive, heavy industrial, resource-exploitative growth—a nation whose cultural hero was first Natty Bumppo, then Horatio Alger, and finally Lee Iacocca—so the legal idea of property changed from private, static rights to public, dynamic ones. Now, as we enter an age of limits, chastened by knowledge that the earth is exhaustible, perhaps the legal idea of property is once again changing, this time to something more compatible with survival. If Owens Valley alfalfa and Mono Lake brine shrimp can pull through, perhaps the rest of us can, too.

---

4 *Los Angeles Water Company v. Los Angeles City*, 55 Cal. 176 (1880).
5 R. Laedabrand, *Owens Valley* 97 (1972).

from "Theory of Contract in *The Merchant of Venice*" (1982)

Included here is an excerpt from another law school paper, written in August 1982, for James Mooney's Contracts course (the complete paper can be found at avoiceforjustice.com).

INTRODUCTION

Contracts in one form or another initiate and then drive forward the plot in several of Shakespeare's plays. *Hamlet* recounts the formation and performance of an agreement between a young prince and his father's ghost. *Lear* examines the consequences of an inept property settlement. *Othello* stems from a nuptial bond and what happens when an intervener convinces one of the parties that the other is in breach. While this jurisprudential jargon does violence to the subtleties and depths of the dramas, it is nonetheless faithful to their spirit: one of Shakespeare's concerns is always the web of obligation and commitment that binds humans to each other. This is nowhere more evident than in *The Merchant of Venice*, where the plot's mainspring, a loan contract between Antonio and Shylock, is echoed by several less-shocking agreements: contracts involving Portia, her father, and her suitors govern the courtship ritual; Antonio and Bassanio arrange a loan agreement, as do Shylock and Tubal; Gobbo breaks one employment contract and forms another; Portia and Bassanio enter into a marriage contract. Shakespeare, writing at a period of history when the mercantile mode of structuring relationships was beginning to expand from the economic realm into all other human activity, examines this phenomenon in *The Merchant of Venice* through the lens of contract theory. Ultimately he sees the present with distaste, the past with nostalgia, and the future with fear.

CONCLUSION

In short, Shakespeare portrays a world that has inverted the classical virtues and vices. To Aristotle and Plato the good life was one of moderation, lived within limits; disregard of limits was hybris and it brought down the wrath of fate. To the Venetians, on the other hand, virtue manifests itself in boundless increase. To the traditional moralist, the love of wealth is the root of all evil: *radix malorem est cupiditas*. To the Venetians, the love of wealth provides the energy that builds empire. To Jesus, the realm of trade was to be bracketed off and kept distant from the realm of love. To the Venetians, the realms are confounded and confused. To Dante, the bond that held together the community and powered the universe was a *moto spirituale*, an ineffable attraction that human beings had toward each other, toward virtue, and toward the godhead. To the Venetians, a bond was something quite different. Shakespeare's Venice is a wasteland where the law of merchants, obeying some inexorable dynamic, has spilled out of its proper bounds, spread from Venice to Belmont and beyond, and infected the essence of human relationships: love.

Within this milieu, two relationships stand out as exceptions: the friendship between Antonio and Bassanio, and the one between Shylock and Tubal. In each, one person willingly—almost instinctively, as a reflex—offers to loan his friend money, with no mention of interest, penalties, or any form of consideration. Antonio responds to Bassanio's request thus: "My purse, my person, my extremest means, / Lie all unlocked to your occasions" (I.i.138–9). Shylock, likewise, relies on a loan from Tubal, and later, when Jessica has fled, it is apparent that Tubal has gone to some expense and effort to help find her. The bond of friendship, then, can survive the commercial setting and override the profit motive. But these friendships are rare, and more significantly, they are doomed. Much has been made of Antonio's alleged homosexual attraction to Bassanio ("I am the tainted wether of the flock") as an explanation for his mysterious melancholia. A more likely explanation is that Antonio, as both a merchant and a noble friend, stands, like Shakespeare, at an historical and geographical spot on the cusp between two eras, looking backwards with nostalgia at the classical and feudal world, governed by an elaborate scheme of obligation, duty, and status, venerating *comitatus* and *virtu* and looking forward on a new world, governed by the laws of contract, venerating competition and cupidity—a world in which we are all Shylock.

PART 4

Writing and Speaking about Law

David Schuman published a number of academic law articles distinguished not only by their rigor but also by their engaging nature—one can enjoy them without being an expert. We are able to reproduce here only a fraction of them, with reduced footnotes and citations. The complete texts can be found at avoiceforjustice.com.

The first article is such a favorite of mine that I have included it in my textbooks. Published in 1990, it uses search-and-seizure law to explore two different ways of explaining the American Constitution: the traditional one focusing on individual rights and emphasizing that "the underlying purpose of the Constitution is to secure individual liberty from the predations of tyranny"; the other viewing individual rights as less important than "mutuality and self-rule" through involvement in the policy-making process. David argues that this latter perspective (known as "communitarianism") produces better search-and-seizure law. Along the way, he refers to and reinforces Oregon Supreme Court Justice Hans Linde's jurisprudence and maintains that in 1990 Oregon courts took a communitarian approach to search and seizure.

The second piece, a speech rather than an academic article, is included here because it updates developments in the Oregon courts since 1990. Unfortunately, these have not been salutary, from David's perspective, because to him they reflect a "relentless deLindification process" that has brought about, among other things, the decay of Oregon's once-acclaimed search-and-seizure laws.

The final piece in the chapter is a foray into the origins of the Oregon Constitution, drafted by a remarkably homogeneous group that comprised mostly small landholders and modest merchants. David reveals here that racism permeated their deliberations as thoroughly as did the group's mistrust of governmental powers and its determination to require frugal state operations. These founders, he says, "produced a state charter remarkable only for its conventionality and small-mindedness" yet ultimately the source of greater individual rights than were conferred by the federal constitution.

—Margie Paris, Emeritus Dean, UO School of Law

from "Taking Law Seriously: Communitarian Search and Seizure" (1990)

This article first appeared in American Criminal Law Review 27, *Georgetown University Law Center.*

I. INTRODUCTION

The conventional story of American constitutional law, the tale we have told our children, each other, and ourselves, has featured the liberty-loving, privacy-seeking, government-distrusting, self-promoting independent individual and the state he[1] has created in his image. We have subscribed to the myth that some benevolent alchemist's invisible hand would transmute a collection of these self-seeking but mutually checking persons into a just and convivial people, and that such private vices as greed and egoism would become, in the aggregate, such public virtues as general wealth and compassion.[2] Increasingly, however, the evidence suggests that the invisible hand lacks alchemical powers: private greed and egoism, summed and accumulated, still translate into pervasive public alienation.[3]

And so a revised story begins to circulate, explaining our constitution—that is, our origins and our make-up[4]—in a more benign voice. In this story, our nation was conceived not in the pursuit of self-interest, but in virtue and interdependence, dedicated not to private individual gratification, but to mutuality and self-rule through inclusive discourse. Although this version of our constitutional origins has gained familiarity and respect,[5] its full acceptance awaits demonstration that it has relevance and utility beyond its function as a comforting fable. This article on search and seizure should contribute to that demonstration. In search and seizure, after all, the essence of any political theory, the government's relationship with its citizens, achieves stark and physical form. It is therefore a legal doctrine that dramatically exposes the theory's strengths and vulnerabilities. My goal in comparing two varieties of search and seizure jurisprudence—one grounded in traditional liberal-individualist theory and the other in the communitarian revision—is to show that the second is not only better, but also possible.

The law of search and seizure deriving from traditional liberal-individualism is expressed in current United States Supreme Court cases. In Part II, I will demonstrate the logical connection between the extraordinary incoherence of these cases and their underlying political theory. In Part III, I will describe what search and seizure doctrine might look like were it to express the republican or communitarian principles of the revised story. I will argue for this version's superiority, and explain why it might best develop as state constitutional law. Finally, in response to those who might label communitarian search and seizure utopian, I will examine the doctrine of one state, Oregon, that seems to be adopting it.

II.   LIBERAL-INDIVIDUALISM AND THE FOURTH AMENDMENT
A.   Liberal-Individualism
1.   Varieties of Liberal-Individualist Thought

In the current scholarly vernacular, "liberalism" refers to a political theory that has nothing to do with the belief in large government, generous social programs, progressive race relations, or any of the other planks in the typical "liberal" Democrat's platform. To avoid confusion, I use the less ambiguous term "liberal-individualism."

Unfortunately, defining this term is more difficult than distinguishing it from its relative. Proponents have reached no consensus about what lies at the logical center of this belief system. Some liberal-individualists have identified strict laissez-faire market economics as the original core tenet.[6] Others, more libertarian in orientation, apply the internal logic of this unregulated market to all areas of human endeavor.[7] More traditional adherents center their theory on the Millian thesis that humans achieve creativity, satisfaction, and fulfillment in inverse proportion to their government's interference with free choice.[8] Community-oriented liberals such as Ronald Dworkin reject strict individualism, recognizing and valuing impulses toward mutuality while continuing to emphasize the primacy of rights.[9] Kantian liberal-individualists like John Rawls also emphasize personal rights and protection from majoritarian tyranny as the centerpiece of their theory.[10]

Despite this variety, it is possible to discern a constellation of premises that has been at the center of American political thought for at least two centuries. These premises concern the individual, associations, politics, rights, and constitutional law.

2.   *The Individual and Associations*

Perhaps the root assumption, the engine driving liberal-individualist theory, is its conception of "human nature." Liberal-individualists believe that the basic unit of human society is the rational, self-interested, self-defining, autonomy-seeking individual. Relationships with those outside the individual's immediate families, while sometimes necessary and emotionally rewarding, are seen as constraining threats to self-determination, forcing compromise and deviation from the individual's self-chosen goals.[11] People join groups for only four reasons: recreation; mutual protection; efficiency in satisfying material needs; and the increased bargaining power that results when people who share similar goals join forces. Groups, in other words, are for the most part interest groups, and one joins them with a sense of *quid pro quo*: one *gives up* a certain amount of freedom and autonomy in order to get benefits. Society is "a scheme of cooperation for reciprocal advantage" (Rawls 33). Or, in Emerson's more radical formulation, it is "a conspiracy against the manhood of every one of its members. Society is a joint-stock company in which the members agree for the better securing of his bread to each shareholder, to surrender the liberty and culture of the eater." The *reductio ad absurdum* of this belief might be found in Kant, who argued (to the astonishment of Hegel) that even the marriage bond was a contract of mutual possession; or in Nietzsche, who wrote "[a] great man . . . what is he? . . . If he cannot lead, he goes alone. . . . He wants no 'sympathetic' heart, but servants, tools; in his intercourse with men he is always intent on *making* something out of them."

3.   *Politics*

A second premise of liberal-individualist theory is that each individual and interest group has its own self-determined goals—its own vision of the good life. The liberal-individualist attitude toward these visions is deontological and pluralist. With only a few exceptions, one vision or set of goals is about as good as any other; there is no single best conception of how people should live (Berlin 28–34). It therefore follows that politics cannot be the search for a common good. Rather, it is the arena in which individuals or interest groups look for ways to achieve their preexisting preferences through a process of bargaining, accommodation, and manipulation. People come to politics as a means to some particular, private end, usually a share of society's privileges or benefits. Politics determines who gets what by a process of interest aggregation or negotiation.

4. Rights
However, not all possible outcomes of this process are legitimate. Because the basic unit in this political theory is emphatically the individual, results are legitimate only if they respect each individual's dignity and autonomy. Consistent with this principle, there is a region within all humans into which the state, this conglomerate of convenience, cannot intrude without an extremely compelling reason, even if a majority of the state's constituent individuals want the intrusion. Such an intrusion would constitute a violation of the social contract. In joining society, individuals surrendered to the state only a portion of their sovereignty— "that part . . . of which the use is important to the community"—retaining for themselves a realm outside "the limits of the sovereign power."[12] This is the realm of rights, which the majority and the political process cannot enter precisely because individuals are by definition inherently and essentially rights-bearing entities (Berlin 121–34).

5. Constitutional Law
In this familiar liberal-individualist paradigm, the underlying purpose of the Constitution is to secure individual liberty from the predations of tyranny, especially the tyranny of the majority.[13] Thus, the Constitution establishes a government in which each branch checks the others, because, by analogy to personal self-interest, each is presumed to be motivated by an inexorable dynamic of self-aggrandizement. The layering of the federalist system and the fragmentation inherent in separated branches serve to control government through the structural arrangement of offsetting ambitions. A legislature of elected representatives guarantees that every interest group will be able to participate in the pitched battle of policy choice, so that whatever policy emerges can be presumed to reflect the will of those able to muster a majority and defeat their opponents.

The legislative will, however, is checked by the Bill of Rights as interpreted by the Supreme Court, designed to protect a core of individual dignity from governmental interference.

This understanding of the relationship between the legislative and judicial branches provides the structure for liberal-individualist constitutional law. The utility of citizen participation through a pluralist legislature lies not in its affirmative creation of an educative, benevolent, value-laden state, but in its maintenance of a neutral and therefore just field upon which individuals and interest groups might fairly compete among themselves for limited resources. The legislative process translates a collection of interests into a maximally efficient distribution of benefits. Furthermore, the individuals and interest groups engaged in this process need give little or no thought to how the pursuit might affect fundamental rights or general welfare; the government is a machine that runs smoothly without altruism or virtue. Concerns about the non-instrumental values inherent in individual or interest-group claims are conceived as constitutional and therefore judicial. Despite their oaths to uphold the Constitution, legislators usually delegate to the judiciary the task of ensuring that the process of policy choice does not incidentally intrude into the meta-political realm of protected fundamental rights.[14] Courts, not legislatures or city councils, are where the discussion of values might occur untainted by majoritarian interest-maximizing, and where individual or minority protections might, as a matter of fundamental policy, be weighed against general utilitarian concerns.

Thus, our liberal-individualist legislatures generally produce laws enabling or regulating private action, while courts deal case-by-case with situations in which the execution of those laws invades protected rights. The judicial method, naturally and logically, is an attempt to "balance" or to mediate among conflicting legitimate claims. Alasdair MacIntyre has explained the connection between liberal-individualism and this type of balancing (169–89). Only in a society that insistently conceives of rights as valid individual entitlements potentially in conflict with another's equally valid rights, or with the aggregated interests of society, must a tribunal mediate between these powerful and legitimate but incommensurable claims. This contrasts with the Aristotelian model, in which law and legitimate assertions of individuality could never conflict because individual virtue consisted of action in pursuit of a single, shared conception of the public good. Disputes would be resolved not by accommodating two valid but conflicting claims, but by declaring which one was right. The Athenian jury, for example, does not balance Socrates's right to express himself against the needs of the polis to preserve its young from corruption; it recognizes conflicting claims and pronounces one legitimate. Only in the post-Stoic or pluralist world, characterized by the absence of shared common goals, can legitimate individual interests clash with each other or with law (MacIntyre 137–53). The idea that an individual's exercise of rights might conflict with some valid social goal in such a way that justice requires mutual accommodation is a distinctly liberal-individualist idea.[15]

B. Liberal-Individualist Search and Seizure
1. *General Approach: Rights First, Law Second*
Liberal-individualism, then, focuses on individuals and regards them as rights-bearing entities whose social and political bonds are instrumental: temporary, intentionally forged, incidental aids to be exploited in pursuit of personal goals. Government serves impartially to provide protection to core areas of personal autonomy and to facilitate individual initiative. Citizens, through their elected representatives,[16] participate in policy choice in order to maximize their own interests, while the judiciary, immune from politics, ensures that such majoritarian policy choice does not unduly intrude into protected privacy. Search and seizure doctrine, in which protection of "privacy" from government invasion assumes actual physical dimensions, presents the archetypal liberal-individualist encounter between the state and its citizens.

Unfortunately, because search and seizure issues arise in the context of motions to suppress incriminating evidence found in the possession of defendants, the citizens seeking judicial vindication of their rights "against" the accumulated weight of the majority's interest are usually guilty criminals. This fact distorts the entire ensuing litigation; the fourth amendment, intended to promote the security and protection of all citizens, is turned against them, assuming the function of a magical incantation that criminals can use to avoid the consequences of their offenses. This phenomenon puts courts in the position of confronting the centerpiece of American liberal-individualist jurisprudence—the pre-political right—within a context where its beneficiaries are people who have demonstrated contempt for the society from which they now seek protection—hard cases, resulting in the predictably bad law. In order to honor the basic fourth amendment right without at the same time depriving the state of its authority to punish a criminal, the court typically genuflects before the constitutional text, and then pronounces a fact-specific "exception" allowing the state to prevail. As the public increasingly sees crime as a ubiquitous threat, these judicially framed exceptions become increasingly profuse and inclusive.

The incoherence, confusion, and intellectual dishonesty of resulting Supreme Court search and seizure jurisprudence[17] is common knowledge, and it is not my intention to pick at that carcass. Still, in the context of accusations that communitarian constitutional law is an unrealistic romantic anachronism, it is worth reciting a brief but representative sample of liberal-individualist fourth amendment doctrine in order to show which theory is realistic and which is fabulist. Liberal-individualist premises have generated a body of law telling us that when police officers peer from a hovering helicopter into an enclosed shed in a citizen's fenced backyard, that action is not a "search" (*Florida v. Riley*, 1989). It is not a search when they look into a private business's outdoor storage area from an airplane, using a telescope so powerful it can detect half-inch pipes (*Dow Chemical v. United States*, 1986), or when they paw through a citizen's bagged garbage (*California v. Greenwood*, 1988). No seizure of the suspect occurs when police block the doorway of an Amtrak roomette, because the suspect is "free to leave" (*New York v. Burger*, 1987). In contemporary fourth amendment jurisprudence, an open field need be neither a field, nor open (*Oliver v. United States*, 1984). A search of a junkyard, conducted by police officers, uncovering evidence of a crime to be used in a criminal prosecution, is not a criminal search but an administrative one (Burger) and a police officer, in order to protect himself from assault, can look in the pocket of a suspect's jacket—even when the suspect is handcuffed outside his car and the jacket is in the back seat (*New York v. Belton*, 1981). Police officials may question a traveler whose only suspicious act is fitting a "drug courier profile" (*United States v. Sokolow*, 1989), which, in some cases, includes such traits as carrying heavy luggage (*Florida v. Royer*, 1983) and, in other cases, includes traits such as not carrying a lot of luggage (*United States v. Ballard*, 1978).

These cases illustrate the "general rule plus exceptions" (*Mincey v. Arizona*, 1978) format flowing inevitably from a rights-oriented premise, with its emphasis on individual protections forged by judges in particular cases. The general rule is that warrantless searches are "per se" unreasonable (*Katz v. United States*, 1967). At the present writing, the list of exceptions to the warrant requirement includes frisks; inventories; administrative inspections; searches incident to arrest; searches by consent; those in emergencies; in hot pursuit; in automobiles; and under generally exigent circumstances (sometimes called "community caretaking"). In addition, a continually growing class of police actions fails even to receive fourth amendment scrutiny because the Court deems them to be non-searches. These "non-searches" include any police intrusion into an area where one has no "reasonable expectation of privacy," including, for example, one's own fenced backyard (*Florida v. Riley*) and police sightings of objects which are in plain view from within a constitutionally protected area to which police have gained lawful admission—even if the intrusion was a mere pretext to gain the sighting they otherwise could not have obtained lawfully (*Horton v. California*, 1990).

Examination of two of these exceptions demonstrates how the theory underlying this non-legislated, rights-oriented, case-by-case method leads to a jurisprudence that is unwieldy and illogical. The "search incident to arrest" cases illustrate the consequences of a system in which general policy choices about fundamental rights emerge from specific encounters presenting themselves as conflicts between individual criminals' rights and general social interests. The "administrative search" cases illustrate the gradual, but ultimately complete, removal of search and seizure policy-making from the political, deliberative arena.

III. COMMUNITARIAN SEARCH AND SEIZURE

A. Communitarianism

1. *Varieties of Communitarian Thought*

Within the last two or three decades, historians, political theorists, and legal scholars have rediscovered or are rebuilding an alternative to liberal-individualism, a counter-theory, which they argue offers a less cynical and corrosive vision of human nature and politics, as well as a more satisfactory account of constitutional history and law. This theory is called, variously, "republicanism," "neo-republicanism," "civic republicanism," or "communitarianism." To avoid confusion with the party of defense spending, deregulation, and restrictive abortion laws, I will usually employ the latter term.

As does liberal-individualism, communitarianism encompasses a variety of strains and subgroups. One, historical and descriptive in its orientation, focuses on the classical communitarian theorists and their early American anti-federalist successors. These communitarians describe a political society based on "virtue," defined as public-spiritedness, political altruism, and the subordination of personal ambition and interest to the greater good. Another strain, more theoretical than historical, puts political participation at the heart of the theory. A related but distinct subgroup emphasizes the values associated with law-making based on rational discourse and deliberation, while still another centers on fostering a pervasive sense of cultural identity and shared context. Localism and smallness are important to many theories. Leading legal communitarians reject the classic republican ideal of a homogeneous citizenry, emphasizing instead the inclusive dialogic articulation of community norms—so-called rainbow republicanism. In a recent and perceptive contribution to legal communitarianism, Frank Michelman lists four characteristic traits of communitarian politics—its focus on the common good, its emphasis on deliberation, its role as a constitutive force in human development, and its rejection of natural rights—but then argues that they are not necessarily linked to each other.[18] The following sketch identifies the most important components of communitarianism, and presents the theory not as a random collection of beliefs but as an internally consistent expression of a unified deep structure.[19]

2. *The Individual and Associations*

The starting point of communitarian theory might be a conception of human nature grounded in Aristotle, who says in the *Politics* that humans are by nature not self-contained units, but polis-dwelling animals, and that the political community is logically prior to the individual. By this he means that defining the community as a collection of individuals or interest groups is to define not a community at all, but a group of isolated, atomized, and alienated pre-humans who happen to be living in proximity to one another. In the communitarian view, groups and other people are not impediments to an individual's fulfillment, but the condition of it. A community is not a necessary evil or an instrumental accommodation; it is authorizing and constitutive. It authors and constitutes people, provides them with identities and roles, determines the very categories into which their sense impressions are organized; it situates them and binds them together in a web of support and obligation, and in so doing, makes it possible for them to be human animals. People, then, are not acontextual self-interest maximizers. They are incomplete organisms who "are meant for [political] association," and thus, in forming associations, create the potential to become fully human creatures. A human, Marx notes, "is an animal which can develop into an individual only in society."

3. Politics

The political community, according to Aristotle the highest form of association, is therefore not a market-like arena into which individuals or interest groups will sometimes venture in order to further their pre-existing private interests. Rather, politics is the process of community self-formation, the shared search for a common good life. Because the public life of the polis is fundamentally constitutive, participation in it through reasoned deliberation is not a duty or burden. It is, rather, the privilege and the birthright of all citizens, the activity in and through which they become human. Politics does not constrain freedom; it facilitates freedom by providing the arena in which a person might carry on the activities that make self-rule possible.[20]

4. Rights

Communitarianism (in contrast to liberal-individualism) de-emphasizes the role of individual rights—those private areas of autonomy beyond the political process into which the state may not go (Michelman 446). By conceiving of freedom not as liberals do—"the inner space into which men may escape from external coercion" (Arendt, "What is Freedom?" 146)—but rather as the opportunity to engage in creative public action, communitarianism expands the scope and the role of public deliberation and, by necessity, reduces in importance and number those situations in which individuals might assert private immunity from the political will of their fellows. Because rights are such an essential part of Americans' self-definition, no realistic American political theory can ignore them. Thus, contemporary legal communitarian thinkers accommodate the particular content of American political life by conceding to rights an important—albeit supporting—role. Communitarian rights are not pre-political natural human possessions, as they are in liberal-individualist theory; rather, as politically generated, traditional, generally acknowledged fundamental decisions, they merely form the background against which the day-to-day deliberative process takes place, or perhaps the safety net beneath it.[21]

5. Constitutional Law

Historians have demonstrated that liberal-individualism was not the only or even the principal political theory driving the Founders, and that in fact the original American constitutionalists were not the Philadelphia

Founders, but the framers of participatory state charters and constitutions. The principal goal of state constitutions and an important goal of the national one, expressed in the concepts of federalism and separation of powers, was to erect a structure that would encourage citizens to participate in a deliberative process leading to the decisions that affected their lives and shaped their values. The principal purpose of checks and balances was to ensure that no measure became law until it had been fully deliberated. This deliberation was not mere interest-bargaining in pursuit of selfish goals and naked preferences, but rather a rational search for common ground guided by "virtue"—a desire to find and promote the common good.

Accordingly, the role of judicial review in this scheme is not to protect certain areas of personal autonomy from repressive or abusive majoritarian or governmental tyranny. Depending on the theorist, the function of judicial review is, variously, to ratify fundamental but informally adopted "structural amendments" that the people have made to the Constitution;[22] to articulate the citizens' ideal by reminding them of fundamental principles on which they already agree; to enforce procedural regularity, or adherence to deliberative methods within the legislative branch; to serve as the last remaining institution within which rational deliberation guides policy formation; or to protect those whose insularity bars them from effective political participation.

B.   Communitarian Search and Seizure
1.   General Approach: Law First, Rights Second
For purposes of search and seizure law, communitarianism has three important features. First, it conceives of public policy as the result of a deliberative, inclusive process seeking to discover a common vision of the good, and not as the outcome of an adversarial bargaining transaction. Second, it conceives of the state as an enabling and constitutive body, and not as a limiting or threatening one. Third, it consequently de-emphasizes pre-political individual rights and judicial review as their guardian, substituting instead a conception of rights as fallback provisions, grounded in tradition and consensus, invoked by courts only when public policy decisions deviate from fundamental constitutive principles.

While federal fourth amendment doctrine is national, rights-oriented, and juriscentric, communitarian search and seizure law must be local and legiscentric. It should maximize the role of public deliberation, preferably at the level of the smallest possible political unit. It should proceed from the assumption that law enforcement is a facet of community self-rule, affecting the relationship between all citizens and their own agents. It should conceive of search and seizure law as a question of political authorization, insisting that searches are presumed unlawful unless specifically authorized by legislation; individual rights should enter the adjudication only if necessary to evaluate the constitutionality of the legislation, not of particular governmental acts. And in determining the scope of rights, the court should focus on articulable, widely shared political and social traditions.

2. Law First

In a communitarian regime, search and seizure would be a branch of administrative law[23] dealing with searches by police as acts by executive agents not unlike tax collectors, schoolteachers, or health inspectors. These agents operate under express legislative authority, and their actions are evaluated first according to whether they are within that authority, and only then according to whether that authority meets some constitutional standard. Neither the courts nor the citizens would assume that police officers, alone among executive agents, operate under an open-ended commission to do whatever they want short of violating the Constitution. Rather, the governing assumption would be that people authorize and define police conduct after rationally deliberating about their own desire to be free from scrutiny, and about the kind of community they want to be. Unlike typical modern administrative agencies, however, police agencies or others exercising authority to search or seize, because this conduct implicates fundamental constitutional protections, would not be permitted to operate by rules the agency itself enacted under a legislative delegation,[24] since their doing so would either circumvent entirely or diminish significantly the public deliberation which communitarian reform is designed to create.

This popular deliberation, involving general, prospective law-making in the context of defining the government's relation to all its constituent citizens, would avoid not only the ad hoc quality of judge-made search law, but would also present the issue outside of the immediate context of a criminal prosecution, a context which necessarily frames it in terms of an individual right against the state. Communitarian search and seizure law, forged in deliberative bodies by politically accountable representatives, would be more likely to perceive the problem as one of self-rule and self-definition involving the citizenry at large and their agents deciding the extent of their own physical privacy in a number of everyday situations, incidentally including law enforcement.[25]

3.   Rights Second

The judiciary in this scheme might have one of two roles. First, it might remind the people themselves of their legislative obligations and prerogatives. This role is necessary not because the logic of search and seizure law-making is strained or bizarre, but because it is unfamiliar. Thus, a court presented with evidence obtained by an unauthorized police search might suppress it, and promise to continue suppressing such evidence in future cases, even if the searches do not violate any constitutional rights. The rationale is the same the court would use to prevent a rogue school board from levying taxes without benefit of legislation, or to prevent a children's services worker from administering unannounced and unregulated parental competence questionnaires. The principle, obvious in other contexts, is that unauthorized governmental action is unlawful regardless of whether or not it would have been constitutional if authorized.

Second, once politically accountable bodies learn to prescribe appropriate investigative practices, the court could resume its institutional role of reviewing this legislation, and not particular police encounters with criminals, for conformity to constitutional requirements. In the case of search and seizure law in jurisdictions whose constitutions contain a "warrant on probable cause" requirement and a "reasonableness" requirement,[26] and assuming that these two requirements are disjunctive,[27] the court would decide whether legislative definitions of "probable cause" meet constitutional minima, and whether the legislatively authorized searches are "unreasonable."[28]

The court would derive these evaluations not from its own balancing tests, but from existing evidence of what the community traditionally and consensually regards as reasonable—evidence such as common-law doctrine or well-established statutes, as well as historical or other data not typically found in law libraries or appellate court opinions. For example, in deciding whether official searches of garbage are reasonable, the court might examine (and counsel discuss) questions of property law (who owns garbage?; at what point does ownership pass from the discarder to the collector?), substantive criminal law (is taking discarded material a crime?; was it a crime at common law?), and tort law (if the searched garbage had caused injury to a bystander, would the discarder be liable?). In evaluating the legality of drug testing by random urinalysis, relevant information would include anthropological and sociological data about shared cultural attitudes toward the privacy of bodily fluid elimination. Only when these sources did not provide an adequate basis for decision—for instance when they were absolutely silent or hopelessly ambiguous[29]—the court could use its own judgment regarding reasonable social norms.

4. The State Constitution:
Vehicle for Communitarian Search and Seizure Law
The judicial role in the creation of search and seizure doctrine, then, is to prod the legislature into policy-making, and then to review that policy for constitutionality. The basis of review is, whenever possible, widely shared and accepted traditional community norms. It cannot be overemphasized that the courts performing these tasks should be construing state constitutional search and seizure provisions, dealing with the fourth amendment only if they determine that state protections fall below the federal minimum.[30] Regardless of its substance, federal judicial review as currently practiced is the wrong procedural vehicle for any kind of communitarian revival. First, it operates at the national level, the very scale of which exacerbates the difficulty of finding shared values. The critics of communitarianism are surely correct when they insist that the modern nation-state is too large a unit in which to discover or nurture a sense of common norms. Second, judicial review at the federal level is not only non-participatory, it is anti-participatory, allowing unelected officials to countermand, in the name of pre-political rights, the actions of the majority's agents. Third, federal judicial review as currently practiced is thoroughly dedicated to various balancing tests setting individual rights against governmental interests—a method of defining constitutional problems that precludes communitarian treatment, because it assumes an adversarial relationship between individuals exercising their rights and the state exercising constraints. State constitutional law, on the other hand, is more local and less committed to a particular judicial methodology.

That state constitutional law is well suited to the expression of communitarian principles is due also to certain historical and structural factors. Existing state constitutions, including state guarantees against unreasonable searches and seizures, trace their ancestry to the earliest state charters. Those documents, predating the federal Constitution, were framed during a period of intense republican sentiment, and gave voice to that sentiment by encouraging citizen participation, creating powerful legislative branches and institutionalizing a number of devices designed to ensure public deliberation. Although this "first wave" of explicitly communitarian state constitutions ultimately gave way to reformed charters reflecting a less participatory, more federalist theory of government, not all communitarian influences were purged. Even today, state constitutions reflect their heritage by seeking "generally to require a more open and deliberative state legislative process, one that addresses the merits of legislative proposals in an orderly and rational manner."[31] Thus, for example, many state charters contain "single subject" provisions to prevent legislative logrolling, and rules that prohibit legislators from proposing amendments that alter a bill's published subject. In interpreting state constitutions as communitarian documents, then, courts would be faithful to the charters' heritage.

Further, and more importantly, the character of contemporary state constitutions makes them appropriate vehicles for communitarian reform. Except on those few occasions when their representatives vote on actual amendments or on controversial Supreme Court nominees, popular participation in federal constitutional law is symbolic at best. For the most part, it is limited to periodic anniversary celebrations, usually highly commercial in tone ("bicentennial moments"), or to assertions of a fictive genealogical link with the original framers and ratifiers. The actual document is a national icon, preserved under glass in Washington, DC, like some fragment of the True Cross. State constitutions, by contrast, have remained relatively demystified and accessible. Between 1776 and 1985, "the states produced about 150 state constitutions"[32] at over 232 state constitutional conventions, thirty-six since World War II alone.[33] The enactment of amendments has reached epidemic proportions; nearly 5,200 have been adopted, for an average of over one hundred per state, many through such popular methods as initiative and referendum. In one biennium, 1984–85, voters in forty-five states deliberated on 238 constitutional amendments. California voters have amended their constitution more than 450 times. Further, state court judges who decide state constitutional cases are usually elected officials, so that even the constitutional glosses made by case law are exposed to an indirect but real popular influence.

Thus, because of their heritage and their present nature, state constitutions are simultaneously *constitutional* and *accessible* to citizens. They are constitutional in that they erect, authorize, and limit a government—they constitute a polity. They are accessible to citizens in that they can be easily rewritten or altered. State constitutions are, as A. E. Dick Howard notes,

> fit place[s] for the people of a state to record their moral values, their definition of justice, their hopes for the common good. George Mason understood that when . . . he wrote that "no free government, nor the blessings of liberty, can be preserved to any people" but by a "frequent recurrence to fundamental principles."[34]

This rhetoric is not merely aspirational. Studies indicate that ordinary citizens participating in constitutional politics sense that the project is exceptional, and respond with conduct that rises above partisan or interest-driven politics.

It is clear, then, that state constitutional search and seizure law provides an auspicious and legitimate opportunity for introducing communitarian precepts. One state court, at least, is taking advantage of that opportunity.

IV. BEYOND THEORY: OREGON SEARCH AND SEIZURE LAW

Recent legal scholarship has demonstrated that communitarian principles can help explain otherwise inconsistent United States Supreme Court doctrine in such areas as substantive due process, takings, public education, and voting rights. Nevertheless, proposals to substitute communitarian legal precepts for traditional liberal-individual precepts have provoked scorn and criticism. Such proposals are labeled romantic, anachronistic, and tyrannical: romantic because they are based on an idealized view of human nature (Simon 89); anachronistic because, although they might have been feasible in a homogeneous small-scale republic where consensus and meaningful participation were possibilities, they could never function in political units of modern proportions;[35]

and potentially tyrannical because, in ceding to the political majority an increased authority at the expense of individual rights, they open the door to majoritarian repression.[36]

Yet, in the state of Oregon, an evolving law of search and seizure suggests that communitarian precepts can be translated into workable and coherent state constitutional doctrine. Oregon has developed an independent interpretation of its constitution's search and seizure provision,[37] and, although it has not done so with any conscious intent to follow communitarian principles, that has been the effect.

Some of these principles manifest themselves in the threshold decision about what qualifies, for constitutional purposes, as a search. Under federal law, police conduct a search when their activity intrudes into a citizen's actual expectation of privacy but only if society is prepared to regard that expectation as reasonable or legitimate. The inquiry begins with the individual and his or her expectations; traditional prerogatives and community norms enter the calculation only after the fact, through a mysteriously derived judicial determination of whether the subjectively held expectation is acceptable. Because it occurs in the context of the individual's alleged criminal activity, this determination tends to be skewed in favor of illegitimacy and unreasonableness.

By contrast, in Oregon, a search is any activity which, "if engaged in wholly at the discretion of the government, will significantly impair [Oregonians'] freedom from scrutiny."[38] This formulation differs from federal law in subtle but significant ways. Most notably, it is wholly objective. The defendant's frame of mind is irrelevant, and the specific facts of a particular case serve only as the occasion for raising the general question. In other words, rather than testing the rights and privacy expectations of an individual criminal defendant against the court's assessment of what society would accept as reasonable and legitimate, the Oregon court begins and ends with a declaration of shared community norms, deduced from such existing evidence as well-settled common-law doctrine, generally accepted and venerable statutes, and even such nontraditional sources as survey research. Such a determination can be made in advance, wholesale or categorically and, for a given type of situation, reduced to a rule. For example, putting beepers on cars is a search because the people do not want police to be able to track their every move; doing so would significantly reduce their freedom from scrutiny.

Beyond the definitional stage, the radical and innovative methods of the Oregon court do not result in a law of criminal search and seizure that is significantly different, in theory, from federal law. Despite repeated exhortations in dissents,[39] law review articles, and committee hearings, the Oregon legislature has assumed responsibility for dictating standards of conduct to police officers only in very few kinds of situations. The greater share of responsibility remains, by default, the court's. Like the United States Supreme Court, the Oregon court insists that a warrantless search is per se unreasonable, unless it falls within one of the few narrowly construed and jealously guarded exceptions to the warrant requirement. Oregon criminal search and seizure law differs from its federal counterpart not in kind but in degree: the exceptions are fewer and more rationally related to exigencies which preclude application for a warrant.

The genuinely radical and communitarian turn in Oregon search and seizure law has occurred in the area of administrative or regulatory searches. When conducting searches for purposes other than the investigation or prosecution of crimes, Oregon officials are guided by a unique set of rules, all of which center on policy-making by legislative bodies.

First, officials may avail themselves of legislatively authorized administrative warrants, such as those suggested in *Camara*, if the legislature would see fit to set up an appropriate application process with stated criteria and goals.[40] The court has suggested "[a] warrant process might be established [by legislation] whereby law enforcement officers obtain a warrant to enter upon premises to seek missing persons or others reportedly in distress."

Furthermore, by a similar process, legislatures or city councils can authorize officials to conduct lawful administrative searches even without such an administrative warrant. The first suggestion of this power surfaced in a case challenging the constitutionality of a warrantless inventory search of an automobile, *State v. Atkinson*. Police, having impounded an abandoned car, discovered contraband while routinely inventorying its contents to preempt later accusations of theft. The court held that "responsible policymakers" could authorize such warrantless and suspicionless searches, if the government agents operated pursuant to lawful authority, conducted the inventory according to an authorized administrative program constrained by administrative rules and designed to eliminate discretion, so long as the scope of the search was consistent with a legitimate purpose. In this case, if a statute or ordinance authorized inventory searches, conducted under rules eliminating the discretion of the officers in choosing whom to search and how, the evidence discovered during such a search would not have been illegally obtained. Because the record did not disclose the existence or non-existence of such authorization, the court remanded the case for more fact-finding.

Within a few years, the court had an opportunity to expand its description of this kind of search and to begin explaining its rationale. *Nelson v. Lane County* involved a constitutional challenge to a drunk driving roadblock. The state argued that its police procedure met the *Atkinson* requirements. First, officers were authorized by statute to enforce the law; second, a police manual outlined procedures to eliminate officer discretion; and third, the search was brief and unintrusive. Holding that the roadblock search was part of criminal law enforcement, and therefore unconstitutional because warrantless, the court nonetheless went on to acknowledge once again that the legislature could authorize warrantless administrative searches without individualized suspicion. The court explained:

> One function of Article I, section 9, [the state constitutional search and seizure provision], is to subordinate the power of executive officers over the people and their houses, papers, and effects to legal controls beyond the executive branch itself. Compliance with the warrant clause . . . itself provides the necessary authorization for searches or seizures intended to discover evidence of crime. In *Atkinson*, we suggested that another method existed for administrative searches. We held that an administrative search conducted without individualized suspicion of wrongdoing could be valid if it were permitted by . . . a law or ordinance providing sufficient indications of the purposes and limits of executive authority, and if it were carried out pursuant to a properly authorized administrative program, designed and systematically administered to control the discretion of non-supervisory officers.

In *Nelson*, the court commented that the legislative authority claimed by the state, a general statute authorizing state police to enforce the law, was too vague to authorize this type of warrantless administrative search without individualized suspicion. According to *Nelson*, when constitutional rights are implicated, the authorization must not be overly general.

Nelson added two requirements to the *Atkinson* analysis. First, the court defined the nature of the required legislative authorization: it must be explicit and specific. Second, and more interestingly, it grounded the requirement for this legislation in the communitarian concept of political authorization by deliberative elected bodies. In *Nelson*, the court rejected the idea that judicial oversight is the sole protector of individual citizens' rights in search situations. Instead, the court supplemented the judicial warrant requirement by ascribing to legislatures and city councils—the politically deliberative organs of government—the duty to articulate rules authorizing certain state interactions with citizens. The *Nelson* court told the people of Oregon that if they wanted to subject themselves and their fellow citizens to random invasions of privacy, if they thought such invasions might be a reasonable price to pay in order to control drunk driving or drug abuse, then the people themselves would have to articulate that policy choice, and not leave it to the discretion of minimally accountable law enforcement professionals. Absent such specific authority or a judicial warrant, government action threatening to diminish protections is presumptively illegitimate. The legislative articulation of authority must be explicit, because according to *Nelson*, at least in the area of legislative delegation of rights-threatening authority to the police, a version of the nondelegation doctrine survives: "[b]efore they search or seize, executive agencies must have explicit authority from outside the executive branch." Vague or standardless delegation of law-enforcement authority will not suffice.

Of course, this does not mean that the citizens could decide to authorize campus security officers to conduct body cavity searches as a condition of admission to football games, or pass legislation allowing for midnight "regulatory" drug raids on private dwellings. Authority from a politically accountable legislative body is necessary but not sufficient; the court retains the power to review legislative authorizations. It does so, however, not through judicial balancing, but by reference to existing evidence of traditional public policy—that is, to well-established statutes, common-law doctrine, or traditions. For example, the determination of what qualifies as a "search" depends at least in part on "social and legal norms of behavior, such as trespass laws and conventions against eavesdropping" (*State v. Campbell*). The point is not that in Oregon police can be authorized to violate constitutional protections; "social and legal norms [alone] . . . cannot govern the scope of the constitutional provision." Rather, the point is that in Oregon the question of proper authority emanating from political deliberations always precedes the question of individual rights: law first, rights second.

This point was confirmed in a subsequent case, *State v. Bridewell* (1988),[41] in which an administrative "community caretaking" search inadvertently led authorities to evidence of a crime. A friend of the defendant, attempting to find him on his isolated mountain property, became alarmed when she noticed signs of distress: chained but unfed dogs, apparently ransacked rooms, and an empty holster. She called the police. After a lapse of twelve hours, which took the case out of any emergency exception, two officers drove to defendant's property and found him in his barn, uninjured, cultivating a thriving marijuana crop. The Oregon Supreme Court sustained suppression of the evidence because the state could cite no statute or ordinance authorizing so-called community caretaking entry onto the defendant's private property. The opinion concisely summarizes the relationship between political authorization, constitutional reasonableness, and judicial review:

> Whether law-enforcement officers have specific functions is a matter of statutory law. Whatever the existence, extent, or nature of community caretaking functions, however, mere exercise of any activity pursuant to one of them does not insure compliance with Article I, section 9. Any intrusion of state power upon a constitutionally protected interest . . . must comply with constitutional standards. The Court of Appeals decided that the intrusion in this case complied with the constitutional standard of "reasonableness" and so upheld the deputies' entry upon defendants' premises. We find it unnecessary to decide the issue because the deputies were without statutory or other authority from a politically accountable body to enter upon defendant's premises pursuant to a community caretaking function.

Thus, the court first questions whether there is authority; if none exists, the court ends the inquiry without confronting a constitutional issue. If authority exists, the court will then examine it for compliance with constitutional standards. Again, law first, rights second.

Although this holding was vigorously attacked in a partially dissenting opinion, it established that *Nelson v. Lane County* (1987), the roadblock case, was not an aberration. Absent a warrant, explicit authorization from politically accountable deliberative bodies must precede police or other governmental action. Before search and seizure questions become questions of a particular individual's rights, they are questions of general public policy.

Thus, the Oregon Supreme Court, interpreting its own state constitution, shows a preference for categorical, prospective, legislative restraints on official discretion, instead of ad hoc judicial limitations cast as rights-based claims against the government. The court sees unlawful administrative searches as unlawful because they do not find their source in some rational deliberative policy choice made by the people or their elected representatives. The Oregon court may or may not be guided by a conscious preference for communitarian, legiscentric doctrine; nevertheless, its search and seizure law has been developing in that direction. Whether this development will flourish, or even survive, remains to be seen.[42] But its mere existence, even if only transitory, proves that communitarian precepts can move from the realm of theory and romance into the real world of police inventories, drunk drivers, and drug testing.

V. CONCLUSION

Liberal-individualism may be a paradigm on the verge of disintegration.[43] Among the many incoherences it has generated, United States Supreme Court fourth amendment jurisprudence is certainly one of the most egregious and most characteristic. At this point, the conventional doctrine can account for the existing state of the law only through convoluted theory that contradicts reality at every turn; in other words, nobody seriously believes that today's fourth amendment law is about rights, individualism, or liberty. Can communitarianism provide a more satisfactory, internally coherent, and logical explanation? Perhaps it can, and perhaps, in one state, it already has.

NOTES

1 I self-consciously use the masculine pronoun here because the mythical hero of liberal-individualist America embodies traits and attitudes stereotypically associated with men—as feminist legal scholars, among others, have argued. *E.g.,* Sherry, *Civic Virtue and the Feminine Voice in Constitutional Adjudication,* 72 VA. L. REV. 543, 544 (1986) (legal and political structure reflects masculine emphasis on individualism).

2 *See generally* B. Mandeville, The Fable of the Bees: or, Private Vices, Public Benefits (9th ed. 1755).

3 R. Bellah, Habits of the Heart: Individuals and Commitment in American Life (1985).

4 Hanna Pitkin reminds us that in ordinary conversation a community's constitution is in one sense its "founding, framing, shaping . . . anew," and, in another sense, its "fundamental make-up . . . the national character of a people, their ethos . . . a product of their particular history and social conditions. . . . When Aristotle wrote his *Constitution of Athens*, he produced primarily a history of that city." Pitkin, *The Idea of a Constitution*, 37 J. Legal Educ. 167–68 (1987).

5 The literature of communitarianism or republicanism is enormous and proliferating. A basic list of texts includes, in the field of American history, H. Storing, The Complete Anti-Federalist: What the Anti-Federalists Were For (1981); W. Adams, The First American Constitutions: Republican Ideology and the Making of the State Constitutions in the Revolutionary Era (1980); J. Pocock, The Machiavellian Moment: Florentine Political Thought and the Atlantic Republican Tradition (1975); G. Wood, The Creation of the American Republic 1776–1787 (1969); B. Bailyn, The Ideological Origins of the American Revolution (1967).

   In the field of political theory, *see* B. Barber, Strong Democracy: Participation Politics for a New Age (1984); M. Sandel, Liberalism and the Limits of Justice (1982); A. MacIntyre, After Virtue: A Study in Moral Theory (1981); H. Pitkin, The Concept of Representation (1967); H. Arendt, On Revolution (1963); S. Wolin, Politics and Vision: Continuity and Innovation in Western Political Thought (1960); H. Arendt, The Human Condition (1958).

   Works in legal scholarship include Michelman, *The Republican Civic Tradition*, 97 Yale L. J. 1493 (1988); Michelman, *Foreword: Traces of Self-Government*, 100 Harv. L. Rev. 4 (1986); Sunstein, *Naked Preferences and the Constitution*, 84 Colum. L. Rev. 1689 (1984).

6 A. Smith, An Inquiry into the Nature and Causes of the Wealth of Nations, *passim* (1776).

7 R. Nozick, Anarchy, State and Utopia (1974); R. Posner, Economic Analysis of Law (1973).

8 J. S. Mill, On Liberty (1859).

9 Dworkin, Law's Empire, ch. 6 (1986).

10 J. Rawls, A Theory of Justice 3–6 (1971).

11 *See generally* I. Berlin, *Two Concepts of Liberty*, in Four Essays On Liberty 118 (1969); R. W. Emerson, *Self-Reliance*, in Prose Works of Ralph Waldo Emerson 243 (1870).

12 J-J. Rousseau, *The Social Contract*, in The Social Contract and Discourse on the Origin of Inequality 32–33 (L. Crocker ed. 1967) (1st ed. 1761).

13 According to Herbert Storing, anti-federalists as well as federalists viewed the preservation of individual liberty as the objective of government. Wilson C. McWilliams, however, argues that the federalists *intended* to impose a tyranny of the majority, defined as a consensus so large that no individuals could believe their participation mattered. W. C. McWilliams, *Democracy and the Citizen: Community, Dignity, and the Crisis of Contemporary Politics*, in How Democratic Is the Constitution? 79, 97 (R. Goldwin and W. Shambra eds. 1980).

14 Commentators have protested this tendency. J. Thayer, John Marshall 106–7 (1901) (judicial review encourages legislative neglect of constitutional issues); *see* Frohnmayer, *Of Legislative Intent, the Perils of Legislative Abdication, and the Growth of Administrative and Judicial Power*, 22 Willamette L. Rev. 219, 229–

36 (1986) (legislative abdication creates vacuum; judicial and administrative bodies fill it); *see generally* Brest, *The Conscientious Legislator's Guide to Constitutional Interpretation*, 27 STAN. L. REV. 585 (1975). Nothing in Marbury v. Madison, 5 U.S. (1 Cranch) 137 (1803), or subsequent cases developing judicial review even remotely implies that legislators are relieved of their duty to evaluate bills for constitutionality before voting on them.

15 *Compare* Plato, *Crito*, in COLLECTED DIALOGUES, at 27 (Socrates goes to his death affirming that laws of Athens are his parents, having given him identity and thereby enabling him to be human) *with* H. D. Thoreau, *Civil Disobedience* (Thoreau treats state and its laws as his enemies).

16 Equating citizen participation with legislation glosses over what is probably the most difficult and important issue in communitarianism: representation. Even with decentralization and increased localism, our world, as opposed to earlier worlds or utopian ones, cannot be restructured to allow meaningful direct participation. The Aristotelian ideal—a polis small enough to allow all citizens to know each other's character—is irrecoverable. Thus, communitarians must develop a theory of representation capable of accommodating citizen deliberation and involvement. Some have argued that modern media technology and the initiative/referendum process, both of which depend on sloganeering and thirty-second sound bites instead of rational, deliberative politics, exacerbate rather than cure this problem. Collins and Skover, *The First Amendment in an Age of Paratroopers*, 68 TEX. L. REV. 1087, 1116 (1990) ("electronic first amendment" limits meaningful public discourse); Linde, *When Is Initiative Lawmaking Not "Republican Government?"*, 17 HASTINGS CONST. L. Q. 159, 169–71 (1990).

More promising suggestions come from the theory of representation developed at length by Hannah Pitkin in H. Pitkin (suggesting, among other things, institutional basis for citizen interaction with political representatives). *See also* Sunstein, *Beyond the Republican Revival*, 97 YALE L. J. 1539, 1576–90 (1988) (suggesting structural changes to representative and electoral institutions to encourage and accommodate deliberation and participation). I plan to address this problem in detail in a forthcoming article on communitarianism and the law of government.

17 *See generally* Amsterdam, *Perspectives on the Fourth Amendment*, 58 MINN. L. REV. 349 (1974); Wasserstrom, *The Incredible Shrinking Fourth Amendment*, 21 AM. CRIM. L. REV. 257 (1984).

18 Michelman, *Conceptions of Democracy in American Constitutional Argument: Voting Rights*, 41 FLA. L. REV. 443, 444–52 (1989).

19 This harmony, I must warn, comes at the expense of nuance. Like any sketch of a venerable and sophisticated political theory appearing in a discussion of substantive applications, my sketch attempts to be useful and accurate rather than perfectly complete.

20 H. Arendt, *What Is Freedom?*, in BETWEEN PAST AND FUTURE: EIGHT EXERCISES IN POLITICAL THOUGHT 148–49 (1980).

21 Sunstein, *Republican Revival*, 1548–51.

22 Ackerman, *The Storrs Lectures: Discovering the Constitution*, 93 YALE L. J. 1013, 1044–72 (1984).

23 This approach, although untried, is not original. For example, the American Law Institute has formulated model legislation defining permissible search and seizure practices. *American Law Institute, A Model Code of Pre-Arraignment Procedure*, art. 210–90 (1975). Many commentators have argued that police practices in general should be circumscribed by rules. *E.g.*, K. C. Davis, POLICE DISCRETION 98–171 (1975) (focusing on need to constrain discretionary arrest and suggesting that police departments promulgate administrative rules); Walker, *Controlling the*

Cops: A Legislative Approach to Police Rulemaking, 63 U. DET. L. REV. 361, 363 (1986) ("[s]tate legislatures or local city councils should enact legislation or city ordinances requiring law enforcement agencies to undertake systematic rulemaking"); Williams, *Police Rulemaking Revisited: Some New Thoughts on an Old Problem*, 47 LAW & CONTEMP. PROBS. 123, 180–81 (1984) (police have authority to develop rules and should use it to provide greater uniformity in decision-making). Several commentators have singled out search and seizure as a subject that would benefit from rulemaking. *See, e.g.*, Dix, *Fourth Amendment Federalism: The Potential Requirement of State Law Authorization for Law Enforcement Activity*, 14 AM. J. CRIM. L. 1, 19–25 (1986–87) (suggesting that fourth amendment may require affirmative state law authorization for state law enforcement activities); Platt, *A Legislative Statement of Warrantless Search Law: Poaching in Sacred Judicial Preserves?*, 52 OR. L. REV. 139, 152–54 (1973) (advocating legislative statements of procedure for warrantless searches).

24 Under federal law and the law of most states, the legislature can delegate rule-making discretion to administrative agencies, providing them with only vague and general standards. This doctrine replaces an earlier one, the "nondelegation doctrine," under which such delegations of legislative power to executive agencies were deemed unconstitutional violations of the separation of powers. Industrial Union Dep't, AFL-CIO v. American Petroleum Institute, 448 U.S. 607 (1980). *But see id.* at 671 (Rehnquist, J., concurring) (suggesting revitalization of nondelegation doctrine).

25 Other benefits to be derived from legislative treatment of search and seizure include (1) The legislative process gives society the opportunity to simplify and modernize the law. (2) It enables the development of the law to be planned, with a design acceptable to contemporary society. (3) If well done, the resulting legislative statement provides a compact, complete, and accessible formulation of the law. (4) It can be subjected to continuous review and revision; its anomalies need not await the haphazard opportunities of judicial correction. (5) Through the legislative process the whole community may become involved in the determination of legal development.

26 Every state has a constitutional guarantee against governmental invasions of physical privacy. In all but six, these provisions, like the original ones and the fourth amendment, have a reasonableness clause and a warrant clause.

27 On the relationship between the two requirements, *see* J. Landynski, SEARCH AND SEIZURE AND THE SUPREME COURT: A STUDY IN CONSTITUTIONAL INTERPRETATION 41–43 (1966) (describing circumstances surrounding development of language of fourth amendment); Wasserstrom, *The Fourth Amendment's Two Clauses*, 26 AM. CRIM. L. REV. 1389, *passim* (1989) (describing competing independent and dependent interpretations of clauses of fourth amendment); Stewart, *The Road to Mapp v. Ohio and Beyond: The Origins, Development and Future of the Exclusionary Rule in Search-and-Seizure Cases*, 83 COLUM. L. REV. 1365, 1371–72 (1983).

28 Unlike Professor Sunstein, I am not arguing that in a communitarian regime the role of the court includes general judicial review for rationality or "virtue." Sunstein, *Interest Groups*, 1731–32. Quite to the contrary, I believe that communitarian judicial review, to the extent that it is not a contradiction in terms, must be as a general matter more deferential to the judgments made by deliberative, politically accountable bodies. Constitutional search and seizure provisions with "reasonableness" clauses, however, present a special case: the constitutional text itself mandates legislative rationality.

29 Many contemporary thinkers argue that all language is hopelessly ambiguous and that "meaning" is radically indeterminate. Legal scholars attempting to demonstrate

the contingency of all utterance offer, by way of example, inventive deconstructions of the apparently unambiguous statement in Article I, section 1, of the United States Constitution, which states that the president must "have attained to the age of thirty-five years." D'Amato, *Aspects of Deconstruction: The "Easy Case" of the Underaged President*, 84 Nw. U. L. REV. 250, 251–52 (1989) (listing legal scholars' different interpretations of age requirement); Peller, *The Metaphysics of American Law*, 73 CALIF. L. REV. 1151, 1174 (1985) (age requirement may signify "certain level of maturity" rather than certain number of years); Easterbrook, *Statutes' Domain*, 50 U. CM. L. REV. 533, 536 (1983) (thirty-five may mean the "number of revolutions of the world around the sun" or "minimum number of years after puberty"). Impressive arguments in defense of meaningful communication also exist. I believe communitarians can have it both ways. Even if the deconstructionists are correct, the premise of communitarianism is that through decentralization and inclusiveness we can create interpretive communities with broadly based shared understandings.

30 Purely as a matter of logic, a court should dispose of all state claims, constitutional and non-constitutional, before confronting a claim under the fourth amendment. If the rights claimant prevails under state law, no federal constitutional issue arises. Until a court decides that the state's law, including its constitutional law properly applied, deprives a claimant of life, liberty, or property, the state has not violated the fourteenth amendment's prohibition. This is the familiar argument underlying the new judicial federalism. The classic formulations occur in Linde, *Without "Due Process": Unconstitutional Law in Oregon*, 49 OR. L. REV. 125, 182 (1970) ("[a] holding that a state constitutional provision protects the asserted claim in fact destroys the premise for a holding that the state is denying what the federal Constitution would assure"); Linde, *First Things First: Rediscovering the States' Bills of Rights*, 9 U. BALT. L. REV. 379, 383–84 (1980) (state court should always consider state constitutions before federal constitution); State v. Kennedy, 295 Or. 260, 267, 666 P.2d 1316, 1320 (1983) (Linde, J.).

31 Williams, *State Constitutional Limits on Legislative Procedures*, 17 PUBLIUS 91, 92 (1987).

32 Friedman, *State Constitutions in Historical Perspective*, 496 ANNALS 33, 35 (1988). Tarr and Porter, in 1987, identify 146 constitutions. Tarr and Porter, *Introduction: State Constitutionalism and State Constitutional Law*, 17 PUBLIUS 1, 5 (1987).

33 Kincaid, *State Constitutions in the Federal System*, 496 ANNALS 12, 14–15 (1988).

34 Howard, *The Renaissance of State Constitutional Law*, 1 EMERGING ISSUES IN ST. CONST. L. 1, 14 (1988) (quoting Mason's language appearing currently in VA. CONST. art. I, § 15).

35 Fallon 1723; Fitts, *The Vices of Virtue: A Political Party Perspective on Civic Virtue*, 136 U. PA. L. REV. 1567, 1627 (1988); Mensch and Freeman, *A Republican Agenda for Hobbesian America?*, 41 FU. L. REV. 581, 610 (1989).

36 Baker, 504; Sandalow, 535; Bell and Bansal, *The Republican Revival and Racial Politics*, 91 YALE L. J. 1609, 1611 (1988); Sullivan, *Rainbow Republicanism*, 1722.

37 The Oregon constitution states:

No law shall violate the right of the people to be secure in their persons, houses, papers, and effects, against unreasonable search, or seizure; and no warrant shall issue but upon probable cause, supported by oath, or affirmation, and particularly describing the place to be searched, and the person or thing to be seized. (OR. CONST. art. I, § 9)

38 State v. Campbell, 306 Or. 157, 171, 759 P.2d 1040, 1048 (1988).

39 *See, e.g.*, State v. Brown, 301 Or. 268, 292, 295–98, 721 P.2d 1357, 1371–75 (1986) (Linde, J., dissenting) (guidelines stating circumstances that preclude waiting for

warrant should be formed by legislature, not court); State v. Tourtillott, 289 Or. 845, 882, 618 P.2d 423, 442 (1980) (Linde, J., dissenting) (officer's decision whether to investigate should be safeguarded by nondiscretionary administration legislative prescriptions), *cert. denied,* 451 U.S. 972 (1981). The dissent in Brown stated: "[w]e continue to see fallacious arguments that police have this or that authority because a court has held that the conduct at issue does not violate the state or the federal constitution. Courts do not authorize executive actions; laws do." State v. Brown, 301 Or. at 296, 721 P.2d at 1374.

40   State v. Bridewell, 306 Or. at 240 n.6, 759 P.2d at 1060 n.6 (politically accountable bodies might provide statutory authority to establish warrant process to be followed by law enforcement officers).

41   In the interest of full disclosure, the author acknowledges that he briefed and argued this case for the State before the Oregon Court of Appeals, where he prevailed, but retired into academia only to see his successor suffer a reversal at the Oregon Supreme Court.

42   I cannot claim that this development will continue; even as I write, the court has under advisement a case called State v. Axsom, 98 Or. App. 57, 777 P.2d 1392, *rev. allowed* (1989), where it is being asked to jettison its innovations in favor of ways that are more familiar. If that happens, a state constitutional law experiment in communitarianism will be abandoned before the nation has had a chance to recognize and evaluate it, and we will all be the poorer.

43   *See generally* Collins and Skover, *The Future of Liberal Legal Scholarship,* 81 MICH. L. REV. 189 (1988).

Remarks on Receiving the Hans Linde Award (2017)

David Schuman gave this speech March 22, 2017, at the American Constitution Society annual dinner at the Portland City Grill.

I have long admired the ACS but refrained from joining, because, despite the fact that Justices Thomas, Alito, and the late Justice Scalia were all active in Federalist Society affairs, I believed that it was not prudent for a sitting judge, even a sitting senior judge, to affiliate with an organization with a constitutional or other policy inclination. However, we no longer live in a country where prudence should frustrate participation; I joined ACS early in the morning last November 9. Last Sunday, I even went to an ACLU fundraiser—without a disguise.

The honor you have conferred on me is magnified in my mind by the fact that it is the Hans Linde Award. I began to admire Justice Linde and to fall under his powerful influence during my first year of law school, when the Supreme Court visited Lane County to hear cases and I observed his incisive questioning of counsel, and then later that year when I took Legislative and Administrative Process, a much-hated-by-almost-everybody-but-me required course that he and Dave Frohnmayer invented. That course for the first time revealed to me that a life in the law could be about much more than participating in private disputes, mostly about money; it could be about participating in the public life of the community; it could be about justice and about forging a public life worth living. At that point, Justice Linde became my idol. Later, when I clerked for him, he became my boss; when I joined the faculty at the UO, he became my occasional colleague as a visiting Wayne Morse professor; when I became deputy AG, he became my incognito co-conspirator in attempts to shape the state's legal positions; and when I joined the Court of Appeals he became my judicial model and my inspiration. Throughout, he has been my champion and advocate; I have had the best jobs that a lawyer can aspire to, and I would not have had any of them but for

Hans. I am proud to claim that, for the past thirty-five years, he has been my friend.

There is much to love and admire about Justice Linde, as we all know. He invented the "new judicial federalism," reminding state courts that they could interpret their own constitutions to confer on their states' citizens more, and more expansive, rights than the minimum guaranteed by the United States Constitution. He demonstrated to us that intellectual rigor is more important than expedience. He urged us, not so much to question authority, but to question unexamined presumptions. He taught us that, to quote Antonin Scalia—I'm pretty sure for the first time ever at an ACS event—that the rule of law should be a law of rules and not amorphous balancing tests that too frequently serve as nothing more than a substitute for rigorous analysis.

I also wish I could talk about Justice Linde's lasting legacy and his continuing influence on Oregon jurisprudence. I regret that I cannot do that with much confidence. It appears to me that the Oregon Supreme Court has embarked on a relentless deLindification process. I mentioned to Hans at one point that I was thinking about writing a law review article exposing and lambasting this process, and calling it "Worst Things First; The Decline and Fall of the Oregon Supreme Court." Hans's response was, "And what do you hope to accomplish by that?" and I had no satisfactory answer. The only answer that I could come up with was that the article would give me a chance to ventilate. Law review articles are not a good forum for ventilation. Annual ACS dinners, on the other hand, . . . So here goes.

- We now live in a state where uniformed and armed police officers, without any individualized suspicion, can approach a law-abiding citizen in, for example, a public park or on a public street, and ask that person to produce identification—so long as the officers ask nicely. Is anybody else reminded of World War II movies, where we recoiled when Gestapo asked people for "papers, please"? Does anybody have any doubts about what demographic is going to be disproportionally questioned in this manner?
- We now live in a state where armed and uniformed police officers can unlawfully trespass onto residential property by climbing over a fence into the back yard, then knock on a bedroom door, confront a half-naked occupant, ask if they can come in, discover contraband,

and have it admitted as evidence against the occupant, because (1) the consent was "voluntary," (2) the "taint" of the unlawful, unreasonable, unwarranted, unconstitutional act of police misconduct was "purged," despite the fact that the request for consent and the discovery of the evidence occurred during the unlawful act.

• We now live in a state where a plaintiff who, according to a jury's fact-finding, has incurred twelve million dollars worth of injuries due to the conceded negligence of a state actor, is going to have to eat nine million of those dollars, despite the constitutional guarantee of a remedy for injury to person and the sanctity of facts found by a jury.

These are only a few of the outcomes from recent cases that would cause Justice Linde, if he were dead, to roll over in his grave. Perhaps even more discouraging, though, are methodological, jurisprudential, and analytical apostasies that have crept into recent Oregon Supreme Court opinions. The court now regularly employs balancing tests in free expression cases like *State v. Babso*n, in equality cases like *State v. Savastano*, in search and seizure cases like *State v. Unger* and *State v. Backstrand*, and in remedy clause cases like *Horton v. OHSU*. The phrase "totality of the circumstances" and the reliance on adjectives like "reasonable" and "substantial" and "compelling," once banished to federal constitutional law where they first spawned, are reappearing in various analytical templates. The word "duty" is even sneaking back into recent tort cases.

Intellectual rigor, as well, is endangered. How else can one explain the following sentence?

We recognize that the damages available under the Tort Claims Act are not sufficient in this case to compensate plaintiff for the full extent of the injuries that her son suffered. However our cases do not deny the legislature authority to adjust, *within constitutional limits*, the duties and remedies that one person owes another.

In other words, we can constitutionally deny this plaintiff the remedy for injury that the jury found she deserved because the constitution permits it. That, ladies and gentlemen, is a classic example of something that

Justice Linde always cautioned against: confusing the conclusion with the premise, also known as begging the question.

Finally, the Linde court's sensitivity to the social context of the law seems to have atrophied. How else can one explain the following sentences, in a case creating a giant loophole in the exclusionary rule:

> We expect that law enforcement officers will act within constitutional limitations in their interactions with Oregon citizens. Civil litigation, tort claims, and training and education help protect Article I, section 9.

Well, the citizens of Oregon deserve more than an expectation of constitutional conduct, and we also understand—or should understand—that relying on civil litigation, tort claims, and training to constrain the few bad actors in uniform is . . . naïve.

How have we come to this? Recent and current Supreme Court justices are not stupid. They are not ideologues. They are not fascists. They are not even Republicans! I've known and worked with many of them. They are good, progressive people trying to do their best. I can only surmise that some of them have a desire to assert their independence, and that they sincerely find fault with various Linde and Linde Court cases and methods. It may also be relevant that legal aid and public defense attorneys, as well as attorneys from the socioeconomic background that public defenders and legal aid attorneys represent, have never had a significant numerical presence on the court.

A more important question is, what can be done? I'm afraid that the answer, at least with respect to jurisprudence and method, is—not much. The prospect of finding, supporting, or promoting a new justice with the experience, the vigor, the brilliance, and the creativity of Hans Linde is remote. We can hold symposia, mentor young lawyers, write briefs and articles, but as the Linde era recedes, these tactics lose force.

As far as substantive outcomes are concerned, as opposed to method, there are more promising possibilities. If the court continues to shrink our constitutional rights and liberties, we can remember a key Linde lesson: constitutional rights establish a floor beneath which the legislature cannot fall, but not a ceiling. I notice that the plaintiff's bar is lobbying for legislation establishing a *statutory* right to a full remedy for injury as found by a jury, in essence superseding recent case law denying such rights as *constitutionally* required. Perhaps the criminal defense bar and other civil libertarians could do the same. The American Law Institute, for example, is working on a statutory code of "policing principles."

Another Lindesque tactic for cases involving police-citizen encounters is to bring those cases in the civil context, where the court is presented with a rights claim in the context of an innocent person's mistreatment, so the rights can be vindicated without "letting the criminal go free because the constable blundered."

So I am not without hope. I can hope, perhaps naïvely, that the inevitable impending backlash against the current administration, including its Trump-Sessions-Giuliani law-and-order cabal, its speech-and-press-stifling paranoia, will generate a revival of concern for rights. If not, and if we survive, we can at least look back with awe and gratitude to an era in which, under the intellectual leadership of Justice Hans Linde, the Oregon Supreme Court, like Oregon public schools and the sane Oregon Republican Party, was a nationally admired state treasure.

from "The Creation of the Oregon Constitution" (1995)

The article excerpted here first appeared in the Oregon Law Review 74. *The full text can be found at avoiceforjustice.com.*

Oregon has had only one constitution, created during a single month in 1857. The sixty drafters, most of whom were farmers,[1] produced a state charter remarkable only for its conventionality and small-mindedness; 172 of its 185 sections were copied from other constitutions, and the thirteen original ones consisted almost entirely of various racial exclusions and measures limiting state expenditures.[2]

Despite this apparent crabbed conservatism, however, the Oregon Constitution has played a key role in the twentieth century's most radical and progressive state constitutional developments: the so-called Oregon System of popular democracy, which grew out of the initiative and referendum provisions of the Oregon Constitution; and the revival of state constitutional rights known as the "new judicial federalism," first and most persistently practiced by the Oregon judiciary. These influential doctrines derive not from the text of the document as drafted in 1857, but from subsequent historical developments: the populist reform politics of the early twentieth century and the revival of state constitutionalism by the Oregon Supreme Court beginning in the late 1970s.

Yet the distinctive political culture that gave rise to those later progressive developments was present even at the founding. Along with meanness of spirit, the original Oregon Constitution reflected a civic-minded people committed to public discourse on important issues, within a bounded universe in which the very terms "public" and "civic" had an intentionally limited and provincial meaning.[3]

I.   PRECURSORS TO THE CONSTITUTION

American settlers, meeting in Champoeg on May 2, [1843], elected a committee to draft a founding compact for submission to the people. As a result of the subsequent plebiscite of July 5, Oregon had its first constitution. The document contained a bill of rights guaranteeing religious freedom, trial by jury, proportionate representation, common law judicial procedure, habeas corpus, public schools, and "good faith towards the Indians." It also banned slavery. The government consisted of a nine-member legislature, elected annually; a three-member executive committee; and a judicial department with supreme, associate, and probate judges. (Robertson 36).

> No sooner had Oregon achieved territorial status than it began to move toward statehood—the development that would require, for the first time, a genuine constitution.

By this time, the issue of statehood had turned partisan. Oregon was quickly becoming politically divided between Whigs, centered in Portland and speaking through Thomas Dryer's *Weekly Oregonian,* and the more numerous and powerful Democrats, centered in Salem and speaking through Asahel Bush's *Oregon Statesman.*[4] Because the Whig administrations of Presidents Taylor (1849–50) and Fillmore (1859–53) filled important territorial positions with Whig appointees, Oregon's Whigs staked out a position in favor of the status quo over statehood, because they knew change would result in Democratic officeholders. Democrats in general, particularly the powerful group surrounding Bush known as "the Salem Clique," espoused statehood because they resented these Whig appointments. The advent of Pierce's Democratic administration in 1853 did nothing to quell the Clique's pro-statehood sentiment, however, because although Pierce did appoint Democrats to Oregon offices, they were non-Oregonians.[5]

Thus, when statehood agitation reappeared in the 1854 legislature, it was known as "the Democratic Dogma of Statehood." By that time, Democrats, swept into office on Pierce's coattails in 1852, had solidified control of both houses (Woodward 76); they managed to pass a bill referring the question of statehood to the people. Statehood lost, 4079 to 3210, after a strident battle in the editorial pages of the *Oregonian* and the *Statesman.* Twice more the legislature referred the matter to the people—in June 1855 and April 1856—with the same outcome, but with statehood losing each time by a smaller margin. Finally, in June 1857, faced with the issue for the fourth time, the people of Oregon voted to hold a constitutional convention and petition to join the Union. Surprisingly, this vote was not close: despite having lost by 249 votes a year earlier, statehood now prevailed by a vote of 7,617 to 1,679. The explanation, ultimately yet obliquely, involved the issue that was dominating national politics at the time: race.

Although it is an understatement to say that early Oregonians were hostile to nonwhites—one of the first acts of the provisional legislature made Black immigration a crime punishable by whipping (Robertson 38), and the territory's most influential Democrat once referred in print to abolitionists as "nigger-struck dames" (Woodward 93)—nonetheless slavery never existed to any significant extent in territorial Oregon.[6] It was contrary to statute,[7] judicially prohibited,[8] and impractical.[9] Perhaps most importantly to the settlers, it would have required proximity to "negroes," and it conjured paranoid nightmares of an antiwhite alliance between rampaging escaped slaves and Indians (Woodward 89). The Missouri Compromise of 1820, in any event, seemed to settle the issue: Oregon, north of the Compromise line, would be free.

Events outside of Oregon, however, conspired to submerge this rift and propel the territory and all its factions toward statehood. Civil strife erupted in Kansas, and federal forces intervened on the pro-slavery side. Oregonians of all political stripes feared that continued territorial status, coupled with deep division over slavery, invited similar federal intervention. Whigs and Republicans feared that any intervention, under the authority of what they perceived as a pro-slavery Democratic administration, would favor pro-slavery forces. Democrats, while divided over the merits of slavery, stood absolutely united on the issue of local sovereignty, preferring any Oregon-determined solution to the problem over any federally imposed one. Thus, the *Oregonian* spoke for nearly the entire population in an editorial on November 1, 1856: "If the power of the regular army is to be used to crush out freedom in the Territories . . . we had better throw off our vassalage and become a state at once" (Woodward 98). To Oregonians, in other words, issues of slavery, patronage and economics gave way to the prior issue of self-determination. After the *Oregonian* editorial had both reflected and helped build a pro-statehood consensus, the people voted overwhelmingly in the next election to convene a constitutional convention.

II. THE CONSTITUTIONAL CONVENTION

A. Organization and Procedures

At the same election (June 1857) the voters also chose convention delegates. Slavery, oddly enough, was not a key issue around which opposing candidates framed their campaigns. Both the Republican and the Whig Party conventions officially adopted free-state positions, while the Democratic convention resolved to endorse candidates regardless of how they stood on slavery, proposing instead that the issue should be decided not by the convention, but by plebiscite afterwards. Only one candidate, Democrat Matthew Deady, ran as an avowed pro-slavery advocate, although contemporary anti-slavery Democrat Judge Williams believed that most of his Democratic colleagues privately supported Deady's position—and indeed the Democrat-controlled convention elected Deady as its president.

Democrats in fact dominated the convention (Seagraves 8). One delegate later estimated that "regular" Democrats—those whose free state stance had not turned them into virtual Republicans—made up three-fourths of the sixty delegates. They came to the convention well-organized and disciplined, having already met in caucus and drafted at least one article (Johnson 172–73). Although Oregon Democrats were by no means obedient soldiers taking marching orders from the national party—that party, after all, took a firm stand against local sovereignty—they did share a basic political orientation. Both the national and local organizations favored strict regulation of corporations, especially banks, and preferred small over big government (Seagraves 5). And regardless of party affiliation—in addition to the Democrats there were Independents, Whigs, and one official Republican[10]—the delegates were all pioneers. "[N]one . . . was wealthy, and many . . . had known the pinch of hard times and had suffered from scarcity of the comforts of life." They mostly came from midwestern states, so that their ideas about state constitutions were shaped by the "reform" charters many of those states had enacted in the 1840s (Johnson 142). Further, they had formed their political ideals in the lexicon of classical republicanism,

valuing independence and civic-minded altruism, while also believing
in the inherently ennobling results of political participation in "face-to-
face relationships, conducted by well-known friends and neighbors." Significantly, these Oregonians had affirmatively chosen the self-sufficient,
rural, noncommercial alternative to the gold-driven dynamism of the
California economy. Thirty-three were farmers, eighteen were lawyers
(including all three of the Territorial Supreme Court justices), five were
gold miners, two were journalists, and one was a civil engineer (McBride
Address 484). Not surprisingly, despite their numbers, "the lawyers
monopolized most of the time and the farmers the least."

The Constitutional Convention opened in Salem on Monday, August
17, 1857. The first sessions were devoted largely to organizational matters. The delegates first elected Judge Deady president and another
Democrat, Chester Terry, secretary. They then received the report of the
credentials committee, debated whether to appoint an official reporter
(they decided not to—an early indication of the convention's obsession
with thrift), whether to use honorific titles in addressing each other (they
didn't), whether to require delegates to swear an oath (motion tabled),
whether to permit smoking (no), whether to have an official chaplain
(no), and whether to impose a forty-minute limit on speeches (passed,
despite this argument from Delazon Smith, a famous orator known to
friends as "the Lion of Linn" and to enemies as "Delusion Smith": "Why,
sir, I could not begin to have a good sweat on by that time. Some men
cannot get their minds off freely until they get warmed up. I am among
that number.").

D. Individual Rights

Individual rights occupied the convention on numerous occasions. The
topic arose as early as the second day, when Judge Williams opposed a
separate Bill of Rights Committee, arguing that "[a] bill of rights is a sort
of Fourth of July oration [that] . . . has been the subject of very much legislation and contention in the older states, as to the effect of certain provisions . . . [and] whether its provisions are directory or not; or whether
they are absolutely binding." Williams proposed instead to work all of
the usual rights guarantees into other parts of the constitution, although

why he believed this would avoid the problems of a special bill is unclear. The discussion was tabled, and arose again the next day, when the terms of the argument and what was at stake became more explicit. Delazon Smith argued in favor of the bill:

> [T]he history of the world teaches us that the majority may become fractious in their spirit and trample upon the rights of the minority; that through the madness of party spirit they may infringe upon the rights of the individual citizen. Then, if the individual is to be protected in this point in which he is endangered, there must be restrictions put into this constitution. The people must say we will limit ourselves in certain principles.

Judge Williams, author of the "Free State Letter" that many credit with dooming slavery in Oregon (Davenport 39), responded with an argument that demonstrates the distinction between anti-slavery sentiment and racial tolerance. Not only did he oppose a separate bill, he also wanted to ensure that the individual rights distributed throughout the constitution did not contain any loose language about "the natural equality of mankind," because "[s]ome say that it means that negroes are equal with whites." Williams's arguments against a separate bill of rights lost, although, as is evident from later developments, not because the convention rejected his anti-negro position. Further, when the committee eventually proposed a bill of rights, the first section declared that "all men, when they form a social compact are equal in right," and this provision passed into the constitution without debate.

Instead, the debates centered on religion and on the powers of the jury. Religion drew the most attention. The committee, using the Indiana Constitution's Bill of Rights as a model ("[i]t is gold refined," declared Delazon Smith), submitted a section declaring that "no money shall be drawn from the treasury for the compensation of any religious services." When a delegate pointed out that literal application of this language would preclude the legislature from employing a chaplain, the topic of the ensuing debate quickly expanded from legislative chaplains per se to church-state relations in general. Judge Deady reminded the delegates that the "theory of our government" on the issue was "that the government shall be separated from churches" because "the country contains persons of all religious denominations, as well as nonbelievers." Other delegates were not so diplomatic in describing Oregon's religious diversity. Mr. Waymire said the people of this country ranged from "the half-crazy religious fanatic to the unbelieving atheist." When Thomas Dryer pointed out that prohibiting a legislative chaplain would make Oregon unique among the states, Lafayette Grover responded with this first example of Oregonian pride in a state constitution that was uniquely rights-generous:

> It is true this constitution goes a step farther than other constitutions on this subject; but if that step is in the right direction, and consistent with the proper development of our institutions, I see no weight in the objection that it is new. Let us take the step farther, and declare a complete divorce of church and state.

The legislative chaplain issue recurred for several sessions. When debate ended, the delegates voted in unambiguous terms: to the prohibition on spending public money on religious institutions, the convention explicitly added, "[n]or shall any money be drawn from the treasury as compensation for religious services in either house of the legislative assembly."

Other than religion, the only provision of the bill of rights to provoke extended debate was Section 16, which provided, "In all criminal cases whatever the jury shall have the right to determine the law and the facts." In another rare departure from pure verbatim transcription, the *Oregonian* reporter commented that this section "elicited one of the most interesting, lengthy and animated discussions" of the convention. That discussion, dominating two sessions, predictably pitted the judges against the populists. Judge Deady began the debate by immediately proposing that the section be amended to read, "In all trials by a jury the court shall decide the law, and the jury the facts." This proposal provided an opening for Dryer, who was still smarting from a remark Judge Deady had made on the floor earlier in the day referring to the press of Oregon, including Dryer's *Oregonian*, as "a running sore on the community." Now, Dryer argued that

> [e]very juryman of sense could understand the law and judge of it just as well as any judge who ever sat upon the bench. Men had

escaped hanging in this territory, because the judge mystified and misconstrued the law. The judges . . . concentrate power in their own hands. . . . They sometimes make awful mistakes.

When the Deady amendment lost, Judge Williams moved to add, "nor shall a judge be allowed to instruct a jury or grant a new trial!" —in order "to make the farce complete." Dryer responded again, reminding the delegates that their duty was to "frame a constitution," not a "judicial monarchy." And so it went, until finally a compromise amendment passed, providing, "The jury shall determine the law and the facts, under the direction of the court as to the law, and the right of new trial as in civil cases."[11]

Although the delegates did not discuss other sections of the bill of rights in any recorded detail,[12] individual rights issues surfaced in several other contexts. For example, one section in the proposed "Miscellaneous" article guaranteed to every married woman "the property and rights she had at time of marriage or obtained afterwards, by means of which the husband was not the meritorious cause." The drafters included this section in response to the Donation Act of 1850, which made available to any married couple 640 acres of free federal land, half in the name of the wife. The section served to insulate the wife's half from creditors attempting to collect judgments against improvident husbands (Bancroft 426). Judge Deady supported a motion to strike the provision. Judge Williams characterized it as a product of "this age of woman's rights and insane theories," which, like the Donation Act itself, "had been the cause of much domestic trouble and many divorces." In defense of the provision and of women in general, Mr. Waymire noted that "his mother was a woman and his wife was one" as well and argued that "if we should legislate for any class it should be the women of this country." Persuaded by this and other arguments, the delegates ultimately approved a strong provision protecting married women's property.[13]

The individual rights topic that most permeated the convention, however, was race. It appeared not only in the context of slavery, but also in discussions of procedure, transition to statehood, suffrage, the militia, and education. It is not an exaggeration to say that the entire convention was obsessed with the question.

Slavery, of course, presented the issue of race in its starkest form. The convention occurred during a time of fierce national convulsion—convulsion that, as discussed above, threatened to divide Oregon. The convention itself took place only because both pro- and anti-slavery forces decided statehood and self-determination were superseding goals; it is not surprising, therefore, that the delegates feared discussion of race would dominate and ultimately paralyze the proceedings. To avoid that result, they did what Oregon lawmakers have done in almost every politically explosive situation since: they referred the issue to the people (Schuman 4). Prior to the convention, Whigs had urged such a plebiscite, and Democrats, themselves divided on slavery, had no incentive to dissent. Thus, on the second day of the convention, Jesse Applegate introduced the following resolution (reported by the *Oregonian* under the caption, "The Nigger Question"):

Whereas, [a] large proportion of the delegates to this convention have been chosen by the people with the expressed or implied understanding that the question of slavery would not be decided for them by this body, but submitted to them in such a manner as to enable them to vote upon it as a distinct issue; therefore,

Resolved, 1st. The discussion of the subject of slavery by this body is out of place and uncalled for, and only calculated to engender bitter feelings among the members of this body, destroy its harmony, retard its business and unnecessarily prolong its session. 2d. That the committee whose duty it shall be to draft rules for this convention be instructed to declare all debate upon the subject of slavery, either as an abstract proposition or as a mere matter of policy, out of order.

This proposal engendered a lengthy debate. Dryer, with what was certainly intentional irony, accused Applegate of wanting "to put the collar and shackles upon the consciences of men." There was much talk of political courage and cowardice, and the session adjourned without a vote. On the next day, the rules committee reported without Applegate's suggestion; its absence was not debated. The next time the issue of whether or not to debate slavery arose was during a discussion of transition to statehood. At that time, no substantive debate on slavery itself occurred, and the issue was tabled, never to reappear. Thus, the convention never reached a formal agreement to avoid debating slavery; nevertheless, it was never discussed. Only once, during debate on the bill of rights, did a delegate even suggest formal action; John McBride proposed adding to that article a provision banning slavery and involuntary servitude. His proposal was defeated without discussion.

The convention's desire to duck the slavery issue did not carry over to other issues implicating race. As already noted, one of the arguments raised in opposition to a bill of rights was that it would likely contain loose language about the equality of men. Although that position did not prevail—the bill was adopted, complete with equality language—the delegates took pains in at least one other section of the bill to indicate that the individual liberties it guaranteed did not extend beyond the white race. At the suggestion of Judge Deady, the convention amended the original text of the section insuring to "[f]oreigners who are or may hereafter become residents of this state . . . the same rights in respect to possession, enjoyment and descent of property as native-born citizens" so that it applied only to "white" foreigners.[14]

This same obsession with race intruded into the discussion of other articles of the constitution, and frequently into the constitution itself. For example, the original Militia Article contained language subjecting all "able-bodied free white citizens" to conscription. This provoked a long and gratuitous discussion of whether it was possible for any white man to be unfree, and whether the indignity of fighting on a battlefield next to a slave derived from the fact that he was a slave, or a Black. To settle the dispute, the delegates amended the section to apply only to male citizens—all of whom, of course, had to be free and white. The Suffrage Article as submitted by the committee specified in Section Two that only white male citizens could vote and in Section Six that no "negro or mulatto shall have the right of suffrage." Apparently these restrictions were not sufficient for Judge Deady, who wondered if Section One, providing that "All elections shall be free and equal," could not be misconstrued. Delazon Smith reassured him that "it did not mean Chinese or niggers." Ever vigilant, the judge then moved that the word "pure" be inserted before "white" in Section Two. Another delegate, in a deft resort to reductio ad absurdum, moved to amend the amendment by inserting the word "Simon" before "pure." After some lighthearted banter regarding who among the delegates might not qualify under such a rigid standard, the various motions were voted down. But another motion to include "Chinamen" among the explicitly disenfranchised groups in Section Six passed. In a similar vein, Judge Deady spoke in favor of an amendment to the Education and School Lands Article that explicitly would have reserved public education to white children, recalling that in Ohio a provision without such an amendment had been construed so as to allow negroes into the public schools. The amendment ultimately lost, but only after Delazon Smith assured the delegates that "negroes and Indians could be excluded without it."

Perhaps the convention's most jarring moment of ethnocentrism, however, occurred during a discussion of the Schedule Article, which dealt with the details of ratification. The article as reported proposed to submit to the people three questions: whether to approve the constitution, whether to approve slavery, and whether to allow "free negroes" in the state. After some quibbling about the proposed election date and without a single voice raised against the propriety of the negro exclusion clause, a major debate erupted over whether or not Chinese should also be excluded. Some favored adding them to the list of excluded groups because their willingness to work for low wages would undercut white labor. Others, like Judge Deady, "saw no reason for making a difference between Chinamen and negroes. The negro was superior to the Chinaman, and would be more useful." Another delegate agreed: "the negroes far surpassed, morally and physically, the Chinamen; if there were any class of thieves who understood their profession thoroughly it was the Chinamen." Judge Williams, author of the "free state letter" (Davenport 233) and of the judicial opinion declaring slavery illegal in the Oregon Territory,[15] the man nearly drummed out of the Democratic Party for his suspected abolitionism (Teiser 266–67), nonetheless supported the motion to explicitly exclude Chinese, and indeed "would consecrate Oregon to the use of the white man, and exclude the negro, Chinaman, and every race of that character." Jonathan Dryer, editor of the free-state *Oregonian*, "would vote to exclude negroes, Chinamen, Kanakas, and even Indians. The association of those races with the white was the demoralization of the latter."[16] Another delegate opposed Chinese because "[t]hey spent very little in the country." The only delegate who spoke in favor of them did so in terms almost as racist as the opponents: Frederick Waymire believed his constituents would "like to have a lot of them" because "[t]hey made good washers, good cooks, and good servants." In sum, one of the clearest messages emerging from the constitutional convention was the delegates' "preference for an all-white state" (Mooney 570–71).

III. THE CONSTITUTION OF 1857

In comparing modern corporate capitalism to servitude, Deady and Boise bring together the convention's great preoccupations—economics and independence, both personal and political—and suggest a paradox. With the exception of the article embracing corporations, the convention and the document it produced define a coherent political culture, a people eschewing luxury, ostentation, and growth, embracing prudence and diligence, distrusting paternalism, hating privilege, and worshipping their own autonomy—sturdy yeoman farmers and small merchants, industrious, stubborn, and somewhat small-minded. Statehood itself and the subsequent convention and constitution finally became popular goals only when they seemed necessary in order to block federal intrusion into local affairs and to attract federal payment of locally incurred war debts. Once in session, the delegates proceeded with a sharp eye for the wasted penny, insisting on modest salaries for public officials, imposing stringent limitations on public indebtedness, and cutting corners wherever possible. They rejected honorific titles and distrusted higher learning. They empowered common jurors and restricted the "judicial monarchy." They forbade special privileges and immunities, special laws, and special taxes. They granted themselves a generous portion of individual rights. Even the rejection of slavery ultimately written into the constitution by the voters stemmed from the belief that it was part of a system founded on caste distinctions and great wealth disparities, a system socially and economically unsuited for a population of small agriculturalists. Their insistent preference for a citizenry composed of others like themselves, a preference that led even to an "English Only" resolution for official state business,[17] demonstrated a desire for classlessness as much as a primitive ethnocentrism. A contemporary observer described this generation of Oregonians as

an exceptionally good people, hospitable, social and fraternal to
a marked degree, as well as being resolute and public-spirited.
. . . [T]he known perils of the overland journey had a selective
effect in bringing to this coast a strong and virile population, . . .
and the four to six months' journey amidst extraordinary trials,
and the communal life incident thereto, disrobed them of social
shams to a great extent and made them all kin. . . . [A]s a general
rule the pioneers were people of moderate means and therefore
unaffected by much disparity in wealth. (Davenport 216–17)

A group of kin, marked by shared hardship, shared values, and a common station in life—it is not surprising that such people would write an
Oregon Constitution marked by moderation, thrift, generous rights for
members, and stingy definitions of membership. They crafted a community in which individuals could have much liberty because, the members
being so much alike, their exercise of liberty did not constitute a threat;
rights received protection and respect because there was little need or
inclination to exercise them.

But the inevitability of progress in the form of a modern industrial
economy, along with its promise of moderately increased wealth for all,
proved too powerful to resist—even as the values of independence and
equality proved too familiar to abandon. As one delegate observed, corporate wealth and development were providential; attempts to impede
them, futile: "Everything is taking that direction, and if we had the dispo-
sition we could not prevent it. The whole mass of community is becoming one great corporation." The Constitution of 1857, then, attempted
simultaneously to preserve the virtues of the past and embrace the
promise of the future, reflecting the ambivalence of those who drafted
it and those who, after a six-week campaign, ratified it, along with a ban
on slavery and free negroes, on November 9, 1857, by a vote of 7,195 to
3,215.

NOTES

1 THE OREGON CONSTITUTION AND PROCEEDINGS AND DEBATES OF THE CONSTITUTIONAL CONVENTION OF 1857, at 28–29 (Charles H. Carey ed., 1926) [hereinafter OREGON CONSTITUTION AND PROCEEDINGS].

2 *See generally* W. C. Palmer, *The Sources of the Oregon Constitution*, 5 OR. L. REV. 200 (1926).

3 David Alan Johnson, FOUNDING THE FAR WEST: CALIFORNIA, OREGON, AND NEVADA, 1840–1890, at 9, 41, 58 (1992).

4 Gordon B. Dodds, OREGON: A BICENTENNIAL HISTORY, 96–97 (1977).

5 Walter C. Woodward, THE RISE AND EARLY HISTORY OF POLITICAL PARTIES IN OREGON, 1843–1868, at 76–78 (1913).

6 One author, T. W. Davenport, *Slavery Question in Oregon*, 9 Q. OR. HIST. SOC'Y 189, 196 (1908), asserts that there were never any slaves in Oregon, but Woodward says that there were never any *legal* slaves, and cites persuasive firsthand accounts of encounters with slave-owners.

7 *See* Sidney Teiser, *The Life of George H. Williams: Almost Chief-Justice*, 47 Q. OR. HIST. SOC'Y 255, 260 (1946).

8 Teiser refers to an 1853 habeas corpus case. Apparently, there is debate on whether the case actually involved a decision on the question of slavery. For further historical interest in the case *Holmes v. Ford*, see *Documentary: The Case of Robin Holmes v. Nathaniel Ford*, 23 Q. OR. HIST. SOC'Y 111 (1922) (compilation of habeas corpus proceedings and Judge Williams's decision).

9 Letter from George H. Williams to the OREGON STATESMAN (July 28, 1857), reprinted in 9 Q. OR. HIST. SOC'Y 254 (1908).

10 John R. McBride, Address Before the Oregon Historical Society (Dec. 20, 1906), *reprinted in* THE OREGON CONSTITUTION AND PROCEEDINGS AND DEBATES OF THE CONSTITUTIONAL CONVENTION OF 1857, at 483 (Charles H. Carey, ed. 1926).

11 As engrossed, the language is as follows: "In all criminal cases whatever, the jury shall have the right to determine the law, and the facts under the direction of the Court as to the law, and the right of new trial, as in civil cases." OR. CONST. art. I, § 16.

12 Apparently the provision on ex post facto laws and laws impairing the obligation of contract provoked "quite a lengthy debate," but neither of the reporters recorded it. OREGON CONSTITUTION AND PROCEEDINGS, 315.

13 Judge Williams's motion to delete the language referring to property "of which the husband was not the meritorious cause" passed; the engrossed section provided that "[t]he property and pecuniary rights of every married woman, at the time of marriage or afterwards, acquired by gift, devise, or inheritance shall not be subject to the debts, or contracts of the husband; and laws shall be passed providing for the registration of the wife's separate property." OR. CONST. art. XV, § 5 (1857).

14 OREGON CONSTITUTION AND PROCEEDINGS, 317–18; *see* OR. CONST. art. I, § 31 (1857) (repealed 1970).

15 *See* Teiser 259–61 (discussing the case of *Robin Holmes v. Nathaniel Ford*). *But cf.* note 10.

16 Dryer was also an accomplished anti-Semite, writing a series of editorials in 1858 accusing Jews of a conspiracy to control the politics and business of the state. Steven Lowenstein, THE JEWS OF OREGON 1850–1950, at 66–67 (1987).

17 OREGON CONSTITUTION AND PROCEEDINGS, 378 ("Resolved, that all laws of the state of Oregon, and all official writings, and the executive, legislative and judicial proceedings, shall be conducted, preserved and published in no other than the English language.").

PART 5

On the Bench

Judge David Schuman, Oregon Court of Appeals (Courtesy of Michael S. Thompson)

The opinions and dissents presented in this section have been shortened by the clerks or justice who selected them. Complete texts can be found at avoiceforjustice.com.

This section highlights four appellate opinions and two dissents that showcase David Schuman's intellectual rigor and delight in the law. McBean, for example, was convicted of reckless burning because he stomped on a fire his friend started, a field burned, and he did not report the fire. Judge Schuman wrote, McBean "has very bad taste in friends" and "a deplorable lack of civic responsibility"—but not the requisite guilty mind that the law requires. Lahmann just wanted to join a club that excluded women. Daniels, Alvarado, and Howard were convicted criminals arguing about governmental searches or seizures in, respectively, a home, a vehicle, and a trash can. And Dufloth owned "Miss Sally's," a nude-dancing business in a city that banned certain types of nude dancing. The Court of Appeals majority rejected her claim to have a constitutional right to free expression by dancing. Judge Schuman dissented, acknowledging that his "dissent is not only swimming upstream, but swimming upstream through water that is over the dam." But it wasn't water under the bridge: the Oregon Supreme Court overturned the Court of Appeals decision, agreeing with Judge Schuman—and Miss Sally.

David Schuman cared about people. He cared about ideas. He dedicated himself to understanding both, which shines through in appellate opinions, dissents, and concurrences that can be understood not just by lawyers, but by the general public. Author E. B. White concluded Charlotte's Web with a thought that, paraphrased, describes Judge Schuman well: It is not often that someone comes along who is a true friend and a good writer.

—Hon. Alycia Sykora, Bend, Oregon

from *State v. McBean,*
189 Or. App. 235, 74 P.3d 1127 (2003)

In State v. McBean, *a man appealed his conviction for reckless burning. At issue was whether stomping on a fire was a reckless act to spread a fire. The opinion demonstrates a clear and concise criminal case, along with David Schuman's wit and literary nature. After reviewing the legal standard (highly deferential to the state) and the unusual facts, Judge Schuman considers whether stomping on a fire is known to spread a fire, as a matter of common knowledge: "On the scale of what is and is not common knowledge, the tendency of stomping on a fire to extinguish it lies, we believe, somewhere between 'the rising of the sun' and 'the fable of the frozen snake.'" The conviction was reversed.*

—Margarita Molina, Judicial Clerk (2003)

Defendant was convicted of reckless burning, ORS 164.335, and appeals, contending that there was insufficient evidence to establish his guilt. *** We reverse.

The facts, presented in the light most favorable to the state, *State v. Cervantes,* 319 Or 121, 125, 873 P2d 316 (1994), are as follows. Defendant and two of his friends, Carreiro and Broderick, lived in an apartment complex in Pendleton near an open grassy field owned by Blue Mountain Community College. On August 19, 2000, defendant learned that Carreiro had set a grass fire in the nearby field and that Broderick was with him at the time. Defendant told Carreiro he thought the act was "pretty stupid." Two days later, he learned that Carreiro had set another fire in the same field.

The next day, defendant and Broderick, knowing that Carreiro was walking through the field on his way back from returning a video, decided to play a prank on him by concealing themselves in the grass and frightening him as he passed by. Carreiro heard them before they could scare him,

144

and the three men had a brief conversation. At that point, Carreiro took out a cigarette lighter and lit the grass on fire. Defendant stomped on the fire in what he later characterized as an attempt to put it out. Instead, the fire spread. Defendant and Broderick then returned to defendant's apartment, where they were joined by Carreiro. They did not report the fire. An employee of the neighboring institution did, but the fire burned a portion of the field before the fire department arrived and extinguished it.

The next day, the assistant fire chief of Pendleton and an Oregon State Police trooper called on defendant to investigate the fires and some unrelated vandalism. After initially denying knowledge of the fires, defendant ultimately told the investigators that his friends had set them. He admitted being present when the last fire was set. After a trial to a jury, defendant was convicted of violating ORS 164.335(1), the "reckless burning" statute[.]

[To] obtain a conviction under the reckless burning statute, the state generally has to prove (1) that the defendant performed an act that caused a fire or explosion so as to damage another person's property; (2) that the act presented such a substantial and unjustifiable risk of damaging the property that only a person demonstrating a gross deviation from a reasonable standard of care would perform it; and (3) that the defendant was aware of the risk and chose to disregard it.

In the present case, the state does not allege that defendant incurred any criminal liability in connection with the first two fires; that he himself set any fires (the uncontradicted testimony of defendant, Carreiro, and Broderick establishes that Carreiro set the fires); or that he aided or abetted in setting a fire. Most importantly, the state does not maintain that defendant intended to spread the fire. The prosecutor expressly disavowed any need to prove intent; in closing, he argued that defendant's intention was to extinguish the fire. He told the jury:

> [Defendant] stands there and watches this man [Carreiro] light the grass on fire. He participates. As he's trying to stomp it out, he spreads the fire. That's reckless conduct.
>
> ****
>
> [Defendant] described the lighter, said [Carreiro] lit the grass on fire with the lighter, then [defendant] said, "I tried to put it out but it went too fast."

Well, it went too fast because when he started stomping on that fire, it spread it. Maybe that was the game. Maybe we'll set it on fire and stomp it out.

The fact is, at that point, he had participated in spreading this fire and, at that point, his conduct was reckless.

Thus, the burden that the state set for itself was to prove (1) that defendant performed an act that caused the spread of the fire that Carreiro started; (2) that his act created such a substantial and unjustifiable risk of spreading the fire that only a person demonstrating a gross deviation from a reasonable standard of care would so act; and (3) that defendant was aware of that risk and chose to perform the act anyway.

The state never specifies which of defendant's acts allegedly amounted to reckless burning. As the transcript portions quoted above indicate, however, the prosecution clearly emphasized that the culpable action was stomping on the fire. In addition to the statements above, the prosecution also argued:

By his admission alone of stomping on the fire and spreading the fire, [defendant's] testimony, he's engaged in reckless conduct and just walks away from it and let it burn.

    ✻✻✻✻

These young men were starting fires. They were playing a game to them. That's reckless.

There are several problems with this theory. For example, the state presented no evidence at trial that stomping on a fire creates any risk of spreading it, much less a substantial and unjustifiable risk, even though one of the state's witnesses was the assistant fire chief. Indeed, it is common knowledge[1] that not stomping on a fire could lead to its

---

1 "[T]he common knowledge of man ranges far and wide, so the doctrine embraces matters so curiously diverse as, e.g., the rising of the sun, the status of the Isle of Cuba, the late Civil War, the contents of the Bible, the character of a camp meeting, the height of the human frame, the fable of 'the frozen snake,' the characteristics and construction of the ice cream freezer, the general use of the diamond stack or the straight stack spark arrester, the habits of those who shave, in fine, 'all things, both great and small.'"
Peterson v. Standard Oil Co., 55 Or 511, 517-18, 106 P 337 (1910) (quoting *Town of North Hempstead v. Gregory*, 65 NYS 867, 689 (1900)). On the scale of what is and is not

spread. A widely used dictionary defines "stomp" as "stamp" and then provides the following definition: "to extinguish, eradicate, or do away with (something) by or as if stamping with the foot . . . usu. used without (one small fire . . . was easily stamped out)." *Webster's Third New Int'l Dictionary* 2222 (unabridged ed 1993). Although this dictionary definition may be of limited utility in defining what a word means in a statute (for example where the word's context implies a different definition), it nonetheless provides an authoritative report of how a word is used in common parlance and therefore serves as an indication of what might be "common knowledge." In any event, we conclude that in the absence of some supporting evidence or, at the least, some argument, no rational trier of fact could find that stomping on a fire presents such a substantial risk of spreading it that the act is a gross deviation from reasonable conduct and, in light of the fact that stomping on a fire is widely believed to be a method of stopping its spread, that the risk was unjustifiable.

However, we need not rely on such an imprecise and historically contingent concept as "common knowledge." Even if we could presume that the jury could find, beyond a reasonable doubt, that defendant, by stomping on the fire, took a grossly unreasonable and unjustifiable risk of spreading it, the state would still have to prove beyond a reasonable doubt that he did so while aware of and in conscious disregard of that risk. ORS 164.335; ORS 161.085(9). Again, no evidence whatsoever supports that conclusion. And although the jury was entitled to disbelieve the participants and to draw reasonable inferences from the evidence, it must have some relevant evidence from which to draw them. *State v. Beason*, 170 Or. App. 414, 423–24, 12 P.3d 560 (2000), *rev den*, 331 Or 692 (2001). The inference must reasonably flow from predicate facts. *Id.* Neither at trial nor on appeal does the state point to (much less establish) any facts that are even remotely relevant to the question whether or not defendant was aware that stomping on a fire presented a substantial and unjustifiable risk of spreading it, even, presuming for the sake of argument, if the state could establish the counterintuitive fact that such a risk existed. Instead, the state relies on defendant's knowledge of the two earlier fires, on the fact that he did not report them or the third, and

---

common knowledge, the tendency of stomping on fire to extinguish it lies, we believe, somewhere between "the rising of the sun" and "the fable of the frozen snake."

on his equivocal testimony regarding an unrelated issue (whether or not he saw Carreiro take a cigarette lighter out of his pocket). Those facts may be evidence that defendant has very bad taste in friends and that he has a deplorable lack of civic responsibility. They may impeach his status as a truth-teller. But they bear no relation to his state of mind when he stomped on the fire that he is accused of recklessly spreading.

****

Likewise, there is no logical connection between any fact in evidence in the present case, including defendant's awareness of the earlier fires and his failure to report the one he allegedly spread, and his awareness and conscious disregard of the risk that stomping on a fire could spread it. In short, no rational trier of fact could conclude from the evidence that defendant was aware of, and disregarded, a substantial and unjustifiable risk that, by stomping on the fire that his friend set, he was going to cause the fire to damage another's property. *Accord State ex rel Juv. Dept. v. Anderson*, 14 Or App 391, 513 P2d 514 (1973) (reversing jurisdictional finding where no evidence supported youth's awareness and disregard of risk of throwing matches in paint thinner).

The state also appears to make a perfunctory argument that defendant's failure to report the fire was a culpable reckless act. We reject that argument. The state never offers any authority or legal argument for the proposition that defendant had a legal duty to report the fire or for the proposition that failure to perform an act that one has no legal duty to perform can constitute criminal recklessness. Instead, it simply asserts the failure and concludes that it is reckless conduct. *But see* ORS 161.095(1) ("The minimum requirement for criminal liability is the performance by a person of conduct which includes a voluntary act or the omission to perform an act which the person is capable of performing."); ORS 161.085(3) ("'Omission' means a failure to perform an act the performance of which is required by law."). If the state's assertion were correct, then a person who sees a grease fire, attempts to extinguish it with water but succeeds only in spreading it, then leaves the scene, is guilty of reckless burning. We are unwilling to affirm a conviction on a theory with such consequences in the absence of argument either below or in this court.

from *Lahmann v. Grand Aerie of Fraternal Order of Eagles*, 202 Or. App. 123, 121 P.3d 671 (2005)

In this case, the Court of Appeals had to determine whether Oregon's public accommodation law, which prohibits discrimination on the basis of gender, could bar the Eagles from excluding women from leadership without running afoul of the Oregon Constitution's guarantee of freedom of association. In other words, can a group escape accountability for discrimination by arguing that the state constitution allows them to associate with others in the way that they please, even when those practices exclude women? According to Judge Schuman, allowing as much "at this stage in our evolution of political community . . . would be cause for alarm." In the court's first interpretation of Article 1, section 26, of the Oregon Constitution, his analysis was assisted by a long (male-dominated) history of freedom of association, which showed that the constitutional right is meant to safeguard assembly for the purpose of deliberating matters of public concern, and not assembly at a fraternal lodge that disallows women from full participation.
—Melissa Aubin, Judicial Clerk (2004–2006)

This case requires us to decide whether the Fraternal Order of Eagles' policy of barring women from membership in its "aeries" violates the Public Accommodations Act, former ORS 30.670 to 30.685 (1999), (1) and if so, whether enforcement of the act so as to compel the organization to consider applications from women would be unconstitutional. ***

Established in 1898, the Fraternal Order of Eagles is a national fraternal organization with over one million members. The group's stated purpose is to promote principles of "liberty, truth, justice, [and] equality, for home, for country, and for God." At the national level, the Eagles have supported the enactment of pension and workers' compensation laws. At the state and local level, members perform community service projects and socialize together.

The Eagles have a national governing body called the Grand Aerie, which oversees state and local aeries. It does so by issuing "statutes," one of which establishes the membership requirement at issue in this case: "No person shall be eligible to be elected to membership in any Local Aerie unless such a person is a male, is of good moral character, and believes in the existence of a Supreme Being[.]" Although that requirement has been in existence since the organization's founding, the Grand Aerie in 1952 authorized the establishment of "Ladies' Auxiliaries" for women at the local and national levels. According to the Ladies' Auxiliary Rules and Regulations, the Grand Aerie retains "complete jurisdiction and control over the Grand [Ladies'] Auxiliary" with limited exceptions, and the "Grand [Ladies'] Auxiliary shall have no purposes that are apart from the aims of the Fraternal Order of Eagles." A local aerie may be affiliated with an auxiliary, but auxiliary members may not attend aerie meetings or vote on aerie matters.

In 1995, the Grand Tribunal of the Eagles, a branch of the national organization charged with interpreting the Eagles' constitution, issued an opinion stating that "the use of the word 'male' in [the membership requirement] is not consistent with prevailing civil law." As a result, the Willamette aerie, along with many others, admitted some women to membership. That practice, however, was short lived. In 1998, the Grand Aerie rejected a proposal to abandon the male-only requirement for aerie membership, and the Grand Tribunal withdrew its opinion concerning the male-only requirement. Since then, the Grand Aerie has not permitted local aeries to accept membership applications from women, and the Willamette aerie has followed that policy.

The Willamette aerie has an auxiliary. The two groups share a lodge, which features a bar, dining facilities, a dance floor, and meeting rooms. In 1999, plaintiff, a member of the Willamette auxiliary, applied for membership in the Willamette aerie, but her application was rejected on the basis of her gender. Thereafter, plaintiff (and two other rejected female applicants who have since voluntarily dismissed their claims) initiated this action under the Public Accommodations Act against the national, state, and local aeries, seeking declaratory and injunctive relief.

The relevant parts of the act are ORS 30.670 and ORS 30.675. ORS 30.670 stated:

All persons within the jurisdiction of this state shall be entitled to the full and equal accommodations, advantages, facilities and privileges of any place of public accommodation, without any distinction, discrimination or restriction on account of race, religion, sex, marital status, color or national origin.

****

We next turn to the question whether application of the act to the Eagles violates their members' rights of assembly under Article I, section 26, of the Oregon Constitution, which states:

No law shall be passed restraining any of the inhabitants of the State from assembling together in a peaceable manner to consult for their common good; nor from instructing their Representatives; nor from applying to the Legislature for redress of greviances [*sic*].

According to the Eagles, application of the act restrains their members "from assembling together in a peaceable manner to consult for their common good[.]" ***

Underlying that argument [is the premise] that the "assembling together" to which the section refers includes assembly whose primary objective is what the trial court found the Eagles' purpose to be—marketing civic or social benefits such as amusement—and is not limited to assembly directed primarily toward determining some political policy or achieving some political objective. ***

The existing case law provides no support for the conclusion that section 26 applies to social gatherings or, indeed, to any gatherings other than those dedicated to political advocacy.

****

An examination of the historical foundation on which section 26 was built also demonstrates that its objective was to protect the people's right to gather for the purpose of deliberating on and promoting political policies. Although we lack documentation of the Oregon framers' purpose for enacting section 26, an examination of the general historical circumstances that led to the creation of similar assembly clauses supports the conclusion that the section was aimed at protecting the people's ability to convene deliberative gatherings for the purpose of promoting the "common good," formulating policy positions, and taking them to the political arena.

****

The right of the people to voice their concerns to governmental representatives is evident in the Magna Carta, but the predicate right to gather in order to deliberate matters appears to have grown out of the historical context of town governance in prerevolutionary America. A useful starting point for appreciating the significance of the right of assembly is eighteenth-century Massachusetts, where town assemblies served a vital role in government, and where British attempts to suppress assemblies would contribute to the declaration and preservation of assembly rights across the young nation.

John Adams's Letter to Abbe De Marly described town inhabitants' practice of gathering and deliberating issues of consequence in colonial Massachusetts:

> These towns contain upon an average, say six miles or two leagues square. The inhabitants who live within these limits are formed by law into corporations, or bodies politic, and are invested with certain powers and privileges, as for example, to repair the great roads or highways, to support the poor, to choose their selectmen, constables, collectors of taxes, and above all, their representatives in the legislature; as also, *the right to assemble, whenever they are summoned by their selectmen, in their town halls, there to deliberate upon the public affairs of the town, or to give instructions to their representatives in the legislature.* The consequences of these institutions have been, that the inhabitants, having acquired from their infancy the habit of discussing, of deliberating, and of judging public affairs, it was in these assemblies of towns or districts that the sentiments of the people were formed in the first place, and their resolutions were taken from the beginning to the end of the disputes and the war with Great Britain.
>
> Charles F. Adams ed., 5 *The Works of John Adams* 492, 495
> (1851) (emphasis added).

In prerevolutionary Massachusetts (then a royal province), the work of the assembly of townspeople was a necessary element of local and regional governance. Margaret E. Monsell, *"Stars in the Constellation* *of the Commonwealth": Massachusetts Towns and the Constitutional Right of Instruction*, 29 New Eng. L. Rev. 285, 288 (1995). The right of representation to the wider, royal provincial assembly "belonged to the town as a corporate body rather than to its inhabitants as individuals," so the deliberation and communication of concerns of provincial import, particularly relations with the crown, rested on the collective shoulders of townspeople gathered in local assemblies. *Id.* at 291. Individuals within the town meeting drew up instructions for the town's representative to the provincial body, "and these would then be debated and voted upon by the entire town meeting." *Id.* In addition to managing the town's internal affairs, townspeople developed positions on matters of regional importance and, at times, instructed representatives to take positions directly opposing the British Parliament. ***

Attempts by the British government to ban town assemblies in Massachusetts catalyzed the Revolution. In 1774, the so-called Intolerable Acts required appointment of council representatives by royal writ rather than election and starkly limited town meetings to a single, annual gathering for the election of assembly representatives. Monsell, 29 New Eng. L. Rev. at 293. The towns continued to meet in defiance of the British mandate. *Id.* That year, representatives from every colony except Georgia met in Philadelphia at the First Continental Congress to protest the Intolerable Acts, define America's rights, and limit British power. *** Shortly thereafter, the Declaration of Independence lamented the failure of the British government to answer the concerns of the colonies, stating that colonists' "repeated Petitions have been answered only by repeated injury," and the Revolutionary War ensued.

In the decades after the war, the colonies-turned-states explicitly reserved to the people the right to assemble and instruct (or petition) their political representatives. For example, Article 19 of the Declaration of Rights in the Massachusetts Constitution of 1780 guaranteed the right of the people to assemble in towns for the purpose of consulting about the "common good," in phrasing very similar to Oregon's Article I, section 26[.] ***

Thus, the drafters of the earliest state constitutions labored under the recent memory of British attempts to suppress town meetings and assert control over representative governments. It is not difficult to infer that those actions figured prominently in colonists' decisions to safeguard the right to assemble, and to fuse it to guarantees of the right of instruction and the right to petition the legislature for assistance in redressing wrongs.

In 1791, the Bill of Rights was added to the federal constitution; the First Amendment guaranteed the rights of assembly and petition:

> Congress shall make no law respecting an establishment of religion, or prohibiting the free exercise thereof; or abridging the freedom of speech, or of the press; or the right of the people peaceably to assemble, and to petition the government for a redress of grievances.

Significantly, the drafters of the federal bill of rights did not parse into separate amendments the rights of free speech and free assembly; nor did they specify that the right of assembly was "for the purpose of" petition. *** Nonetheless, the federal right of assembly was construed in the nineteenth century as the right to gather for the express purpose of consulting to petition the federal government. *See, e.g., Slaughter-House Cases*, 83 US (16 Wall) 36, 118, 21 L Ed 394 (1872) (Bradley, J., dissenting); see also Jason Mazzone, *Freedom's Associations*, 77 Wash. L. Rev. 639, 742 (2002) (addressing associations protected by the assembly clause and noting "we have largely overlooked [the] political aspect of associations that lay at the core of their treatment in the early Republic.").

In time, the right of assembly and the right of free expression were conflated in the First Amendment. *** Ultimately, federal constitutional law came to include a guarantee of expressive association, as we discuss in the next section. But no similar development has occurred in Oregon constitutional law. At most, the rights of free expression and assembly or instruction have been simultaneously invoked in certain fact situations and the claims disposed of either separately or together in an almost summary fashion. *See, e.g., Ausmus*, 336 Or at 508.

In sum, from an examination of assembly clauses in their initial social and political contexts, we conclude that they were drafted in literal terms as a reaction against attempts to limit the ability of colonists to assert themselves politically. Assuming that the framers of the Oregon Constitution appreciated the import of the right of assembly for consultation on the common good to the communities that employed it in the late-eighteenth through the mid-nineteenth century, we conclude that the framers intended the assembly clause to accomplish what it recited, that is, to ensure the right to assemble in order to deliberate on matters of public concern as a part of the political process.

We therefore cannot conclude, as the Eagles would have us do, that section 26 confers a right of association that applies to organizations such as the Eagles. No Oregon court has construed the provision in that manner. The text does not address assembly for expressions apart from those directed specifically for the "common good." Nor does the initial political purpose of assembly clauses indicate that the framers of the Oregon Constitution understood section 26 as an expansive guarantee of expressive association or purely social assembly divorced from matters of public concern. Although it is true that, at the national level, the Eagles have on occasion apparently been known to support particular political objectives, nothing in the record before us, and nothing suggested by the Eagles, indicates that discourse about matters of public concern or political importance occupies anything more than an insignificant amount of aerie time or resources. And to the extent that such matters are a part of the Eagles' mission, nothing in the record suggests that allowing women to join aeries would interfere with that function.

****

The Public Accommodations Act applies to the Eagles because, as the trial court found and the Eagles do not dispute, the organization provides amusement and civic services, and it offers them unselectively to the male public. Enforcing the act so as to require the Eagles to consider women for membership on the same terms that they consider men does not violate the organization's members' rights under the state constitution's guarantee of religious freedom, nor does it violate their right freely to assemble to consult for their common good; neither case law, text, context, nor history provides any reason to apply section 26 to groups engaged principally in activities outside of the political realm. Moreover, applying the act will not violate the members' right of expressive association because admitting women will not require the Eagles to send a message contrary to one of the organization's core values, and, even if it did, that interference with associational rights would be justified by the state's compelling interest in eliminating gender discrimination.

****

At this stage in the evolution of our political community, laws permitting the opposite of that conclusion would be cause for alarm.

from *State v. Daniels*, 234 Or. App. 533, 541, 228 P.3d 695 (2010)

In this case, James Daniels appeals his conviction for child sexual abuse and pornography by attempting to suppress evidence collected through a search warrant, granted by a judge, partly on the basis of the "training and experience" of the police officer whose affidavit supports the warrant. Although the court ultimately upholds the conviction, this opinion expresses considerable skepticism about "training and experience" as a catchall justification for police behavior. The message is loud and clear that "training and experience" is "not a magical incantation with the power to imbue speculation, stereotype, or pseudoscience with an impenetrable armor of veracity." This classic Judge Schuman statement reveals an acerbic wit that could surface at any moment.

—Sara Einowski, Judicial Clerk (2010)

After the court denied defendant's motion to suppress evidence that police seized from his residence pursuant to a search warrant, defendant was tried on stipulated facts and convicted. The motion to suppress was based on defendant's argument that the application for the warrant did not contain facts that were sufficient to justify a search for incriminating photographs and videotapes. He renews that argument on appeal. We affirm.

The warrant at issue was based on the affidavit of Creighton, the Port Orford Chief of Police. The court issued the warrant, and officers subsequently searched defendant's house and found videotapes that contained, among other things, children engaging in sexually explicit conduct and images that defendant had surreptitiously recorded through his bathroom window showing nude young girls. Defendant was indicted on 33 counts of encouraging child sexual abuse in the second degree, ORS 163.686; two counts of invasion of privacy, ORS 163.700; and one count of sexual abuse in the third degree, ORS 163.415.

The question on appeal is whether the court erred in authorizing the search for and seizure of the videotapes.

A judge may issue a search warrant if, after reviewing an application and supporting affidavit, the judge finds that "there is probable cause to believe that the search will discover things specified in the application and subject to seizure." ORS 133.555(2). "Probable cause" is a more rigorous standard than mere suspicion; even a well-warranted suspicion does not suffice, because "a suspicion, no matter how well founded, does not rise to the level of probable cause." *State v. Verdine*, 290 Or. 553, 557, 624 P.2d 580 (1981). At the same time, "there is a vast difference between proof of probable cause and proof of guilt ***." *State v. Tacker*, 241 Or. 597, 600, 407 P.2d 851 (1965).

To determine probable cause, the judge may rely on facts asserted in the affidavit as well as reasonable inferences to be drawn from them. In reviewing a judge's determination that a warrant is supported by probable cause, we examine the information in the supporting affidavit in a "commonsense and realistic fashion." *State v. Villagran*, 294 Or. 404, 408, 657 P.2d 1223 (1983). Doubtful cases should be resolved in favor of allowing the warrant. *Tacker*, 241 Or. at 602, 407 P.2d 851 (quoting *United States v. Ventresca*, 380 U.S. 102, 109, 85 S.Ct. 741, 13 L.Ed.2d 684 (1965)).

In the present case, the issuing judge had the following relevant information. According to defendant's daughters, defendant repeatedly sexually abused them when they were children, the last incident occurring in 1990 when the younger daughter was in college. On one occasion, one of the daughters recalled that defendant attempted to videotape the act, but the attempt was unsuccessful. Beyond that incident, neither daughter recalled any instances of videotaping, nor did either recall that defendant possessed videotapes or photographs. No charges were ever filed against defendant for the acts involving the daughters.

For a period of time ending nine months before the warrant application, a male child living with defendant at the time had regularly witnessed defendant sexually abusing the boy's sister, then 13, by rubbing her crotch and vaginal area. Further, the boy recalled that defendant occasionally took the 13-year-old girl into the bathroom and bedroom, closed the door, and became angry when disturbed. The boy did not recall seeing pornographic videotapes or photographs.

Finally, the judge learned that the affiant, Creighton, had training and experience causing him to believe that pedophiles "often retain *** movies in reference to their deviance," that the retention "may span several years," and that "pedophiles rarely dispose of their sexually explicit material."

We agree with the state that, even without the information supplied by Creighton based on his training and experience, the affidavit established probable cause to believe that some evidence of inculpatory sexual activity between defendant and his foster daughter—for example fluids on bedding or undergarments—would be found in defendant's residence. Such evidence, unlike drugs, is not consumable or marketable, nor is it likely to dissipate (DNA, for example, lasts for millennia); therefore, it is not necessarily "stale" after a short time. *See State v. Corpus-Ruiz*, 127 Or. App. 666, 670, 874 P.2d 90 (1994) (staleness depends on the nature of the thing to be seized; an item that can be consumed in short time becomes stale quickly); *State v. Kirkpatrick*, 45 Or. App. 899, 903, 609 P.2d 433 (1980) (staleness is to be determined by the kind of evidence sought).

However, without the information derived from Creighton's training and experience, the affidavit is undeniably deficient with respect to the videotapes. It contains very old allegations of sexual abuse from two victims and a more recent allegation from a witness, but only one person recalled anything that is per se relevant to videotapes that could be evidence of the suspected crimes. That recollection was at least 20 years old, and it involved only an unsuccessful attempt to create such material. Because of its age, its lack of corroboration, and its lack of anything connecting defendant to the actual creation or possession of inculpatory videotapes, that old information adds very little to the quantum of information relevant to the search for and seizure of that material. To link defendant to the inculpatory videotapes, an additional fact is necessary: that people who have at some point engaged in sexual abuse of children possess and retain videotapes of live children, unclothed or engaging in sexual acts. Without that fact, the affidavit creates at most a tenuous suspicion that defendant might possess illegal videotapes. As noted, however, mere suspicion is not enough. We must therefore consider the weight to be given to Creighton's training and experience information.

It is well settled that determinations of probable cause involve the totality of the circumstances in any given situation and that a law enforcement officer's training and experience are among the circumstances that can be considered. It is also well settled, however, that an assertion of "training and experience" is not enough by itself to create probable cause. *State v. Jacobs*, 187 Or. App. 330, 333, 67 P.3d 408 (2003). In order for an attestation regarding training and experience to support probable cause, it must connect a defendant's particular conduct or circumstances with the specific evidence that police seek, and it must be supported by "objective facts derived from other sources." *State v. Goodman*, 328 Or. 318, 328, 975 P.2d 458 (1999). As we have explained, if an officer testifies that, for example, his training and experience have taught him that "paperfolds of a particular shape are often used for drugs," and the officer also testifies that "the defendant possessed a paperfold of that particular shape," the training and experience create "a basis to believe that the defendant's paperfold contained drugs." *State v. Miglavs*, 186 Or. App. 420, 432, 63 P.3d 1202 (2003), aff'd, 337 Or. 1, 90 P.3d 607 (2004) (citing *State v. Herbert*, 302 Or. 237, 242, 729 P.2d 547 (1986)). Put another way, the training and experience information (paperfolds contain drugs) supplies the major premise on which the conclusion (defendant possessed drugs) depends, and that major premise must be followed by a minor premise (defendant possessed a paperfold) that is supported by objective facts derived from other sources. *See id.* at 432, 63 P.3d 1202 (describing connection between facts, training and experience, and conclusion as a syllogism).

In the present case, Creighton's affidavit states that, in his experience, pedophiles (that is, people who are sexually attracted to children) own and often retain "deviant" movies. That is the major premise. The affidavit also contains information that, as recently as nine months before the date of the warrant, defendant was seen in his home sexually abusing a child, and the child was still living there—in other words, that defendant is a person who is sexually attracted to children. That information is the minor premise, a fact supported by independent evidence (D.'s statement). Creighton's statements about his training and experience, therefore, adequately supply the necessary major premise that, along with the independent objective fact regarding defendant's conduct, logically leads to the conclusion: there are probably inculpatory videotapes in defendant's residence.

That conclusion alone, however, does not mean that the affidavit was legally sufficient. A syllogism can be logical without yielding a true or dependable conclusion ("All automobiles have six wheels; my 2008 Honda is an automobile; therefore my 2008 Honda has six wheels."). The value of the conclusion depends on the accuracy of the major premise. In the context of statements regarding training and experience, that means we must not only ensure that the officer's knowledge is connected to the facts of a particular case; we must also examine the knowledge itself. The phrase "training and experience," in other words, is not a magical incantation with the power to imbue speculation, stereotype, or pseudo-science with an impenetrable armor of veracity.

In many cases, what the officer states that he has learned from train-ing and experience reflects common sense—for example, that hunters keep their rifles at their homes, *State v. Clapper*, 216 Or. App. 413, 422, 423–24, 173 P.3d 1235 (2007), or that people who possess stolen property hide it in their homes or vehicles, *State v. Henderson*, 341 Or. 219, 225, 142 P.3d 58 (2006). However, as the information becomes more esoteric, specialized, counter-intuitive, or scientific, increasingly persuasive explanation is necessary. The extent to which an officer must explain the basis of his or her "training and experience" knowledge, in other words, varies from case to case across a broad spectrum. At one extreme is knowledge such as the fact that a person who stole property is likely to keep it at his or her home—knowledge that, in fact, need not be justified by any reference to training and experience. At the other end of the spectrum is knowledge such as, for example, the fact that anhydrous ammonia is a precursor chemical used in the manufacture of methamphetamine and that a brass fitting that has been in contact with that substance will turn blue. *See State v. Heckathorne*, 347 Or. 474, 478, 223 P.3d 1034 (2009). Knowledge at that end of the spectrum, in order to count in the magistrate's probable cause calculus, requires more of a foundation than the bare assertion of training and experience.

In the present case, Creighton provided the following details about his training and experience: After stating that he had 24 years of law enforcement experience, his affidavit continued:

> Part of my duties as a police chief include the investigation of sex crimes, including, but not limited to, crimes committed against minor children. I have received approximately thirty-five hours of advanced training and expertise in sexual abuse crimes, in which children are victimized.

Additionally, I have had on the job experience in investigating sexual abuse crimes while employed with The City of Port Orford Police Department as well as several other agencies ***. The training and experience that I've received in the course of my employment has familiarized me with the methods of operation of persons committing the crime of sexual abuse against children.

During my employment as a Law Enforcement Officer, I have investigated numerous sexual abuse allegations involving the sexual exploitation of children. I have interviewed numerous children who have been victimized by sexual exploitation and furthermore, I have conducted numerous interviews of perpetrators involved in the sexual exploitation of children.

It is true that, in several particulars, this recitation could provide more detail to demonstrate the value of Creighton's training and experience. Did the 35 hours of advanced training include studies or other documentation about the habits of pedophiles, in particular with respect to videotapes? Did the interviews with perpetrators include people who had made videotapes? Did the interviews with victims include people who had been filmed? Had he ever actually been involved in a case in which a pedophile had made or kept an inculpatory videotape?

In the final analysis, however, and in light of the precept that searches under warrant are favored by the law, *Henderson*, 341 Or. at 225, 142 P.3d 58, we conclude that this is not a case that requires a precise calibration of the affiant's knowledge and its underlying foundation. Creighton's knowledge is neither so obvious that it could be accepted without reference to training or experience, nor so technical that it requires elaborate detail. The explanation that he provided was sufficient to justify the magistrate's reliance. Creighton's affidavit provided facts from which the judge could issue a warrant authorizing police to search for and seize videotapes in defendant's home.

from *State v. Alvarado,*
257 Or. App. 612, 307 P.3d 540 (2013)

*Like the Fourth Amendment to the US Constitution, the Oregon
Constitution protects individuals from unreasonable searches and
seizures. Both constitutions also provide that court-issued search warrants must be based on probable cause and must particularly describe
"the place to be searched, and the persons or things to be seized."
Nevertheless, under many circumstances, police have broad powers to
conduct warrantless searches and seizures. Judge Schuman's opinion
in State v. Alvarado is one of the many instances during his judicial
career when he wrestled with the implications of those powers for a free
society. The opinion reflects two key tenets of his judicial philosophy
about warrantless police searches: that the Oregon Constitution requires
that officers provide a convincing justification for any warrantless
search; and that it prohibits police from engaging in suspicionless fishing
expeditions for evidence.*

—Eamon McCleery, Judicial Clerk (2012)

Defendant appeals his convictions for unlawful obliteration of the
identification number on a firearm, ORS 166.450, and unlawful possession of a firearm, ORS 166.250. The firearm that precipitated these convictions was discovered when police searched defendant's vehicle after
stopping him for speeding and for failing to display a front license plate.
On appeal, defendant asserts two assignments of error. First, he asserts
that the trial court erroneously denied his motion to suppress the evidence obtained from the search of his vehicle. Specifically, he argues that
the evidence against him was found after a traffic stop was unlawfully
extended without reasonable suspicion. Second, defendant argues that
the trial court erroneously denied his motion for a judgment of acquittal
on the obliteration charge. According to defendant, his conviction for

intentionally obliterating a firearm's identification number was based upon the court's application of an unlawful evidentiary presumption. For the reasons that follow, we conclude that, although the court did not correctly apply the obliteration statute, it properly denied defendant's motion for a judgment of acquittal; however, we also conclude that it erred in denying his motion to suppress. We therefore reverse and remand.

****

We begin by briefly reciting the facts relevant to defendant's motion to suppress, which we state consistently with the trial court's ruling. *State v. Ehly*, 317 Or 66, 75, 854 P2d 421 (1993) ("A trial court's findings of historical fact are binding on appellate courts if there is constitutionally sufficient evidence in the record to support those findings."). As previously described, defendant was pulled over during a traffic stop by Patrol Sergeant Turner; the facts relevant to the motion to suppress concern the circumstances of that stop. After spotting defendant's vehicle, Turner pulled onto the highway and drove his cruiser directly behind defendant's van. Defendant reduced his speed so that he was traveling 20 miles below the speed limit. Turner then stopped defendant's vehicle.

As Turner approached the vehicle, defendant rolled down the passenger side window. A strong odor of cologne emanated from the vehicle. Turner observed two bottles of body spray on the front passenger seat and numerous air fresheners scattered throughout the vehicle. Lying next to the body spray were a cell phone and a pager. An open energy drink was sitting in the center console. Turner also noticed "religious symbols" in the vehicle.

When asked, defendant provided Turner with his license and registration. Turner observed that defendant was from Washington but driving a van with Oregon license plates. The van was not registered to defendant. Turner asked defendant where he was traveling, and defendant replied that he was going to Pendleton to pay his cousin's taxes. Turner then returned to his patrol car where he ran license and warrants checks. These checks revealed that defendant had no outstanding warrants, that defendant's license was valid, and that no one had reported the vehicle as stolen. Nevertheless, Turner remained suspicious that defendant was involved in some illegal activity so he called in a request to have Senior Trooper Chichester come to his location with a drug detecting dog.

Turner returned to defendant's vehicle and noticed that defendant had moved the pager from the front seat to the glove box and was holding his cell phone in his right hand, looking at it repeatedly. Turner asked defendant if he had any controlled substances in the vehicle. Defendant became nervous, and his cheek began to twitch. He told Turner that he did not want his vehicle searched because it did not belong to him. Approximately 10 minutes after Turner made the request for a drug detecting dog, Chichester arrived at the scene. Chichester brought the dog up to the vehicle and it alerted—erroneously, as it turned out—to the presence of controlled substances. The officers then searched the vehicle and discovered ammunition and the pistol with the obliterated identification number.

On appeal, defendant argues that the evidence discovered during that search should have been suppressed, because Turner extended the stop without reasonable suspicion, thereby violating defendant's rights under Article I, section 9, of the Oregon Constitution. The state responds that reasonable suspicion supported the extension of the stop ***.

****

Officers may "stop and briefly detain motorists for investigation of noncriminal traffic violations." *State v. Rodgers/Kirkeby*, 347 Or 610, 624, 227 P3d 695 (2010) (emphasis omitted). However, "[p]olice authority to detain a motorist dissipates when the investigation reasonably related to that traffic infraction, the identification of persons, and the issuance of a citation (if any) is completed or reasonably should be completed." *Id.* at 623. When police have all of the information necessary to complete their investigation into the traffic infraction, but instead of citing the driver or ending the encounter, they choose instead to launch an investigation into a matter that is unrelated to the infraction, they have unlawfully extended the stop. Police must provide some other justification for continuing a traffic stop beyond that point. *Id.* at 624 n 4 (rejecting the argument that a de minimis delay while processing a traffic violation does not violate Or. Const., Art I, § 9).

In this case, the state argues that defendant's continued detention was justified because Turner reasonably (but erroneously) suspected defendant was involved in drug trafficking. An officer's reasonable suspicion that an individual has committed a crime permits that officer to temporarily stop that individual and make investigatory inquiries. *Nguyen*, 176 Or. App. at 262. Whether a suspicion is reasonable depends on the totality of the circumstances and requires an officer to "point to specific and articulable facts that gave rise to the officer's suspicion that the individual committed a crime." *Id.*

The state argues that the following facts support a reasonable suspicion that defendant was involved in drug trafficking: (1) defendant slowed his vehicle after spotting Officer Turner; (2) defendant was traveling interstate in a car owned by someone else; (3) defendant explained to Turner that he was on his way to Pendleton to pay his cousin's taxes; (4) defendant's vehicle contained numerous air fresheners, two bottles of cologne, and smelled strongly of both; (5) defendant had "religious symbols" in his vehicle; (6) defendant had an open energy drink; (7) defendant was traveling with both a cell phone and a pager; (8) during his conversation with Turner, defendant looked down at his cell phone; (9) defendant moved the pager to his glove box; (10) defendant became nervous when asked about the presence of drugs. We consider these facts individually before determining whether taken together they support a reasonable suspicion that defendant had committed a crime.

As an initial matter, we conclude that defendant's looking at his cell phone, moving the pager to the glove box, and nervous response when asked about drugs could not figure in the reasonable suspicion calculus, even if they were suspicious—which they are not. Whether an officer has reasonable suspicion is determined as of the time that the stop becomes unlawfully extended; here, that occurred when the officer, having determined that defendant's license was valid, his vehicle was not stolen, and he had no warrants, chose to pursue a criminal investigation instead of citing defendant. The circumstances mentioned above occurred after that point. We also conclude preliminarily that defendant's consumption of an energy drink or the fact that he slowed his vehicle after speeding add nothing to the reasonable suspicion calculus. Likewise, the reason defendant gave for his travel—going to Pendleton to pay his cousin's taxes—may be unusual, but it does not suggest criminal activity; Pendleton is a county seat, and people pay taxes there. The state offers no explanation of the connection, if any, between these facts and the crime of drug trafficking. *See State v. Maciel,* 254 Or. App. 530, 541, 295 P.3d 145 (2013) (finding no connection between defendant's "bizarre story" and the crime of drug trafficking). We also decline to consider the fact that defendant had religious symbols in his vehicle. The officer's explanation—that people carrying drugs have religious symbols in order to falsely create the impression that they are good people—simply holds no water. Further, the fact that defendant was driving a van with out-of-state plates is of no significance, in that the plates were from Washington and defendant was driving on I-84 just across the Columbia River from that state.

We also conclude that defendant's anxious behaviors contribute very little to our reasonable suspicion calculus. We have held that "there is nothing inherently suspicious about *** being nervous when pulled over by a police officer." *State v. Berry*, 232 Or. App. 612, 618, 222 P.3d 758 (2009), *rev dismissed*, 348 Or. 71 (2010). Moreover, there is nothing in the record before us that would lead us to conclude that defendant's nervousness was uniquely suspicious.

This leaves three facts for us to consider: (1) the car defendant was driving was owned by somebody else; (2) defendant was carrying a cell phone and a pager; and (3) the car contained multiple air fresheners and two bottles of cologne. The state argues that these facts are consistent with the transportation of narcotics. That may be true. However, a set of facts will not always create a reasonable suspicion just because those facts are consistent with, but do not necessarily suggest, a crime being committed. Wearing clothing while driving, to use an extreme example, is also consistent with the transportation of narcotics. Less extremely, so too (for all we know) is wearing cologne. This consistency, however, would not be enough to support reasonable suspicion. *See Maciel*, 254 Or. at 539 (holding that notwithstanding officer's testimony that people engaged in criminal enterprises often use prepaid cellular phones, the presence of two prepaid cellular phones carried little weight because such phones can be easily lawfully acquired by criminals and noncriminals alike). Moreover, there are several traffic stop cases where we considered those same factors and determined that officers lacked reasonable suspicion. *See State v. Juarez-Godinez*, 135 Or. App. 591, 900 P.2d 1044 (1995), *aff'd* on other grounds, 326 Or. 1, 942 P.2d 772 (1997) (holding that facts, including (1) a vehicle with a heavy odor of air freshener; (2) third-party registration of the vehicle; and (3) nervous occupants with salon-styled hair, gold jewelry, and new clothes were insufficient to establish reasonable suspicion of a drug offense). *See also State v. Meza-Garcia*, 256 Or. App. 798, 303 P3d 975 (2013) (holding that factors, including (1) a vehicle traveling interstate; (2) the presence of two cell phones; (3) the strong odor of air freshener; (4) the defendant's nervousness; and (5) third-party registration of the vehicle were insufficient to establish reasonable suspicion).

During the hearing on the motion to suppress, Turner did not explain why he found it suspicious for defendant to be traveling in a car owned by a third party. He did, however, testify that the smell of cologne and air freshener was significant because "oftentimes people who are transporting contraband, controlled substances, or unlawful items in their vehicle, they use these things as a cover scent, so that it masks the odor of anything that's illegal in their car that could be emitting an odor." With respect to the cell phone and pager, he explained: "[I]t is again something that's seemingly normal. Oftentimes people will have one cell phone or two cell phones, but when you're carrying both of them it—it says to me that boy, this person really needs to get contacted. So unless one is for work and one is for business, it's really odd that somebody would have two modes of communication to be contacted."

However, the record does not provide details about any particular training or experience that might help explain how Turner knows that carrying both a cell phone and a pager and using cover scents are tactics that drug traffickers "oftentimes" employ. It is, of course, fairly intuitive that cell phones, pagers, and cover scents might be used by drug traffickers. Accordingly, we would afford these factors some minimal amount of weight under the totality of the circumstances even without the invocation of an officer's training and experience.

We do not, however, find that Turner's bare assertion of "training and experience" adds any additional weight to these factors. An officer's training and experience are relevant to, and may help explain why, a particular circumstance is suspicious. *State v. Jacobs*, 187 Or. App. 330, 333, 67 P.3d 408 (2003). We have also recognized, however, that "[t]he phrase 'training and experience' *** is not a magical incantation with the power to imbue speculation, stereotype, or pseudoscience with an impenetrable armor of veracity." *State v. Daniels*, 234 Or. App. 533, 541, 228 P.3d 695 (2010). As relevant here, the invocation of training and experience, without more elaboration describing what that training and experience consists of, does little to prove that otherwise innocuous facts—carrying a cell phone and a pager, wearing cologne, and having air fresheners—are evidence of criminal activity. *Id.* at 541–42; *see also State v. Morgan*, 230 Or. App. 395, 215 P.3d 120 (2009) (reasoning that the officer's testimony about direct, relevant experience with the suspected crime should be afforded more weight than a general invocation of training and experience).

We find that, taken together, the facts cited by the state are not a sufficient basis to conclude that Turner had reasonable suspicion to detain defendant until the drug dog arrived. As soon as police were able to issue defendant a citation, their authority to detain defendant evaporated. The extension of the traffic stop, therefore, violated defendant's rights under Article I, section 9. Because there is no dispute that the evidence defendant sought to suppress was discovered as a result of that extension, we find the trial court erred in denying defendant's motion to suppress.

In sum, we conclude that, when rejecting defendant's motion for a judgment of acquittal and subsequently convicting him of intentionally obliterating the identification number on a firearm for an unlawful purpose, the trial court failed to consider whether defendant intentionally committed the alleged act and whether the alleged act was done for an unlawful purpose. For that reason, we reverse. However, there was sufficient evidence from which a rational trier of fact could have found those elements beyond a reasonable doubt. For that reason, we remand. We also conclude that police did not have reasonable suspicion to extend the traffic stop, so, on remand, all evidence discovered as a result of the unlawful extension, including the firearm, must be suppressed. We therefore reverse the trial court's denial of defendant's motion to suppress, reverse defendant's conviction under ORS 166.450, and remand.

from Dissent: *City of Nyssa v. Dufloth,* 184 Or. App. 631, 57 P.3d 161 (2002)

At issue in this case was whether a city ordinance that required nude dancers to remain at least four feet away from the audience violated the free expression guarantee of Article I, section 8, of the Oregon Constitution. In State v. Robertson *(1982), the Oregon Supreme Court held that a law that regulates expression on the basis of the content of that expression violates Article I, section 8, unless it is wholly contained within a "historical exception" to the constitutional guarantee. In* State v. Ciancanelli *(2002), the Oregon Court of Appeals concluded that a state law regulating public sexual conduct was wholly contained within such a historical exception because of widespread regulation of such conduct at the time of the adoption of the state constitution. The defendant in* Ciancanelli *sought review in the Oregon Supreme Court. While review was pending, an appeal in City of Nyssa came before the Court of Appeals. That court concluded that* Ciancanelli *was controlling and upheld the ordinance. Judge Schuman, only recently appointed to the Court of Appeals, had not participated in the* Ciancanelli *decision. The City of Nyssa appeal was his first opportunity to express his views on the subject. In brief, Judge Schuman's dissenting opinion suggested that* Ciancanelli *had been wrongly decided. He explained that merely because certain behavior historically was forbidden does not necessarily mean that the framers of the state constitution did not intend Article I, section 8, to apply to that behavior, a position that the Oregon Supreme Court ultimately adopted in reversing* Ciancanelli.*

—Justice Jack Landau, Oregon Supreme Court

The City of Nyssa, Oregon, enacted an ordinance that requires nude dancers to remain at least four feet away from the audience. The municipal court convicted defendants, the operators of nude dance clubs, of violating that ordinance, and the circuit court upheld the convictions.

On appeal, defendants argued that the city's ordinance violated Or. Const. art. I, § 8. The court of appeals disagreed. Laws regulating nude dancing fell within a well-established historical exception to Or. Const. art. Nude dancing was, of course, entitled to all the protection that the First Amendment afforded, but defendants did not raise a First Amendment claim in the case.

SCHUMAN, J., Dissenting.

Neither the majority opinion nor the concurrence persuades me that a law requiring nude "adult" entertainers to remain four feet away from their audience survives scrutiny under Article I, section 8, of the Oregon Constitution as construed by binding Oregon Supreme Court precedent. I understand that the majority finds support in an opinion of this court.[1] For that reason, this dissent is not only swimming upstream, but swimming upstream through water that is over the dam. The arguments have been made here before; I will therefore be brief.

The majority holds that this case is controlled by *State v. Ciancanelli*, 181 Or App 1, 45 P.3d 451; 181 Or. App. 1, 45 P3d 451, *rev pending* (2002). 184 Or. App. at 634–35. That may or may not be accurate.[2] Assuming that it is, I dissent because I believe that case, and I neither want nor intend to reopen the thorough debate between its majority and dissents. Suffice it to say that, in my opinion, the *Ciancanelli* majority's historical research does not demonstrate that, at the time the Oregon Constitution was written and adopted, a widely known and well established statute of common-law principle prohibited people from putting on, participating in, or observing shows including nudity, when the nudity was not exposed to view by the general, unwilling public. The research does demonstrate that exposing the genitals to the general, unwilling public was widely banned. And from the research we can probably infer that, had the framers been asked whether lawmakers could ban limited-admission sex shows, they would unhesitatingly have said that they could. They might well have said such shows were already unlawful. But the crucial

---

1 *State v. Ciancanelli*, 181 Or. App. 1. 45 P.3d 451, rev pending (2002).

2 Ciancanelli sustained a statute prohibiting live sex shows. This case involves only nude dancing. The Ciancanelli majority opinion did, however, flow necessarily from the predicate conclusion that "public exposure of the genitals" was widely regulated at the time the Oregon Constitution was adopted and therefore could be regulated now. 181 Or. App. at 16. It is therefore at least arguable that the conclusion regarding nudity was a necessary part of the conclusion regarding live sex shows and for that reason part of the holding.

fact is, nothing in the majority's historical research shows that such a ban did exist and that it was well established and widely known. That is what *State v. Robertson*, 293 Or. 402, 649 P2d 569 (1982), and subsequent Supreme Court cases require. Further, even if historical research could uncover a well-settled law banning limited-admission nude shows, that is not the kind of historical exception that *Robertson* envisions: that case uses the carefully chosen phrases "conventional crime," *id.* at 433, and "historical exception that was well established," *id.* at 412. It provides examples: "perjury, solicitation or verbal assistance in crime, some forms of theft, forgery and fraud and their contemporary variants." *Id.* at 412. Laws regulating nude dancing or sex shows, whether we approve of them or not, are not the kind of well-established conventional speech crimes that the *Robertson* court envisioned.

****

For the foregoing reasons, I dissent.

from Dissent: *State v. Howard,*
204 Ore. App. 438; 129 P.3d 792 (2006)

*At issue in this case is whether Article I, section 9, of the Oregon
Constitution requires police to obtain a search warrant before examin-
ing the contents of garbage set out at the curb for pick up. A majority
of the Oregon Court of Appeals concluded that a search warrant is not
required, based on Oregon Supreme Court case law holding that an
individual who discards property loses any constitutionally protected
interest in it. Judge Schuman dissented. He argued that the Supreme
Court case law was factually distinguishable and that the proper test is
whether police action "will significantly impair the people's freedom from
scrutiny." Applying that test, he concluded that, in light of the significant
amount of private, personal information that may be gleaned from
garbage, the state constitution requires a search warrant. A decade later,
in* State v. Lien *(2019), the Oregon Supreme Court essentially adopted
Judge Schuman's view that the court's precedents were distinguishable
and that, under the proper test, a search warrant is required.*

—Justice Jack Landau, Oregon Supreme Court

SCHUMAN, J., Dissenting.

Police, apparently recognizing that they lacked authority to go on
defendant Howard's property in order to seize her curbside garbage
container, arranged to have her garbage collection service pick up the
container and immediately turn it over to them. The officers then took
the container away, extracted its contents, and inspected them. The state
contended at trial that the seizure of the container, extraction of its contents, and inspection did not amount to a violation of defendant's possessory or privacy interests and, for that reason, that the police conduct
was not subject to any of the limitations imposed by Article I, section 9,
of the Oregon Constitution.

The state, in other words, argued below (and continues to argue on appeal) that the provision of the Oregon Constitution guaranteeing "the right of the people to be secure in their persons, houses, papers, and effects, against unreasonable search" leaves government officials free to have people's garbage seized from their property—without telling them, without a warrant, and without any reason to believe that they have done anything wrong—and then to harvest from the garbage whatever personal information it may yield. The trial court agreed. So does the majority. I do not.

Under a well-settled and frequently repeated precept first announced in *State v. Campbell*, 306 Ore. 157, 171, 759 P.2d 1040 (1988), government officials (usually but not always police officers) interfere with a person's privacy so as to implicate constitutional limitations when they engage in a "practice" which, "if engaged in wholly at the discretion of the government, will significantly impair 'the people's' freedom from scrutiny[.]"

***

Later cases have clarified that the "practice" is not evaluated in the abstract, but with respect to the context in which it occurs. *State v. Meredith*, 337 Ore. 299, 307, 96 P.3d 342 (2004). Thus, attaching a "beeper" to a private citizen's car is a search, whereas attaching one to a public employee's publicly owned car is not. *Id.* Emphatically, however, whether the act implicates protected privacy interests can never depend on whether the person searched is a criminal suspect: Article I, section 9, protects "the people," and our determination whether an act is a "search" must always be made with the awareness that it is all Oregonians' freedom from unwanted government scrutiny that is at stake—even though we are called upon to make that determination in a context where the practical effect of our decision could be that incriminating evidence of a criminal act will be suppressed and, because the "constable has blundered," the criminal will go free. *People v. Defore*, 242 NY 13, 21, 150 NE 585, 587, *cert den*, 270 U.S. 657, 46 S. Ct. 353, 70 L. Ed. 784 (1926) (Cardozo, J.). As Justice Harlan famously noted in the context of electronic eavesdropping,

> since it is the task of the law to form and project, as well as mirror and reflect, we should not, as judges, merely recite the expectations and risks without examining the desirability of saddling them upon *society*. The critical question, therefore, is whether under

our system of government, as reflected in the Constitution, we should impose on *our citizens* the risks of the electronic listener or observer without at least the protection of a warrant requirement.

United States v. White, 401 U.S. 745, 786, 91 S. Ct. 1122, 28 L. Ed. 2d 453 (1971) (Harlan, J., dissenting) (emphasis added).

Thus, the inquiry in the present case is this: Did the police do something that, if they could do it in similar circumstances whenever they wanted, would diminish the freedom from unwanted government scrutiny to which an Oregonian is entitled? In less abstract (but no less relevant) terms: If police officers (or tax collectors or OR-OSHA inspectors or SAIF investigators), without your knowledge and without cause to believe that you had done anything wrong, had your garbage collectors give them your curbside container immediately after pickup, and then the officers took the container to their office, dumped the contents out on the floor, and went through them with the proverbial fine-toothed comb, in the process discovering your social security number, your bank account numbers, your credit card account numbers, your diet, where you shop, what you buy, what medications you take (birth control pills? Viagra? Rogaine? Prozac?), what cosmetics you use, what congenital diseases your DNA might disclose, what periodicals you read, what the discarded drafts of your reports or correspondence say, whom you telephone, how much alcohol you drink, whether or not you threw away that atrocious necktie Aunt Sally gave you for your birthday, and other details of your personal and professional life—in that situation, would you feel that your privacy had been violated? That is the question, and the answer can only be yes.

Put another way, if the state's rule becomes law, then—as the state itself acknowledges in its brief to this court—people who do not want to give government officials unchecked authority to go through their garbage and discover intimate details of their personal and professional lives are left with four choices: They can haul their own garbage to the dump; they can try to negotiate a side agreement with their scavenger service; they can try systematically to render their refuse incapable of revealing personal information (although that might be difficult with used tampons, which is what police inspected and analyzed in *State v. Galloway*, 198 Ore. App. 585, 589, 109 P.3d 383 (2005)); or they can trust government officials not to avail themselves of all the power we will have conferred on them. I believe that imposing one or another of those options on the people of Oregon would unconscionably burden their ability to avoid loss of freedom from unwanted scrutiny.

The state's argument that people can take steps to avoid having their garbage officially scrutinized and inventoried might also be made with respect to, for example, outgoing parcels that they leave on their doorstep for a UPS or Fed-Ex truck to pick up. As the trial court noted, "when garbage is delivered to the curbside, common sense dictates that it is with the intent that it be taken to a landfill or garbage dump." So too when a parcel is left for the carrier to pick up and deliver; that act of faith is performed with the intent that the parcel be taken to a recipient. In both situations, a person deposits a closed item in a publicly accessible place with confidence that a particular person or entity will pick it up and deliver it to a destination. Like the sanitation company, the parcel delivery service is an intermediary and a carrier. Prevailing social norms give us confidence that the carrier will not open the item or divert it to somebody who will. Although a prudent person might well deposit parcels only in a secure collection box or a hand-to-hand transaction, or, for similar reasons, shred or haul his or her own trash, social norms make that prudence optional. If inspections or diversions were to become commonplace and unregulated, "the people" would have suffered a significant loss of their freedom from unwanted scrutiny.

The majority frames the issue in this case as "whether police invaded defendants' protected possessory or privacy rights under Article I, section 9, of the Oregon Constitution by searching their garbage after the sanitation service collected it and voluntarily turned it over to police." Ore. App. (slip op at 1). It then relies on *dictum* in *Galloway* to demonstrate that defendants had no possessory interest in their garbage and on *State v. Purvis*, 249 Ore 404, 438 P.2d 1002 (1968), to demonstrate that defendants had no privacy interest.

Neither of those cases compels the majority's conclusions. The *Galloway dictum* is not controlling because, in that case, we did not reach the dispositive question here; *Galloway* implies that a person has no possessory interest in refuse after it is picked up, but the case does not address the question whether people might retain a privacy interest[.] ***

To demonstrate that defendants lost their privacy interest, the majority relies on *Purvis*. In that case, police recruited hotel housekeepers to collect trash from the defendant's room and turn it over to them. The housekeepers found and turned over a marijuana cigarette butt that the defendant had left on the floor. The Supreme Court held that, in those circumstances, the police did not violate the Fourth Amendment. 249 Ore. at 411. *Purvis* does not apply to the present case for two reasons. First, the police conduct in *Purvis* differed materially from the conduct in the present case. In *Purvis*, the defendant apparently casually discarded the evidence and left it exposed to anybody who happened to be in the room. The garbage in the present case, in contrast, was placed in a closed container with the expectation that it would remain obscured until it was commingled with other garbage and therefore not easily retrieved and identifiable. *Purvis* would be relevant, in other words, if police had seized and inspected loose trash that defendants had strewn about their lawn.

Second, *Purvis* is clearly a Fourth Amendment case: there is only one passing reference to the state constitution ("the Fourth Amendment and its counterpart in our own constitution," *id.* at 409), and that reference occurs in the context of a statement about what hypothetically would be unconstitutional in a different case[.] ***

In sum, I am unwilling to endorse a rule under which government authorities—for good reason, bad reason, or no reason at all—are free, through the expedient of recruited civilians, surreptitiously to arrange for the seizure and subsequent inspection and analysis of the contents of garbage containers that people leave at curbside for pickup and delivery to the dump or recycling facility. Such a rule would result in an unwarranted and significant reduction in the people's freedom from unwanted scrutiny. For that reason, I conclude that officials may not engage in such conduct without a warrant or circumstances justifying an exception to the warrant requirement. It bears repeating that if police have good reason to believe that the garbage will yield the fruits, evidence, or instrumentalities of crime, then they can obtain lawful authority to search by using the procedure that the framers established to ensure that the people would be secure against unreasonable searches: they can obtain a warrant from a neutral and detached magistrate. Police in this case had no warrant, and the state does not argue that some exception to the warrant requirement applied. The search was unlawful, and the evidence derived from it should have been suppressed. I therefore dissent.

David Schuman accepting Frohnmayer Award for Public Service from Chief Justice Martha Walters 2014 (Courtesy of Jack Liu)

Speech at Frohnmayer Award Dinner 2014 (Courtesy of Jack Liu)

David Schuman with Attorney General Ellen Rosenblum (Courtesy of Jack Liu)

David Schuman with Justice Jack Landau (Courtesy of Jack Liu)

Jack Landau, Hans Linde, and Hardy Myers (Courtesy of Jack Liu)

Dave Frohnmayer, Martha Walters, David Schuman, Michael Moffit, Melissa Aubin, Garrett Epps (Courtesy of Jack Liu)

PART 6

Speeches and Tributes

The speeches and tributes included here represent a wide range of situations and personal connections, but all reflect David Schuman's power to engage listeners. From becoming a judge to exploring his Jewish roots to welcoming new students at the UO law school, receiving awards, or expressing his admiration for others, each occasion gave him an opportunity to think about the qualities he most admired and sought to embody.

—Sharon Schuman

Remarks, Oregon Court of Appeals Investiture (2001)

This speech was delivered by David Schuman on April 23, 2001, in the Oregon Supreme Court courtroom in Salem, Oregon, on the occasion of his investiture as a judge of the Oregon Court of Appeals.

I understand that protocol at these events calls for the newly invested judge briefly to introduce a few relatives, humbly to thank and acknowledge a few mentors, and modestly to promise diligent execution of duty, all within, say, ten or fifteen minutes. As a professor, however, I was unaccustomed to relinquishing the podium in anything less than a full hour. You will be happy to know—especially those of you who are standing—that this afternoon I intend to adopt the traditional practice of my new calling.

One nontraditional topic I want to mention briefly is the robe. You may be surprised to learn, as I was, that a new judge has to choose a robe from among a variety of different styles, fabrics, and makers, including one company that encloses with its illustrated catalog a testimonial from Judge Lance Ito. I am not making this up. After careful deliberation and a thorough canvass of my colleagues, I made my first decision as a judge: to splurge on a silk robe, of the so-called Geneva cut. I placed my order with the Ito-endorsed company, only to discover last week that there is a worldwide shortage of robe-quality silk. My first judicial decision, in other words, was overruled by worms.

A reliable source who wishes to remain nameless assures me that this was not the last time in my judicial career I would suffer this fate.

In any event, by the time I reordered it was too late to obtain a robe of my own for this ceremony. Justice Linde, who is about my height—six-feet-two—generously offered to let me use his, and I was honored to accept. Some of you who regard this act as symbolic may be encouraged and others may be terrorized, but I assure you that no symbolism was intended.

Let me begin in earnest by citing some authority, which after all is what judges on intermediate appellate courts do most. I use the word "authority" in its original sense, in the same sense that Dante used it when he called Virgil his "authority": our authorities are those who have *authored* us, whose example of wisdom and whose willingness to pass it on have helped to make us who we are and who we hope to be.

We are most obviously authored by our families. Allow me to introduce mine.

My father you have already met. Now allegedly retired, he was a lawyer in Chicago. He was also the starting center for the University of Michigan football team immediately before that position was occupied by Gerald Ford. He was also a Scoutmaster, a village official, the founder of a synagogue, and in general such a prolific contributor to the public life of his community that its leaders have named a park after him. To me he has been both a hard act to follow and a gentle inspiration in my endless attempts to follow it.

A quick story about my father and me. This may explain something. After undistinguished freshman and sophomore years in high school, I finally brought home what I thought was a good report card: three A's and a B. When I showed it to my father, he looked it over for a moment and said, "That's wonderful. You got a B in English?" The next semester I did better and brought home four A's. When I showed it to my father, he looked it over for a moment and said, "That's wonderful. You only took four courses?"

A month ago, I called to tell him that the governor had appointed me to the Court of Appeals. He was quiet for a moment and then said, "That's wonderful! Is that the highest appellate court in Oregon, or do they have a supreme court?" I am certain that if I had called to tell him that I had been appointed to the supreme court, he would have been quiet for a moment and then said: "That's wonderful. Oregon or United States?"

In my earlier life as a nonlawyer, I was inspired and, I hope, shaped by people who are not familiar to most of this audience but whom I must acknowledge anyway: Nick Lovrich and his parents, Randall Reid, Jack Schaar, Jeff Lustig, Alan Barahal.

In my profession I have been blessed to learn from and to work for lawyers like Pete Swan, Jim O'Fallon, Les Swanson, Hans Linde, Dave Frohnmayer, Gini Linder, Mike Reynolds, and Hardy Myers. Nobody could imagine a better exposure to legal knowledge, intellectual rigor, political courage, personal kindness, professionalism, and integrity.

Finally I want to acknowledge, as an authority—as an *authoring* force in my life—not a person but an institution: the University of Oregon Law School. My life has revolved around that institution since August 21, 1981, when I attended first-year orientation as an already-middle-aged ex-English teacher. Fifteen years later, when I left to become deputy attorney general, I conceived of myself as holding office while on temporary leave of absence from my true identity. One day last fall, for the first time, I was introduced at a conference without the "professor on leave" description, and I was suddenly forced to think of myself as having a persona separate from the academy. I decided on the spot to go back—to go "home." And now I have left again, for another vocation, another calling.

But not really; because even when I learn to think of myself as a judge, it will be as a judge who is professing the law. To profess is to avow, to promote, to declare, to disseminate. Of all my authorities, the absolute highest must always be the laws, the community's values made manifest, as they have been forged within the frame of the constitution by the community's lawmakers and expounded by its judges. Socrates calls the laws of Athens his mother and his father, even as he is about to die under their edict, because they formed him and created the web of allegiances and obligations that are the necessary precondition for being human. In promising to profess law, I pledge faith to law's authority even when doing so will disappoint those who have been my supporters, disconcert those who have been my detractors, and disregard those who will be my constituents. I make this pledge because I know that strong judges stand between a people and misrule; that to stay strong, judges, who have neither the sword nor the purse, must protect their only capital, which is their integrity; and that we can have integrity only by rendering fair judgments, explained clearly by reasoned discourse, eschewing expedience and influence. To do otherwise would be to squander the legacy that my colleagues and my predecessors in the Oregon judiciary have so carefully earned over the years.

And further, I will try to profess law under the familiar biblical injunction from the Book of Micah, which still strikes me as the best guidance for any judge: "What doth the Lord require of thee, but to do justly, and to love mercy, and to walk humbly with thy God?"

This command sets us on a hard path: We must elevate our duty to the laws over our impulse to be merciful, but to do that without stifling our sympathetic impulses. We must remain vulnerable to fellow-feeling even as we manipulate abstractions and draw bright lines and impersonally dole out reward or punishment. In this respect Micah's command echoes the God of Deuteronomy, who says, "And I charged your judges at that time, saying, . . . ye shall not be afraid of the face of man."

And so when I sit in judgment I will try to do so in a way that is faithful to the law *and* informed by the knowledge that the decisions we render involve real people and, almost always, their suffering. I will not flinch from the face of man or woman. I will try to remember that beneath the surface of any case, behind the pleadings and the briefs and the antiseptic dialogue of oral argument, there are real people who feel love and betrayal, humiliation and anger, desperation, pride, and pain.

So much for justice and mercy. That is the hard part of the command. The easy part is "to walk humbly"—easy because the task is so daunting and so much is at stake in doing it right. Here is my humble conclusion.

Socrates says that no evil can ever befall a good person. Socrates was not a fool; he knew as well as you and I that a good person is as likely as a bad one to be felled by a bolt of lightning or a random virus or a rogue cell. What he meant was that the only evil of importance is acting without virtue. Whether or not I will merit the judicial office that Governor Kitzhaber has given me and for which I now express my gratitude—whether I will be a virtuous judge—remains to be seen. If I fail, though, it will not be for lack of knowing what's expected of me: I am expected to render fair, clear, and reasoned decisions that follow law without forgetting the faces of those whom the decisions touch. Nor will it be for lack of help: I will be surrounded by brilliant, industrious, and generous colleagues on the Court of Appeals. Nor will it be because I have been badly prepared: nobody could want better authorities, better virtue-models, than I have.

Beyond the Wasteland:
Being a Lawyer in the 2010s (2013)

This speech was given to the members of Solomon's Legacy Society,
an affinity group of Jewish attorneys, judges, and law students in the
Greater Portland area.

Thank you for inviting me to Solomon's Legacy. I never met Judge Solomon, but I've read Harry Stein's biography and, like all Oregon lawyers, I know him by reputation. Like all Jewish lawyers in Oregon, I work in his shadow and under his continuing influence, and it's an honor to address this group that is named for him and for the biblical judge of whom he was the namesake.

Although the publicity for this event announces that the title of my talk is "Beyond the Wasteland: Being a Lawyer in the 2010s," it goes on to say that I'm going to "reflect on my career path and the ways in which a Jewish perspective informs my work." Now, asking me to talk about myself is like asking Chris Christie if he'd like a donut. It's like asking Joe Biden if he'd like to say a few words. There's nothing I enjoy more, or should avoid more, than talking about myself. Nor can I imagine that the bar would award CLE credit for listening to me reflect on my career path. So, insofar as possible, I'm going to revert to form and offer some observations about being a lawyer in the 2010s.

The title of this talk echoes one that I gave in April 1990, when I was asked to deliver the keynote address at a conference sponsored by the Oregon State Bar called "Law in the '90s." At the time, I was a professor at the University of Oregon Law School, and I promised the bar that I would avoid talking about topics that I knew almost nothing about, such as, for example, law in the '90s. I promised instead to offer some unsystematic observations from the perspective of a professorial observer. I followed through on that threat with a speech quoting, among others, Plato, Aristotle, Socrates, Emerson, Boccaccio, Dante, Chaucer, Shakespeare, Shelley, Melville, Dostoevsky, and Hannah Arendt—all of whom

I had taught during my former life as a literature professor, and some of whom I had actually read.

That was then, as the saying goes, and this is now. I am no longer a professor; I am now a judge, the difference being that not only law students, but also actual practicing attorneys, many of whom are much smarter, richer, and more important than I am, have to pretend that they like me even if they don't. So this morning, I promise to cut way back on the classical allusions; in 1990, I was twenty-three years closer to my days as a professional teacher of literature and also I had a much better memory. These days, I am more apt to quote *PGE v. Bureau of Labor and Industries* and other classics from the annals of Oregon appellate jurisprudence, or, perhaps, from the indispensable key to that jurisprudence, the third edition of *Webster's Unabridged Dictionary*.

However, some things have not changed. I noted then, and I continue to note, that practicing our profession can make us susceptible to adopting a certain corrosive or soul-bruising way of looking at the world. By our training and experience, we are steeped in a complex of ideas that, when left to grow unchecked, can be inappropriate and dysfunctional. The model of that complex of ideas is the typical legal dispute as it appears in the appellate opinions that I write and that law students confront from the first day of their legal training. Smith and Jones find themselves with different accounts of what is right. Each of them is represented by a zealous advocate who has presented a skillfully crafted argument to a panel of neutral adjudicators. The opinion is the court's explanation of why one argument more closely conforms to the rule of law implicit in the existing universe of precedent, legislation, and other relevant legal materials. There is a winner and a loser. The traditional defense of this model is that, in a clash between competing arguments, the better argument prevails. The traditional critique of this system attacks the presumption that prevailing arguments win because they are better, suggesting instead that they often win because they fit more comfortably within the dominant ideology or were propounded by the party with more skill or resources.

I have an additional critique. The law as it's taught and practiced can too frequently lead us to lose sight of the fact that, behind its abstractions, lie real human beings. Legal study and the legal profession tend to reward students and practitioners—and judges—precisely to the extent we can refine out of every situation all of those motley and unpredictable elements like personality, sentiment, and compassion, and deal instead with pure cold abstractions—and with people only as "plaintiffs" or "defendants" or "parties" or "witnesses" to be subjected to impersonal, mechanical, and neutral formulas. For example, we can learn everything the bar exam and our careers will require us to know about *Brown v. Board of Education* without learning who Brown was, or what particular scars segregation might have left on her soul. We can learn about *Roe v. Wade* without learning the real name of the plaintiff, or if she agonized over whether or not to carry her pregnancy to term. What we do learn, more subtly and indirectly, is that for the purposes of "pure" legal analysis, her name and who she was and what suffering she might have endured do not matter.

During law school, and even more so afterwards, this model undergoes refinements and complications. But its pervasive structure survives to color nearly everything a lawyer does, even a lawyer who never sees the inside of a courtroom. The presumption underlying almost everything that lawyers do is that the world of others is hostile, waiting to attack at the first sign of vulnerability, and that prudence requires us to be equally hostile or, at least, defensive. Our metaphors betray us: the highest praise a legal document can earn is to be called "ironclad" or "bombproof," terms from the lexicon not of civil discourse, but of warfare.

It is small wonder that lawyers, who are trained in the ethic of the jugular attack and immersed in a system that increasingly forces complex, multidimensional problems with subtle gradations of moral nuance into the form of allout battles, find it difficult to sustain stable, convivial, and collaborative work groups, not to mention families. After all, we are the ones who invented the pit bull deposition, the sadistic crossexamination, the discovery avalanche, the document dump, and other forms of hardball litigation. Emerson once noted,

The religion in which we worship writes its name on our faces, be sure of that. And we will worship something—have no doubt of that either. . . . That which dominates our imagination and our daily thoughts will determine our life and character. Therefore it behooves us to be careful what we are worshiping, for what we are worshiping we are becoming.

The civil religion that we lawyers and judges practice eight, ten, or twelve hours a day is worship of aggressive disputation and defensive living: the arrangement of human transactions in such a way as to make them invulnerable to the aggression, greed, and selfpromotion we presume are the engines driving all people. If we had to invent from scratch our own version of a world characterized by emotional detachment and alienation, by failures to connect, we could not invent a more effective one.

What can we do to inoculate ourselves against this professional peril? Let me answer that by citing authority, which is what those of us on intermediate appellate courts do best. Only here, by "authority" I don't mean precedent; I use the term more literally: an authority is a person who *authors* us, who shapes us through example or wise counsel. If you will indulge me, I'd like to talk about two of my authorities, and what they might tell us about how to avoid some of the professional pitfalls to which we are vulnerable. As it happens, they are both Jewish lawyers.

The first is my father. He was born in 1915 in Chicago, the son of a Russian immigrant father and a second-generation mother. He grew up in the North Shore suburb of Winnetka, where he was an all-state center on the New Trier High School football team and spent his summers as a counselor at a wilderness camp in Canada. He went to college at Michigan; I have a photograph at home of the Michigan Wolverine's 1935 lineup of centers—my father, Gerald Ford, and some other guy. After three years as an undergraduate, he entered the Michigan law school, thereby ending his football career, the lasting relics of which were a moth-eaten navy blue letter sweater emblazoned with the yellow letter M (which my mother insisted stood for mazel tov) and a nose that showed the effect of having been broken at least twice. (This was before the era of face masks. It was also an era in which a five-foot-nine-inch 200-pounder could be a starting interior lineman in the Big Ten.) After law school, his legal career was almost immediately interrupted by World War II; he served in the anti-aircraft corps in the European theater. When he returned home to his wife and two children, he incinerated his uniform and never talked about the war.

Over the next sixty years, beginning at a firm called Kixmiller, Barr and Morris, which subsequently morphed into a firm called Foss, Schuman and Drake, he built a practice, ultimately specializing in major construction transactions involving shopping centers and high-rise building projects. He represented, for example, the general contractor of the Sears Tower, which for a period was the world's tallest building.

What I want to emphasize about his life, though, is what he did outside of serving his clients. He was for a time the president of the Men's Club at the local synagogue, North Shore Congregation Israel, in Glencoe, Illinois. When that temple became too big, too institutional, and too image-conscious for him, he and some like-minded friends started a new one, Am Shalom. He served as its first president. He started, and was the first president of, the Glencoe Human Relations Committee. When the local African Methodist Episcopal church was ready to buy a permanent home, he handled the real estate transaction pro bono, and, over the years, he provided so much more pro bono service to that organization that, in 1996, the congregation presented a choir concert in his honor. He chaired the real estate section of the Chicago Bar Association. He helped draft and lobby for the Illinois Landlord Tenant Act. He was president of the Illinois Amateur Speed Skating Association. He was a precinct captain for the local Republican Party, a party to which he remained affiliated right up to the nomination of Barry Goldwater. He was a member, and ultimately chair, of the Glencoe Park Board; today there is a small Lake Michigan overlook area that is named after him. He was the longtime scoutmaster of Troop 22. He single-handedly reestablished the tradition of town July Fourth and Memorial Day parades and picnics. He organized an annual Greenleaf Avenue block party. When he died in 2007 at the age of ninety-two—he drowned in the Skokie Lagoon, when the canoe in which he was paddling stern capsized and he'd given the only life jacket on board to the family dog—the local newspaper referred to him as Mr. Glencoe, and the flag at city hall flew at half-mast for a week.

My second Jewish lawyer authority, Hans Linde, is, thankfully, still very much alive. In fact, I'm having coffee with him this afternoon on my way home. His story is of course more familiar to you. Born in Berlin, 1924; emigrated to Denmark in the early thirties at the age of nine; emigrated again to Portland in 1939 at the age of fifteen. Lincoln High School; Reed College; United States Army in World War II; law school at Boalt Hall, where he was editor in chief of the California Law Review; law clerk to Justice William O. Douglas; lawyer in the State Department; legislative aide to Senator Richard Neuberger; professor, University of Oregon Law School (first teaching assignment: tax); and justice, Oregon

Supreme Court. Justice Linde is universally recognized as one of the most important and influential constitutional law scholars and state judges of the twentieth century.

Again, though, I want to focus on neither his scholarship nor his opinions. Instead, I would like to note his career-long passionate involvement in law reform and government. As I noted, he began his post-clerkship in the political branches. Early on, he was a prominent member of the ill-fated Oregon Constitutional Law Revision Commission, created in 1959 and doomed to draft a model revised Oregon Constitution that the legislative assembly failed, by one vote, to refer to the people. He was the moving force behind the creation, by law, of the Oregon Law Revision Commission, before it withered away for lack of funding, and then he was the moving force behind its reestablishment. He served on that commission for many years. He also served on numerous task forces and work groups, including one to overhaul the law of judicial review of local government action and one to reform judicial selection. As a member of the Council of the American Law Institute, he has worked on reform legislation in the field of corporation law and torts. Even in his teaching and his scholarship, he has insisted that a focus on appellate opinions as the source of what we lawyers call "law" is misguided.

So what do these two authorities—one, a Midwestern mesomorph, a facilitator of real estate developments, the other a cerebral scholar-jurist—have in common, and what might we learn from them? To answer that question, I'll go back on my word and allude to a classic. In *Democracy in America*, Alexis de Tocqueville observed that Americans had more or less invented a new way of being in the world, and he called it "individualism." Before Tocqueville, that word did not exist; he invented it in an attempt to capture the uniquely American and democratic trait that "is a mature and calm feeling, which disposes each member of the community to sever himself from the mass of his fellow-creatures," and to believe that "they owe nothing to any man, [and] expect nothing from any man," leading them to "imagine that their whole destiny is in their own hands." Individualism also translates into the belief that the best way for a society to advance is for individuals—real or corporate—to aggressively pursue their own ends. If unchecked, this attitude, according to Tocqueville, "saps the virtues of public life."

To counteract that tendency, Tocqueville observed, Americans have developed democratic political institutions, and what he called "associations," by which he meant "associations of a thousand . . . kinds—religious, moral, serious, futile, extensive or restricted, enormous or diminutive. The Americans make associations to give entertainments, to found establishments for education, to build inns, to construct churches, to diffuse books, to send missionaries to the antipodes; and in this manner they found hospitals, prisons, and schools."

The practice of law is in many ways a highly individualistic enterprise. By that, I do not mean that lawyers don't work in or represent groups; I mean that, in their roles as advocates and representatives, lawyers must focus on producing an outcome that is beneficial to the client, without regard for some collective good. In Tocqueville's terms, that can "sap the virtue of public life." But Tocqueville also famously noted that lawyers, whom he called the aristocrats of a democracy, were specially qualified to participate in the political and civil institutions that helped prevent the decay of public life. I suggest what my authorities demonstrate is that one way to counteract some of the perils of a life in the law is active participation in political institutions and civil associations. My authorities—and I am certain that, had I known him, Judge Solomon would have been in the lineup—might teach that a life in the law should not only promote the private interests of disputants, but should forge and partake of a public life worth living; that a fully formed Jewish lawyer will not only represent combatants, but try to heal a broken world.

A Lecture for New Law Students (2014)

David Schuman had recently retired from the Oregon Court of Appeals and was a senior judge of the Oregon Judicial Department when he delivered this speech at the University of Oregon Law School Convocation on August 21, 2014.

You have now been subjected to almost a week of advice, some of which has probably been confusing, intimidating, and inconsistent—but all of which has been well-intended. By tradition, the last convocation speaker is expected to continue in that vein, only with an extra portion of pomposity and condescension. I plan to continue in that tradition, and I beg your indulgence for just a few more moments. I would like to offer some advice about apparent failure, and apparent success.

For my advice about apparent failure, I offer my own personal experience. I started as a first-year law student on this campus thirty-three years ago, to the day. At the time, I was a thirty-seven-year-old college professor of English with a fancy degree from the University of Chicago and a long list of publications—not long enough, apparently, because my presence as a 1L derived from the fact that I could not get the kind of college teaching job that I wanted, and I didn't want the kind of job that I had. Despite that fact, I was still pretty confident that, what with my status as a card-carrying, certified PhD, I could more or less cruise through law school, where my fellow students were not nearly as experienced, wise, or educated as I was.

You can therefore imagine my shock when my first semester grades were, to put it generously, not stellar. To put it less generously but more accurately, they were barely mediocre. I was particularly galled by my grade of C+ in Contracts, where I felt a special affinity with the professor, whose first reading assignment had been Shakespeare's *The Merchant of Venice*, a play I had frequently taught.

The day I picked up my shocking grades, still reeling, I went to the professor's office and asked if we could go over my exam. We did, and when we were done, he said, "Mr. Schuman"—I had been hoping he'd call me Dr. Schuman, but no such luck—"there's nothing really wrong with this exam, but there's nothing particularly right about it either." Succumbing to temptation, I replied, "Sort of like your lecture on *Merchant of Venice*." Fortunately, he took that comment as the joke it was probably not intended to be, and, in later years, we became—and are still—very good friends.

In any event, following my "joke," he made a generous offer: he offered to confer with me periodically throughout the second semester, to give me practice exam questions, and to go over my answers. I took advantage of that offer. I studied Contracts extra hard. And when second semester grades came out, I can report that I received the highest C in the class.

Now flash forward thirty-three years. Looking back from this vantage point, I can say with confidence that I have been lucky enough to have had the most rewarding, most intellectually challenging, most satisfying jobs that a lawyer can hope for. (I have been a clerk to one of the best state supreme court justices in the country; an appellate litigator for the state; a law professor; the state's deputy attorney general; and a judge.) I have never had to send a bill to a client. In fact, I don't think I've ever even *had* a client. The moral to this story is, if you suffer setbacks, and most of you will, see them for what they are: they are setbacks, not failures. A bad grade in a class, or a bad GPA for a semester, or even a low ultimate class rank—none of these things is an accurate predictor of your success as a lawyer, and, more importantly, none is a reflection of your worth as a human being.

So much for failure that is not really failure. I now want to shift my focus. Most of what you have heard this week, including what you just heard from me, has been designed to prepare you for the obstacles and perils that stand between you and success in law school—what they are and how to avoid them. Yet the fact is, the overwhelming majority of you will succeed in law school. That is a statistically verifiable truth. That is why I now want to talk about the *perils* of success. In particular, I'm going to talk about two unfortunate unintended consequences of an apparently successful legal education—a tendency to abuse power and a tendency to develop a certain coldness of heart—and what you can do to avoid them over the next three years and beyond.

Let me begin with abuse of power. Many people, perhaps you among them, come to law school because they correctly understand that attorneys have a state-granted monopoly on access to the forces that can move social and political systems and make them do good things. Law school is where we come to obtain the power to promote our values. But during our three years of legal education, as we become more and more adept in the mysteries of power, too often a mysterious change takes place. Power corrupts—or in any event, *something* happens to the idealism even as the empowerment proceeds.

I am not talking about the champions of progressive causes who suddenly begin appearing in dark suits and power haircuts for on-campus interviews with law firms whose list of major clients looks like the Who's Who of Corporate Crime. I refer more generally to what happens to our values when we begin to confuse what is *legal* for what is *right*, what we can lawfully *get away with* for what we *should do*, as though any action, no matter how obstructionist, obnoxious, dishonorable, deranged, or cruel that is not literally prohibited by some rule of law or code of legal ethics therefore carries an ethical seal of approval, especially if done in service of a paying client.

Meanwhile, as the distinction between what is right and what we can legally get away with blurs and the superego atrophies, the empowerment continues and grows. When you graduate from law school and pass the bar exam, you will receive not only a diploma and the functional equivalent of a union card, but you will also receive the proverbial keys to the city as well. You will not only have access to the levers that move the political, social, and economic systems—the forms and rituals of transaction, administration, and litigation—you will also have a quantity of power that can only be called magical and terrifying. If you were a member of a different culture and you had this power an anthropologist would call you a witch or a wizard, and you would be either venerated or ostracized, but in either case you would be feared. Because you will have the power to utter a few special words of hocus pocus, or make a few marks on paper, or punch a few buttons on a telephone or a computer, and by those actions alone inflict pain, humiliation, and personal financial disaster. By those actions alone, you will be able to invoke the official machinery of the judicial system, knowing that this machinery itself, with you now licensed to operate it and to deploy it against others, can maim all who are involuntarily drawn into its range.

True, you can use your power well. But only a constant and active exercise of self-discipline will prevent you from corrupting it.

Now let's talk about coldness of heart. Legal study and the legal profession tend to reward you precisely to the extent you can refine out of every situation all of those motley and unpredictable elements like personality, sentiment, and compassion, and deal instead with pure cold abstractions—and with people only as "plaintiffs" or "defendants" or "parties" or "witnesses" to be subjected to impersonal, mechanical, and neutral formulas. For example, you can learn everything the bar exam and your career will require you to know about *Brown v. Board of Education*, the landmark 1954 case making racial segregation illegal, without learning who Brown was, or what particular scars segregation might have left on her soul. You can learn about *Roe v. Wade* without learning the real name of the plaintiff, or if she agonized over whether or not to carry her pregnancy to term. What you *will* learn, more subtly and indirectly, is that for the purposes of "pure" legal analysis, her name and who she was and what suffering she might have endured do not matter. I suggest that "pure" legal analysis of this type is typical but it is also dangerous to your soul, and wrong. I urge you to remember that, every case you read and, later, in practice, every case you work on, involves at least one person for whom the case was among the most important things in his or her life.

Abuse of power and coldness of heart. These are among the dangers that you will confront when you successfully complete your legal education and enter your new profession. I want to ask you now to grasp some knowledge that you already have and to hold it close during the next three years and beyond, because it can protect you from these perils.

As of now, since you are not yet JD impaired, you probably believe that "law" is much more than the result of litigation. It is principally the rules forged in the public arena by ourselves and our elected representatives. Ideally it should be the sinew of the community, the community's values made manifest, the fruit of public discussion and debate about what constitutes or promotes a life of virtue—and not what some judge says about who wins some private dispute, usually about money. Socrates from his prison cell calls the laws of Athens, under which he is about to die, his mother and his father—that which gave him his identity and his roles, which bound him to others in a web of support and obligation and in so doing made it possible for him to be a human and not a beast. I urge you to try to see your legal training not only as a process by which you become a certified pit bull but also as preparation for the profession of law in the larger sense, to see your access to the machinery of the system not only as a means to promote the private interests of litigants but to forge a public life worth living. I urge you to enlarge your sphere of concern so that it includes not only argument in the service of private wealth, but debate over the nature of the public good.

I am also urging you, in the words of the prophet, to do justice *and* to love mercy, to let your devotion to the rule of law remain open always to the heart's way of knowing. When you read about an oil spill or a freeway pileup and the first thing you think about is proximate cause or strict liability; when you hear of a racist or sexist or homophobic practice or policy and the first thing that comes to your mind is the equal protection clause of the Fourteenth Amendment or the Civil Rights Act—then you have probably over-learned your law school lessons. This opening up of yourselves, I suggest, can be your inoculation against that perversion of power and coldness of heart which are the hazards of our business.

Socrates, again, tells us that no evil can ever befall a good person. Socrates was no fool and neither am I and neither are you. We all know that a good person is as likely as a bad one to get hit by a truck or a kidney failure or an errant cancer cell. What Socrates meant, I think, was something like this: A person with a well-ordered soul is immune from the only kind of evil that matters, which is a disordered value system. To what extent you have and maintain a well-ordered value system remains to be seen. Some would say that your three years in law school will reduce your chances. I disagree. I believe that if you attend to the difference between what is right and what is merely legal, and if you see the law as what ties each of us to our fellows, and you remember that those fellows have faces, you can enjoy a rich professional life in which you wield principled power and do it with abundance of heart. Good luck.

Remarks on Receiving the Frohnmayer Award for Public Service (2014)

This speech was presented on November 7, 2014, in Portland, Oregon, at a dinner celebrating the recipient of the Frohnmayer Award for Public Service, an award given annually since 2002 by the Law School Alumni Association. Named in honor of the family of University of Oregon President Emeritus and Law Professor Dave Frohnmayer, the award recognizes a graduate, faculty member, or friend of Oregon Law whose public service brings honor to the school.

I was hoping to find an appropriate quotation from Shakespeare to begin these brief remarks about public service. This would have been an homage to my older brother Sam, a Shakespearean scholar who has managed to rope a line or two from the Bard into all of his speeches. The only quote I could find that appeared relevant to the topic of public service comes from Othello, who says in Act V, "I have done the state some service and they know it." Unfortunately, the line comes right after he has strangled his completely innocent wife, and seventeen lines before he kills himself. So I've decided instead to begin, Academy Award style, with some thank-yous.

I am moved and honored to receive this recognition. The honor is particularly moving for me because earlier recipients include many people under whose leadership I worked, whose wise counsel I had the good fortune to receive, and to whom I remain intellectually and morally accountable: Martha Walters, who, along with Tim Sercombe and Les Swanson, supervised me when I was a summer associate at the Harrang firm thirty-one years ago—believe it or not—1983 (when Martha and Tim and I were twelve); Justice Hans Linde; Attorney General Dave Frohnmayer; UO law school Dean Dave Frohnmayer; UO President Dave Frohnmayer; and Attorney General Hardy Myers.

Although I am honored and moved, I have to protest that, in giving me this award for public service, the law school has it exactly backwards. It is I who should be thanking the public, in the form of the state's public law school, for serving me. True public service involves sacrifice and is driven by altruism. I am reminded of the Oregon lawyers who went to Mississippi in 1965 to provide legal services to civil rights workers. I have sacrificed nothing, and, to the extent that my career path resulted in some service to the public, that was an incidental by-product of what was, in essence, a self-indulgent decision to pursue a career doing the kind of work that I found fascinating.

As a result of that decision, and of the education that the people of Oregon largely subsidized (this was before the era of tragic disinvestment), and also the result of being in the right place at the right time, I have had the most enjoyable and rewarding jobs that a lawyer could be lucky enough to experience. I have never had to bill a client. In fact, I have never *had* a client. I have never had to experience the pit-bull depositions, the paperwork avalanches, the billable hour pressures, or the intra-firm rivalries that plague so many in our profession. To the contrary: I have enjoyed engaging, challenging, and consequential work, under the direction of inspiring mentors, and with wonderful colleagues, students, and, for the last thirteen years, an astonishing array of brilliant judicial clerks—all of whom, I might add, have been UO law school alums.

And so it is with gratitude, but with a nagging sense of fraud, that I accept this award for public service. Perhaps I can come actually to merit the honor going forward. The public in general, and the legal profession in particular, could certainly use some services. I will quickly mention only three.

First, the bar is still too homogeneous—I know you're tired of hearing this, and so am I, but I'm tired of hearing about the crisis in the Middle East, too, but that's no excuse to ignore it.

Second, the bar must do something to address the ironic situation we find ourselves in, with too many new lawyers unable to find work while too many people are unable to find affordable lawyers. Perhaps we could lobby for the creation of something analogous to Teach for America. We could call it Plead for America.

And third, we need to support institutions like the UO law school, which has provided many people, as it has provided me, with a legal education that teaches students that there is a place in the law for them even if they are more interested in advancing debate over the nature of the public good than they are in the pursuit or protection of private wealth.

These are worthy goals, and I will do what I can to promote them as I limp off into my golden years, sustained by one artificial hip, two repaired hernias, trifocals, and four false teeth. I hope you will join me.

But, in the meantime, I want to express my gratitude once again. I will remember tonight as a highlight of my professional life. Based on that life, and on the family I was lucky to be born into, and the family that my wife Sharon and I have been lucky enough to form—my two children Ben and Rebecca, my granddaughter Milly, and my soon-to-be second grandchild known for the present as Schu-Fetus—I can say with only a few reservations, as my brother Sam said recently in quoting Lou Gehrig, that tonight, I consider myself the luckiest man on the face of the Earth.

Introducing Hardy Myers

Serving six years as Oregon deputy attorney general for Hardy Myers
was a job David Schuman relished, in part because it was such an inspi-
ration to work with the Oregon attorney general.

There are politicians, that is, people who choose to make a career out of running for and holding public office, and who enter the private realm only reluctantly, when they lose elections; and there are public servants, citizens with careers in the private realm who, from time to time, are called to serve in the political realm. Politicians are a relatively new breed. The profession was unknown, for example, to Periclean Athens, where a citizen was defined as a person who could rule and be ruled in turn. More relevant to us here tonight, the framers of the Oregon Constitution consciously created a state that would be governed by "citizen legislators," public servants who would temporarily abandon their regular employment to meet for only a few months every other year. Subsequent legislatures have followed suit by setting compensation for themselves and other high elected executive officials at rates that can hardly provide a comfortable standard of living for a sustained period and ludicrously low in comparison to what such talented individuals could earn in the private sector if they so desired.

The reasons for favoring public servants over politicians were always idealistic. It was believed that a government of public servants would be less likely to foster the creation of a closed and insulated governing class, to fall prey to the corruptions of power and the temptations of self-aggrandizement; they would more faithfully respond to the needs and preferences of the citizenry of which they were a part. As governing becomes more complex, the ideal of the public servant has not survived wholly intact. Our legislative assembly now meets annually, and we can all think of examples of professional Oregon politicians—some characterized by talent and virtue, others . . . not so much. But the ideal survives. And one of its best examples is our speaker tonight, Hardy Myers.

Hardy was born in Electric Mills, Mississippi. Shortly thereafter, however, he rectified that mistake by moving to central Oregon, where he went to the public schools. Briefly recidivating, he returned to Mississippi for his undergraduate education, before recovering his senses and returning permanently to Oregon—first to Eugene, where he earned his law degree at the University of Oregon law school and then, on graduation, to Portland, where he first clerked for a federal judge and then joined the law firm now known as Stoel Rives. Soon thereafter, he heeded the call to public service, first as the president of the Portland City Planning Commission, and then, for ten years, as a member of the Oregon House of Representatives, including two terms as its Speaker. During that time, the *Oregonian* twice named him the most outstanding member of the legislative assembly.

After his time in the House, Hardy returned to private practice, but he did not retreat from public service. He chaired the Oregon Criminal Justice Council, developing sentencing guidelines, and he was a member of the State Sentencing Commission; he chaired the Portland Future Focus strategic planning committee; and he was active in civic affairs. And then, after twelve years out of office, he gave in to the urging of his party leaders and ran successfully to become the attorney general of Oregon. He was reelected to that office twice and served for a total of twelve years. During those twelve years, it is worth noting, he received, without complaint, a legislatively determined salary that was approximately 50 percent of what a starting twenty-six-year-old attorney earns at a big urban law firm.

Hardy's accomplishments as attorney general were many, which is why the National Association of Attorneys General in 2008 awarded him its highest honor, the Kelley-Wyman Award. The National Association of Attorneys General, by the way, is often referred to as the National Association of Aspiring Governors, because traditionally the office is seen as a stepping-stone to higher office—which is why so many attorney general candidates, mostly in other states, campaign on a platform of strict enforcement of criminal laws and aggressive consumer protection, and then, when in office, issue a torrent of press releases touting their accomplishments in those areas. Now, law enforcement and consumer protection are important objectives, and Hardy pursued them with vigor, innovative use of limited resources, and remarkable success. He was co-chair of the NAAG Consumer Protection Committee, and chair (and founder) of the Oregon Attorney General's Sexual Assault Task force. For his work on that task force, he was recently honored by Oregon Women Lawyers. But under Oregon statutes, criminal law enforcement and consumer protection are not the primary duties of the attorney general. Law enforcement is in the first instance the duty of elected county district attorneys, and the legislative budget for consumer protection allows for the employment of no more than a handful of assistant attorneys general. Under Oregon law, the attorney general is tasked primarily with the unglamorous and non-self-promoting duty of providing the people of the state, their officials and agencies, with high-quality, ideologically unbiased legal services. Hardy's greatest accomplishment as attorney general was his steadfast determination to fulfill that obligation and his undisputed success in accomplishing it.

David Frohnmayer—A Tribute (2016)

After the death of David Frohnmayer in 2015, an issue of the Oregon
Law Review *(vol. 94, no. 3) was devoted to tributes in his memory,
including this one from David Schuman.*

Dave Frohnmayer hired me in 1985 as an assistant attorney general in
the Oregon Department of Justice, my first job as a practicing lawyer.
Shortly thereafter, I left the department and joined the University of
Oregon law school faculty where, in 1991, I was on the search committee that persuaded Dave to serve as our dean. I would like to characterize these two events—his hiring me, my "hiring" him—as reciprocal or
symmetrical. That would not be accurate. In both cases, it was I who
was the petitioner, trying in the first instance to persuade Dave that I
was qualified enough to hire, and in the second, trying to persuade him
that we were qualified enough to be the beneficiaries of his intelligence,
judgment, and energy.

In any event, I worked for Attorney General Frohnmayer, Dean
Frohnmayer, and President Frohnmayer for twelve years. During that
time, our professional relationship morphed into what I flatter myself
to call a friendly relationship between our families. During these years,
Dave—and it was always Dave, never General Frohnmayer or Dean or
President—made incomparable contributions to the life the University
of Oregon, the state, and, by virtue of his nationally recognized leadership as both an enormously influential state attorney general and flagship university president, to the entire country.

Other writers in this volume of the *Oregon Law Review* discuss
these contributions with respect to Dave's legal and academic accomplishments. Demonstrably, these professional accomplishments derived
in large measure from two of Dave's character traits: first, his faith that
individual and societal well-being flourish when citizens are more concerned with the justice of their community than with maximizing their
own self-interest; and second, that the proper response to any seemingly

insurmountable obstacle was to unleash energy in search of a solution and to inspire others to do the same. The degree to which he brought these precepts to bear in his professional life is extraordinary. But that accomplishment occurred in a context. In Dave's case, that context was an unspeakably cruel onslaught to his daughters. It would have been extraordinary if Dave had simultaneously endured that onslaught and maintained a minimal professional life. The fact that he devoted himself to battling that private curse, while simultaneously and energetically excelling as a public servant, magnifies his accomplishments in both arenas.

The curse to which I refer, of course, is Fanconi anemia (FA), an incurable (at least for now) and inevitably fatal (at least for now) inherited disease that has taken two of Dave and Lynn's daughters and threatens a third.[1] Where most of us would have responded to such a curse with despair, or impotent anger at an unjust God, or passive faith that a just God's apparent sadism serves some unknowable divine plan, or self-anesthetization by drink or drugs—I myself cannot imagine even getting out of bed in the morning—Dave, along with Lynn, attacked the disease with the same relentless vigor and confidence in the altruism of others that he brought to bear on the challenges confronting Oregon's government, its law school, and its flagship university. As attorney general, he (for example) guided the state through a period in which a religious cult threatened to take over an entire county in eastern Oregon and attempted to poison a variety of elected officials. As law school dean, he mollified influential and wealthy interests who threatened harm to the institution based on their perception that its environmental activism was harmful to their business interests, while simultaneously refusing to stifle or insist on the moderation of that activism. As president of the University of Oregon, he not only guided the institution through a period of unprecedented legislative disinvestment, he also cultivated private generosity leading to an improved built environment and a solid academic reputation. As Jews recite at every Passover Seder, *daiyenu— that much by itself would have been enough.*

But along with these accomplishments, he also, as a parent, working with Lynn, attacked Fanconi anemia. First, they organized a Fanconi

---

1   Amy Elizabeth Winn, Dave and Lynn Frohnmayer's youngest daughter, died in 2016. In 2021, Fanconi anemia remains incurable and inevitably fatal.—S.S.

Anemia Family Support Group, which (among other things) provided FA families with the opportunity to interact, support each other, and exchange information about treatments. Next, Dave became a founding director of the National Marrow Donor Program, which created and maintains a voluntary international register of people who could donate hematopoietic cells to help children with FA and other bone marrow or immune system disorders—a register that lists more than 10.5 million individuals and has facilitated more than 55,000 transplants. And finally, in 1989, he and Lynn founded the Fanconi Anemia Research Fund. That organization, which began in Dave and Lynn's living room, has grown exponentially. It now sponsors annual expense-paid summer camps where FA patients and families gather to exchange information and support and to learn of the latest developments in FA research. The fund also sponsors annual international symposia attended by leading scientists. Most significantly, it raises and distributes funds—so far more than $18,000,000—to researchers whose proposals meet rigorous, peer-reviewed scientific standards. The immediate purpose of the research fund is to improve the treatment of FA and to search for a cure. This research has produced advances that are relevant not only to FA but to several cancers as well. And although a cure has remained elusive, the fund has contributed to the significant improvement of life expectancy for FA patients, who now typically live into their mid-thirties and sometimes into their forties and fifties.

Beyond this immediate goal, Dave identified a mode of operation and a larger mission, both of which reflect the traits that made him such a successful public servant. Addressing researchers at a ceremony giving him and Lynn an award for "outstanding contributions to biomedical research," Dave emphasized that, "While competition is healthy and Nobel fever may be unavoidable, there is an irreducible need . . . for combinations of brains, not division of intellects into competitive and warring or secretive camps."[2] And he also identified the larger mission: "We simply are trying to solve a problem and alleviate some quantum of misery in the human condition."

---

2 *The Fanconi Anemia Research Fund Story: Building Something from Nothing* (2008), at https://www.fanconi.org/images/uploads/other/The_Fanconi_Anemia_Research_Fund_Story.pdf.

In Memoriam, James M. O'Fallon, 1944–2017 (2017)

At the memorial service in 2017 for James O'Fallon, Emeritus Professor of Constitutional Law at the University of Oregon School of Law, David Schuman delivered this tribute.

Those of you who are part of the academic community know that the university expects its faculty to meet high standards in scholarship, service, and teaching. In each of these areas, Jim O'Fallon's career at the University of Oregon law school serves as an example to which the rest of us can only aspire.

His scholarship includes a 1994 *Stanford Law Review* article, one of the most influential and important works about *Marbury v. Madison*, the most influential and important Supreme Court opinion in the history of the nation. The article has been cited and discussed by other scholars more than ninety times, including two times this year alone. Jim also wrote leading works on the jurisprudence of Justice Holmes, Justice Douglas, feminism, equal protection, and legal history. His writing was lucid but never simplistic, authoritative but never arrogant, original but never disrespectful of the canon, rigorous but never obtuse.

Jim's service to the law school and the university was legendary. Most conspicuously, he was the university's long-serving faculty athletic representative, and within the law school, he took on the thankless position of associate dean. That job requires the ability to process a daunting amount of paperwork, to provide counsel to the dean and other administrators, to mollify numerous constituencies whose demands are frequently in tension, if not at war, with each other, all the while trying to promote and sustain institutional vitality. Jim navigated these difficult waters with good will and cheerful diligence, and with the unprecedented skill of a canoeist shooting Class 4 rapids. In other official committee work—admissions, appointments, and promotion in particular—he was a passionate advocate for excellence. The passion, however, was always modulated, reasoned, and thoughtful. I never heard Jim raise his voice and I never heard him launch an *ad hominem* attack on a colleague, student, or applicant.

Jim's most remarkable service, however, was neither committee work nor associate dean work. It was his informal service to his colleagues. This took many forms. An anecdote related by our colleague Ibrahim Gassama most accurately captures this quality:

> I recall that after one rather awful presentation of my first work in progress, I retreated to my office to contemplate whether I had any business here. Shortly, there was a knock on my door and there was Jim with a short volume by one of the giants of international law. Jim, with that ever-present gleam in his eyes, handed it to me, saying something like, "Your talk reminded me of this." I accepted it gratefully and built my early writings upon the ideas expressed in that slim text.

And teaching. . . . I first knew Jim when he was my Constitutional Law professor in 1982. Since that time, he has been my colleague, my mentor, my counselor, and my friend. In every role, to me and to everybody else who had the good fortune to come within the expansive sphere of his influence at the law school and beyond, he was always a teacher. He taught that there is room in the study and practice of law, not only for analysis and craft, but for ideas and values. I do not mean doctrinal ideas like, for example, the relationship between constitutional text and structure. I mean ideas like the nature of citizenship in a democracy, the concept of civic virtue, the quality of justice, the meaning of equality. And I do not mean doctrinal values like, for example, the value of judicial restraint or legal precedent, or even the value of a written constitution. I mean values like equal respect for the dignity of all people, the value of reasoned discourse, the value of integrity in private and civic life. He taught these things using the traditional tools of pedagogy, but more importantly, he taught them by living them. Again paraphrasing Ib Gassama, Jim O'Fallon was a person who, by his very presence and without uttering a word, inspired you to be your best self. Our greatest tribute to Jim would be if, in his absence, his memory continued to exert that influence. As Hamlet says about his father in Shakespeare's play, "He was a man, take him for all in all. We shall not look upon his likes again."

Hans Linde Dedication (2009)

David Schuman wrote this dedication to Hans Linde for the Oregon Appellate Almanac, 2009. The volume begins, "The Appellate Practice Section of the Oregon State Bar dedicates this 2009 edition of the Appellate Almanac to Hans Linde."

Born in Berlin, Hans Linde moved with his family to Copenhagen at the age of seven. He attended school there until the family once again moved when he was fifteen, this time to Portland. He attended Lincoln High School, where he met his future wife, Helen, and quickly came to the attention of his English teacher, Maurine Neuberger, later a United States senator. Despite the fact that English was his third language, he quickly acculturated and became the editor of the school newspaper. When he finished high school, he went on to Reed College (senior thesis: a study of Hans Kelsen, Georg Jellinek, and Carl Schmitt, three German philosophers of law). He served in the US Army during World War II and went to law school at Boalt Hall, where he was editor-in-chief of the *California Law Review* (and supervised publication of one of Professor Prosser's seminal articles on torts). Upon graduation, he and Helen moved to Washington, DC, so Hans could serve for a year as law clerk to Supreme Court Justice William O. Douglas (and play in a weekly poker game with other clerks, including William Rehnquist and Abner Mikva). After his clerkship, he served in the state department and as legislative aide to Senator Richard Neuberger, the husband of his high school English teacher.

Having achieved the trifecta of federal government service—serving in all three branches—he returned to Oregon and, at the request of then-Dean Orlando Hollis, he joined the faculty of the University of Oregon law school (to teach torts and tax). He remained at Oregon for seventeen years, with visiting appointments to Stanford, Boalt, and other law schools, until Governor Robert Straub appointed him to the Oregon Supreme Court in 1978. He "retired" in 1991. The quotation marks around "retired" are in recognition of the fact that, since 1991, he has been Distinguished Jurist in Residence at Willamette University College of Law, where he energetically maintains a teaching, writing, correspondence, and advising schedule that would fatigue a person whose capacity for work was merely normal.

In the world of constitutional scholarship—a world beset by trends, fads, and fashions—Professor Linde's work remains as important (and as frequently cited) today as when it was first published. By now, several generations of scholars have studied, admired, responded to, argued about, criticized, but always recognized the seminal importance of such articles as "Due Process of Lawmaking," 55 *Nebraska Law Review* 197 (1976), and "Judges, Critics, and the Realist Tradition," 82 *Yale Law Journal* 227 (1972). Among his past and current professorial colleagues, he is regarded as a pragmatic, grounded analyst with a respect for common sense, a disdain for high theory, and an insistence on questioning long-accepted first principles.

The readers of this *Almanac* need no reminder of Justice Linde's influence on the substance of appellate law in Oregon, particularly his reintroduction of state constitutional law as an independent and primary source of individual rights. Nearly two decades after his retirement, Article I, section 8, cases are still elaborations of *State v. Robertson*, 293 Or. 402, 412, 649 P.2d 569 (1982); and equality cases are still elaborations of *State v. Clark*, 291 Or. 231, 630 P.2d 810 (1981). Less recognized are his contributions to administrative law (*Megdal v. Board of Medical Examiners*, 288 Or. 293, 605 P.2d 273 (1980) still remains foundational), torts (*Fazzolari v. Portland School District No. 1J*, 303 Or. 1, 734 P.2d 1326 (1987) still defines negligence), and public financing (bond lawyers around the country still love "the WPPSS case," *DeFazio v. Washington Public Power Supply System*, 296 Or. 550, 679 P.2d 1316 (1984)).

Regardless of the subject matter, his opinions were notable—and nationally noted—for their intellectual rigor, their willingness to question assumptions, and their intolerance of formulaic thinking.

And yet, if Hans Linde were to make a list of what he would want a dedication like this to mention, I suspect it would not contain the things for which he is most famous. Rather, and somewhat ironically, it would emphasize his dedication to the principles that law is not made in appellate opinions and that scholarship must always resonate in the untidy world of politics. He would point, not to his careers as professor and judge, but to his participation in law reform, from the Constitutional Revision Commission in the late fifties and early sixties to the Oregon Law Commission, which he helped bring into existence and on which he served since its inception. And, whether he wanted it to or not, the dedication would not be complete without mentioning the incalculable influence he has had on generations of students, friends, and law clerks, as well as his loyalty and generosity to them.

EPILOGUE

Legacy

Justice Hans Linde's ninetieth birthday (unknown photographer)

Cycling in Bend (Photo by Alycia Sykora)

After a ride, 2018 (Photo by Robert Rocklin)

David Schuman with family in Italy, 2018 (Photo from Schuman family)

Jack L. Landau, Justice, Oregon Supreme Court

Judge David Schuman was a skilled advocate, a gifted teacher, a nationally recognized scholar of state constitutional law, a conscientious judge, and a valued colleague and friend.

As a judge, David was the best of us. He brought a scholar's insight to the development and application of legal doctrine. He brought a poet's eloquence to his writing. He offered a teacher's gift of clarity and accessibility to his reasoning.

David's work as a judge reflected an unwavering sense of impartiality. He never failed to follow binding precedent, even when he disagreed with it. That is not to say that he always did so without grumbling a bit. He chafed especially at the Oregon Supreme Court's case law requiring very close—if not literal—interpretation of statutes. In *State v. Chilson*, for instance, he upheld the lawfulness of a traffic stop based on a statute requiring a driver to signal one hundred feet before turning, even when it is physically impossible to do so. David wryly observed: "If this were a jurisdiction where we could construe a statute so as to avoid the plainly absurd results of a literal interpretation that the legislature could not possibly have intended—that is, every other jurisdiction in the United States—the outcome of this case would be simple and straightforward. . . . Not here." But, having voiced his concern, he dutifully followed the law.

His work likewise demonstrated a fearless sense of integrity. David did not shrink from disagreeing with his colleagues, if he felt principle required it. In fact, it is in his concurring and dissenting opinions that his work as a judge was in some ways most influential. In *State v. Howard/Dawson*, for example, he dissented from the court's *en banc* decision that police do not need a warrant to search an individual's garbage left at the curb. Ten years later, the Oregon Supreme Court adopted his view, in *State v. Lien/Wilverding*. Likewise, in *City of Nyssa v. Dufloth*, David dissented from the court's decision upholding the constitutionality of a local ordinance that regulated nude dancing. The Supreme

Court ultimately sided with David's view of the scope of free speech protections under the Oregon Constitution.

David's work as a judge also reflected a deep commitment to state constitutional law. A former law clerk to Justice Hans Linde—one of the founders of the field—and a leading scholar in his own right, David persistently reminded the bench and bar of the importance of resolving disputes based on state law before resorting to federal constitutional principles. And his careful descriptions of what that state law required became templates for future decisions.

Finally, David's work revealed a constant concern not just for doctrinal details, but also for how the law produces just and sensible results. He was particularly skeptical of such technicalities as preservation of error rules, which, as David complained in his dissent in *State v. Vanornum*, "primarily preserves injustice."

David Schuman was indeed the best of us. He is greatly missed.

Ellen Rosenblum, Oregon Attorney General

Long before we served together on the Court of Appeals, I knew and genuinely appreciated David Schuman. He was a protégé of Hans Linde, from whom he learned—and then expounded upon—the special place state constitutional law has in our jurisprudence. He'd also been a beloved, award-winning professor at the University of Oregon's School of Law (our shared law school alma mater even though we'd both grown up in Illinois) and had performed important legal and policy work at the Oregon Department of Justice—that I now lead—for Attorneys General David Frohnmayer and Hardy Myers.

Though Judge Schuman graduated from law school a decade after me, he was by age my senior, and I always viewed him as one of the court's wise judges—and treated him, as we say in the law, "with due deference." More important, I loved working with him. He was welcoming, fun, wise (as noted), and could even be a little gossipy if you caught him when he wasn't in mid-thought, writing, or meeting with his clerks (all of whom adored him).

There was a special quality about David's approach to the law—and to the opinions he wrote, which is the way judges are remembered. Personal biography goes a good way to explaining and deepening our understanding of a person's uniquenesses, and David's certainly was a fascinating life story—including his early years as a competitive speed skater. (He came in second in the North American finals in the 220-yard competition at the age of seventeen.) Interestingly, his early relationship with law school was clearly one of ambivalence. (He had dropped out after only six weeks the first time.) But you never would have imagined that history upon meeting him as a judge. The David Schuman you encountered in that role was a judge's judge—born to the law—or so it seemed.

None of this, though, does much to help explain the David Schuman so many knew and loved. Rather, it was another of his lives—as an

English teacher and writer of fiction—that helps get at what made him so special to so many of us. Writers have to be able to understand deeply the lives of others—and to imagine and empathize with people, including some who never actually existed but are their own special creation.

Teaching, too, calls for empathy—for the material and the students. A good teacher has to listen intently to his students—and even to engage in a similar kind of deep imagining as a writer of fiction—to be able to understand what's really going on with them. Perhaps most important, the best teachers are able to put their own biases aside, in order to make better sense of their material and to relate more effectively with their students.

I always felt David was a great teacher when I sat on the court with him. One of my brothers, now a college teacher himself, thought so, too. He recalls with near-messianic fondness his days as an English student of David's at Deep Springs College, where he (and Sharon) taught for seven years beginning in the mid-1970s. Once David had arrived at the University of Oregon, incoming law students in Eugene always clamored to meet him at his annual appearances at OLIO (Opportunities for Law in Oregon)—due to his amazing reputation.

More to the point of this remembrance, David was a careful and beautiful judicial writer. To understand and appreciate his generous spirit, one experience, in particular, stands out in a way that highlights his special qualities. He and I, and a third judge, were on a panel in a case that gave us all fits. We just kept going back and forth, and at the end of the day we still didn't know how it would come out. But we were judges, for whom deciding was the essence of our work. David offered to take the assignment to write the opinion. I remember so clearly what transpired next. What he crafted wasn't just a proposed majority opinion in the case; he also wrote and shared with us a dissent he'd written, opposing his own majority opinion. Now, who does a thing like that? David. Why? Probably because it was his way to work through his own angst about the case—and to help us with ours. It was also a welcome surprise, a sort of gift to us as his co-panelists.

In this day and age, when it feels as if all too many judicial appointments are designed to predetermine the outcomes of important legal issues, my experience with Judge Schuman is a bright and shining example of what judges should do: imagine, empathize, understand what's at stake, use these special skills in applying the law to the facts, and—yes—then write the result in clear, meaningful prose that can serve as a powerful guide for future judges, lawyers, and the public.

There is no better time than the present to reflect on—and appreciate—those qualities that made my former colleague so special in the annals of the law in Oregon.

James C. Egan, Chief Judge, Oregon Court of Appeals

In this book you will find words written by David Schuman, who was one of the finest scholars of state and federal constitutional law in a generation. While there are other more recognizable names among those scholars, here you will find a hidden gem forged deeply under the solid ground of psychology, English language, and English literature. There are other hidden gems from different generations whose names you will find if you poke around libraries and explore the dusty pages of obscure journals—names like Hans Linde and Derrick Bell.

David Schuman worked with Justice Linde and Dean Bell. He did not hesitate to stand on the shoulders of the giants in his life. By standing in that position with the advantage of his extraordinary training at Stanford, University of Chicago, and the University of Oregon law school, David identified new paths of constitutional analysis. Around the time of his untimely death, I had a copy of David's 1995 *Oregon Law Review* article entitled "The Creation of the Oregon Constitution" opened on my desk. I was reading the article for some academic confirmation of the intersections between Oregon's foundational law and race. Of course, David did not disappoint. Now, younger scholars stand on David's shoulders.

So, here you will find the echoes of prior scholarship and the resonant voice of current scholarship. As a judge on the Oregon Court of Appeals with David, I watched him use that voice to train the young lawyers that he chose as chamber clerks. As a senior judge teaching constitutional law at the University of Oregon law school, he recommended law students for clerkships. Those students were always clever, bright, and intelligent, with a bent toward my way of thinking. David and I did not always agree on outcomes; his students might not agree with him either; but none of that mattered to him. What David cared about was the quality of reasoning and the challenge that the disagreement and advocacy presented.

In my experience, David enjoyed a good challenge. By challenging all of those around him, he elevated our thinking even if that made his own task more difficult. I hope that you find here what I found in David: gems of brilliance, a resonant voice, and the joy of a good challenge.

Martha Walters, Chief Justice, Oregon Supreme Court

In "Lawyers in Hell," the commencement address that begins this book, David Schuman proposes three principles: that to serve the law, we must see not only abstract general rules, but also the real people who occupy them; we must beware of two professional dangers—perversion of power and coldness of heart; and we must forge a public life worth living. David lived by those principles. His carpool mates, including me, referred to David as the Shoe; we did so because he walked through life in those truths, abiding by those principles, every day, in both his life and in his work.

On the frozen rivers of justice, Judge Schuman skated like a Chicago speed-skater—with eyes open to the real world about him. On the constitutional parchment, Judge Schuman wrote as a Chicagoan does—bluntly and with an understanding of the ways in which power can be abused. On the streets of our town, Judge Schuman engaged and educated. He spoke like a Chicagoan—with skill and strength. He believed in our democracy and our system of justice. He spoke out about how that system should work and our obligation to ensure that it does—for everyone.

Judge Schuman was a brilliant jurist who appreciated the law, but who was not limited by its strictures. In the commencement speech I referenced, he describes the laws of Athens as giving Socrates "his identity and roles, which bound him to others in a web of support and obligation, and in doing so made it possible for him to be a human animal." He describes Dante's Beatrice as representing "his transcendence of self, his connection with the human community." David Schuman was a revered judge, but that did not set him apart. He knew so well that our mutuality is inescapable and that it is our human connections that set us free.

During his life, the Shoe walked in shoes that were deliberately ordinary, but he was no ordinary man. He was, by Dante's definition, an authority—someone whose example enlightened and enabled. He was an authority like no other, and I loved him.

Kristen Bell, Assistant Professor of Law, University of Oregon

My focus here is on one piece of unfinished business in his life: In an opinion written by Judge Schuman in 2013, the Court of Appeals overturned Jerrin Hickman's murder conviction on the ground that the testimony of two eyewitnesses should never have been admitted.[1] The Oregon Supreme Court then reversed and reinstated that conviction in 2014.

The testimony of two witnesses who identified Mr. Hickman as the shooter was the central issue on appeal. The two witnesses, D. and N., were young white women who lived in the suburbs and came to Portland to celebrate New Year's Eve. Around midnight, they drove up to a party and saw twenty-five to fifty men, all African-American, gathered outside. From inside their car, they saw men fighting; "they didn't feel comfortable" and "want[ed] to leave." D. and N. then heard and saw shots fired. A man whom they believed to be the shooter then came up to their car and tried to get in. Another passenger repelled him, and they drove away.

When police questioned D. and N. that night, D. said "she didn't see the shooting" and N. could describe only basic features of the shooter. In the two years before trial, neither witness was asked to identify Mr. Hickman in a lineup, photo array, or other process. Shortly before trial, the district attorney met with each woman. D. told the prosecutor that she could not give details about the shooter because "[a]ll black men look the same to her." The prosecutor said he would ask D. to identify the shooter at trial only if she signaled with her eyes that, having seen him in court, she could answer that he was the shooter.

The Court of Appeals held that the process leading up to the identification was too suggestive to be admitted into evidence. Judge Schuman

---

1 *State v. Hickman*, 298 P.3d 619 (Or. App. 2013). Judge Wollheim and Justice Nakamoto were also on the panel.

analogized the process to a "show-up" in which the police bring a suspect to the station and simply ask whether the witness can identify the suspect. That process has been held "inherently suggestive ... because the witness is always aware of whom police officers have targeted as a suspect." The Supreme Court disagreed with the analogy on the ground that a show-up occurs before trial, and the witness identification here occurred at trial.

But there is perhaps a larger issue over which Judge Schuman and the Oregon Supreme Court disagreed: the relevance of race. Judge Schuman twice cited research that "[w]itnesses are significantly better at identifying members of their own race than those of other races." The Supreme Court did not mention anything about cross-racial identification; on the contrary, it cautioned against relying too heavily on any research about eyewitness testimony. The differences in how the opinions characterize race are subtle, and remarkable. For example, in characterizing the description that N. initially gave to police, the Oregon Supreme Court said that "N. described the shooter in some detail, including his age, race, build, and apparel." In Schuman's words, "N. could tell Beniga [the police officer] only that the shooter was an African-American man wearing a 'do-rag,' had a stocky build, and was in his mid to late twenties." In describing D.'s testimony about the shooter, the Oregon Supreme Court said, "D. testified that the shooter had particular facial features." In Judge Schuman's words, "[D.] was able to give a physical description of the shooter, albeit one that was couched in racially stereotypical terms ('close Afro or braids,' 'broadish nose and big lips')."

Judge Schuman and the other judges on the Court of Appeals had the courage to name race as an explicit issue in the case rather than talk around it. Given the established and ever-growing body of evidence about the unreliability of cross-racial identifications, and Mr. Hickman's continued claim that he is innocent, the case warrants a second look. Jerrin Hickman remains in prison serving a life sentence.

Nicholas Lovrich, Emeritus Professor of Political Science, Washington State University

Solving the world's problems—who does that as a college student? As roommates, David Schuman and I set aside mundane matters such as preparing for exams and dealing with exploitative landlords to engage in lofty debates about the existence of God, racial and economic justice, civil liberties, and world peace. I did not know then that David would go on to find his place among the select few jurists whose words and actions would move us all closer to democratic government's noble goal of producing wise law for posterity. David's approach to our debates was unfailingly gentle, considerate, and humane—but deeply penetrating and rigorous.

After college David and I shared academic interests in judicial selection and administrative law, benefiting greatly from the work of Justice Hans Linde. In 2009 the Seattle University law school hosted a conference about state judicial selection. Then recently retired Justice Sandra Day O'Connor addressed the gathering, focusing on the challenge to judicial independence posed by massive judicial campaign funds. The reaction panel comprised chief justices from the supreme courts of Washington and Texas, and David. While the justices criticized O'Connor's advocacy of independent judicial commissions and defended judicial elections, David's defense of Justice O'Connor's more compelling argument was characteristically erudite, exquisitely supported, and artfully delivered.

Over the course of a lifetime, few people make a profound impact upon one's thinking and actions in all aspects of life, personal and professional. David was such a person for me. From the tributes to him collected for this remarkable book it is good to learn that his noteworthy contributions to the long arc of history bending toward justice are appreciated by such wise public servants. May his good work live long in the opinions he wrote, a few of which are collected here, and in the many students', interns', and colleagues' lives he touched during his all-too-brief life.

Hans A. Linde, Justice, Oregon Supreme Court, 1977–1990

What follows here is a summary by Judge Rex Armstrong and Judge Henry Breithaupt of an interview they conducted with the Honorable Hans A. Linde shortly after his ninety-sixth birthday in 2020 and before his death on August 31, 2020. Judge Armstrong, a former Linde clerk, currently sits on the Oregon Court of Appeals; Judge Breithaupt, a former student of Justice Linde, is a retired Oregon Tax Court judge.

Justice Linde first met David Schuman at David's interview to clerk for him during the 1984–1985 court term. The interview took place during an election campaign in which the justice had been challenged by two other candidates. David got the job. Justice Linde won the election. David celebrated the victory with others whom Justice Linde had taught and mentored, including Hardy Myers, then a lawyer and member of the Oregon House of Representatives, and future Judge Armstrong—a group that would become David's professional colleagues and friends.

Justice Linde took into account David's academic resume and experience, especially his PhD in English from the University of Chicago, which indicated that he had the academic talent, confidence, and discipline to pursue a career of thinking and writing. Justice Linde remembers fondly David's work as his clerk.

The justice formed long-lasting attachments to his clerks, and David was no exception. Like Justice Linde, David continued in public service after his clerkship. In his scholarly work on the Oregon Constitution, David focused on that constitution as a living document. This work developed the importance of state constitutions championed by Justice Linde, who had restored their power in both his academic and judicial writings. David's clerkship was no doubt where the seeds of later work were planted. Importantly, David understood that the study of the Oregon Constitution was something different from the study of court opinions interpreting the

Oregon Constitution. That distinction, constantly pointed out by Justice Linde, has eluded many judges and lawyers in Oregon.

Justice Linde and his wife, Helen, forged a friendship with David and his wife, Sharon. They very much enjoyed visits with David and Sharon, whether in Salem or Portland, and especially appreciated that David and Sharon came to see them as advancing age made it more difficult for them to travel to see others. Visits were, among other things, chances to appreciate David's sense of humor—sharp but not raucous.

David Schuman was one of many lawyers and judges inspired and mentored by Justice Linde. He built on Justice Linde's work to protect rights and civil liberties. Without question, David's teaching, scholarship, and judicial actions reflected that devotion to law and the Oregon Constitution. Justice Linde was and remains extremely proud of David's work, his legacy and their professional friendship.

The Dog Contract

This "contract," written by David Schuman in 2009, was presented by a friend of Sharon Schuman, with introduction and conclusion by Sharon, at his memorial, October 19, 2019, at the Knight Law Center, University of Oregon.

Only once did the worlds of law and family overlap for the Schuman family. That was when David found it necessary to draft the Dog Contract. To understand this document, you need to know that David did not like dogs, in spite of the fact that when he was a toddler his neighbor's boxer saved David's life by standing behind that neighbor's car and barking, to prevent it from backing over the baby. Instead of being filled with gratitude, at the age of ten David embarked on a terror campaign against the dogs on his paper route. He used his Little League skills to aim each paper at a dog. One day a gate got left open, and he got bit. Failing to see the justice in this retribution, from that moment forth David hated dogs. So it was not a surprise that he requested from me a prenuptial promise to never bring a dog into our home. I had grown up with, and loved, dogs, but the glow of romance made me agree.

Fast forward forty-three years. About eight years ago, David asked me one day, "What is it that you want?" I think he was expecting an answer like, "to see Africa!" or "to write another book!" Instead, I said, "A dog." He laughed. But the next day, he said, "You were joking about the dog, right?" When I responded, "Not really," you could see that he was irritated. He said, "But we had an agreement!" I responded, "Statute of limitations." I let it go, though. That was when Ben and Rebecca began their campaign: "Mom needs a dog!" They did not get very far until one day Rebecca said, "Dad, you know how mom likes to micromanage everything? If she had a dog, she would leave you in peace." That argument must have carried weight, because when Hanukkah came, among my presents was a small package that contained a dog leash. Tacit

230

consent. At this moment, before the dog actually entered our house, I was presented with the Dog Contract.

DOG CONTRACT

Whereas important family decisions involving David Schuman (hereafter Husband) and Sharon Schuman (hereafter Wife) have been made by consensus; and

WHEREAS for 43 years, Husband has blocked the acquisition of a dog by withholding his agreement; and

WHEREAS Husband has been subjected to a ceaseless 43-year nag-athon attempting to secure Husband's agreement, an attempt into which Wife has recently conscripted Husband's and Wife's children Benjamin and Rebecca, numerous other relatives and family friends, and Husband's and Wife's granddog Charlie, and

WHEREAS Husband has decided that prudence and familial tranquility require a reevaluation of his longstanding refusal to agree;

THEREFORE:

I.   Husband's agreement:

I.A Husband hereby agrees that Husband and Wife may acquire a dog.

****

I.C Although Wife has primary responsibility for selecting the dog, husband, in conformity with the longstanding policy of consensus in important family decisions, reserves the right to veto any selection for any reason whatsoever, including but not limited to size, breed, gender, temperament, age, or aesthetics. Husband agrees that his veto power will not be unreasonably exercised. Disputes as to what is "reasonable" will be resolved as set out in Section IV.A.

In consideration of Husband's agreement, Wife agrees as follows:

II.A Wife agrees to take sole responsibility for the care, feeding, and maintenance of the dog, including but not limited to training, walking, grooming, transporting, making medical decisions, cleaning up after, and making temporary lodging arrangements. Although Husband may, in his sole discretion, volunteer to take on such tasks, asking Husband to "volunteer," either directly or indirectly, by word or deed, shall be considered a breach of this Dog Contract, thereby allowing imposition of any of the remedies described in Section III.A, below.

****

II.D Wife, on behalf of dog, agrees that dog will not bite Husband or any other person over the age of 10 more than one time in any 12 month period. "One" means the sum of bites to all persons over the age of 10 and not the sum to any one person. Thus, for example, if dog bites Husband once and a stranger once, dog has breached this provision. Dog may bite Wife at will.

II.E Wife, on behalf of dog, agrees that dog will not bite a child 10 years of age or under. Period. No second bite. No exception for bites that are allegedly provoked by the child.

II.F Wife, on behalf of dog, agrees that, after dog has been with family for six months so as to permit training, dog will not habitually chase bicyclists or newspaper delivery personnel.

II.G Wife, on behalf of dog, agrees that dog will not unreasonably bark during Husband's normal sleeping hours. If dog does so, husband reserves the right to isolate dog in some place where dog's barking will not be heard by Husband or the family's neighbors. If the only way to stop dog from such barking is for some person to get out of bed without delay and devote attention to dog, Wife agrees to be that person.

Remedies for material breach:

III.A The remedies for breach of this agreement by Wife or dog include, but are not limited to, placement of dog with (a) another family, (b) a dog rescue association, or (c) a Humane Society.

III.B The remedy for breach of Husband's promise to agree that the family may acquire a dog under the terms set out in this contract is as follows: Wife may acquire a dog without limitation.

Miscellaneous

IV.A Any disputes arising under this agreement will be resolved by submitting the dispute to a neutral arbitrator to be mutually agreed upon by Husband and Wife. If Husband and Wife cannot agree on a neutral arbitrator, Husband will select one person to serve as arbitrator, Wife will select one person, and the two people selected will select a third. The arbitrator's decision shall be final and nonappealable.

IV.B. This agreement is the complete agreement between the parties until revoked in writing. It replaces any prior agreement, written or oral.

Since the Dog Contract was created, about once a year, when the dog has done something especially egregious, David has reminded me of it. But my response has always been something like, "I never signed that contract," or "Didn't you get a C+ in Contracts from Jim Mooney?" Meanwhile, on more than one occasion, I caught David sitting on the TV room couch, possibly petting Billy Budd, while he watched the Tour de France.

I have no idea how long it took the author of more than six hundred appellate opinions to create this contract, but I'm sure he had fun. His sense of humor was a great defense against the absurdities of the world. In the face of power abused, exploitation of the vulnerable, and assaults on justice, equality, and the rule of law, David felt an obligation to try to protect democracy itself. I hope that we can all use our own very different skills and passions to continue this work. The path is not terribly easy. What David knew was that we make it bearable by our ability to laugh.

David Schuman with Billy Budd (Photo by Sharon Schuman)

Writings of David Schuman
(excluding Judicial Opinions)

1965
"Saturday Night." *Workshop* 1 (1): 1–6. Stanford University. From author's collection.

1973
Heiress and Architect: Idiosyncrasy and Form in the Poetry of Thomas Hardy. PhD dissertation. University of Chicago.

c. 1975
"The History of Western Civilization." Unpublished short story. avoiceforjustice.com.

1976
"Good Work If You Can Get It: The Experience of One Academic Couple." *Careers and Couples: An Academic Question* 1: 32–35. Modern Language Association of America.

1977–1978
"Cold Turkey," to Sam and Nancy.

1981
"Education and Solipsism." *CoEvolution Quarterly* 29 (Spring): 1: 32–139.
"Show Business." *Webster Review* 6 (2): 95–101.
"Tracy." *Four Quarters* 30 (4): 24–31.

1983
"The Winner." *Four Quarters* 3 (2): 3–13.

1984
"The Political Community, the Individual, and Control of Public School Curriculum." *Oregon Law Review* 63 (2): 309–334.

1986
"Oregon's Remedy Guarantee: Article I, Section 10 of the Oregon Constitution." *Oregon Law Review* 65 (1): 35–72.

1988
"Discretion in Oregon Public Law." *Oregon Law Review* 67 (4): 859–69.
"Evaluating State Supreme Courts." Review of *The Role of State Supreme Courts in the New Judicial Federalism,* by Susan Fino. *Judicature: The Journal of the American Judicature Society* 71 (4): 220–21.

"The Right to Equal Privileges and Immunities: A State's Version of Equal Protection." *Vermont Law Review* 13 (1): 221–46.

1989

"Advocacy of State Constitutional Law Cases: A Report from the Provinces." *Emerging Issues in State Constitutional Law* 2 (1): 275–97. National Association of Attorneys General.

"Lawyers in Hell: A Law School Commencement Sermon." Commencement Charge to 1989 Graduates of the University of Oregon School of Law; reprinted in *Old Oregon*, University of Oregon (Autumn).

"*State ex rel. Ray Wells, Inc. v. Hargreaves*: Welcome to the Twilight Zone." *Oregon Law Review* 68 (1): 217–26.

1990

"Taking Law Seriously: Communitarian Search and Seizure." *American Criminal Law Review* 27 (4): 583–618. Georgetown University Law Center.

"Beyond the Waste Land: Law Practice in the 1990s." *Hastings Law Journal* 42 (1): 1–14.

1991

"Our Fixation with Rights Is Dysfunctional and Deranged." *Chronicle of Higher Education* (April 1). Reprinted as "What's Wrong with Rights?" *Old Oregon* (Winter).

1992

"The Right to a Remedy." *Temple Law Review* 65 (4): 1197–228.

"A Failed Critique of State Constitutionalism." *Michigan Law Review* 91 (2): 274–80.

1993

"Packwood: The Case of the Pizza Boy." *Washington Post,* May 6.

"Give Oregon Voters a Real Choice: Should Candidates Have More License to Deceive Than a Used Car Salesman?" *USA Today,* May 11.

1994

"Common Ground." *Oregon Quarterly* (Summer): 16–19.

"Daniel Bell, *Communitarianism and Its Critics.* New York: Oxford University Press, 1993." *Journal of Legal Education* 44 (2): 297–303.

"The Origin of State Constitutional Direct Democracy: William Simon U'Ren and the Oregon System." *Temple Law Review* 67:947–64.

1995

"The Creation of the Oregon Constitution." *Oregon Law Review* 74 (1): 947–63.

1998

"Law and Life: Breathing Life into an Ideal." Review of *Archibald Cox: Conscience of a Nation*, by Ken Gormley. *Oregon State Bar Bulletin* 59 (1).

1999

"Professionalism: A Sermon." *Journal of the Oregon Trial Lawyers Association* (Summer).

2000

"Deputy Attorney General Weighs Initiatives." Interview. Eugene *Register-Guard*,
    August 21.

2009

"Hans Linde Dedication." *Appellate Almanac* 2009. Oregon State Bar.

2011

"Using State Constitutions to Find and Enforce Civil Liberties." *Lewis and Clark Law
    Review* 15 (3): 783–97.

2014

"Women Deserve Yes on Measure 89." Eugene *Register-Guard*, October 16.

2016

"Remarks: Investiture of Justice Lynn Nakamoto." Salem, Oregon, January 25.
"David Frohnmayer—A Tribute." *Oregon Law Review* 94 (3): 673–76.

2017

"Travel Ban Rulings Based on Law." Eugene *Register-Guard*, February 22.

2018

"Comments on Robert Williams's *State Constitutional Protection of Civil Litigation*."
    Rutgers University Law Review 70 (4): 975–78.

2019

"Jack Landau: A Tribute." *Oregon Law Review* 97 (3): 579–82.